THE TARASOV SAGA

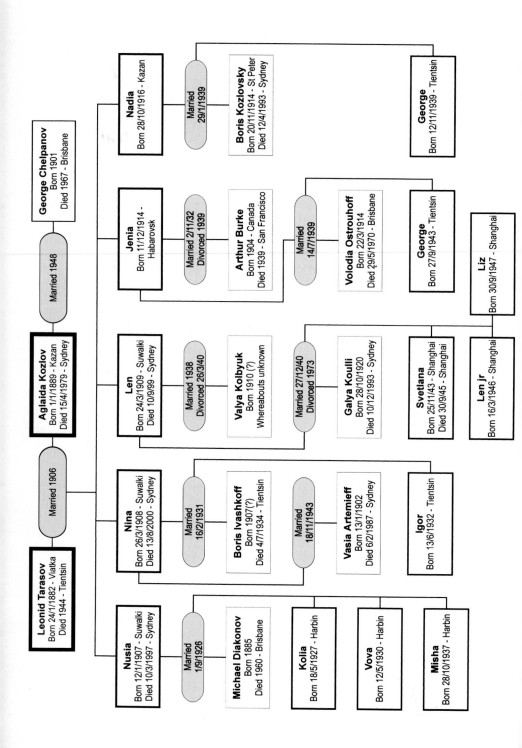

THE TARASOV SAGA

From Russia through China to Australia

Gary Nash

MAY YOU LIVE IN INTERESTING TIMES...

Ancient Chinese curse

ROSENBERG

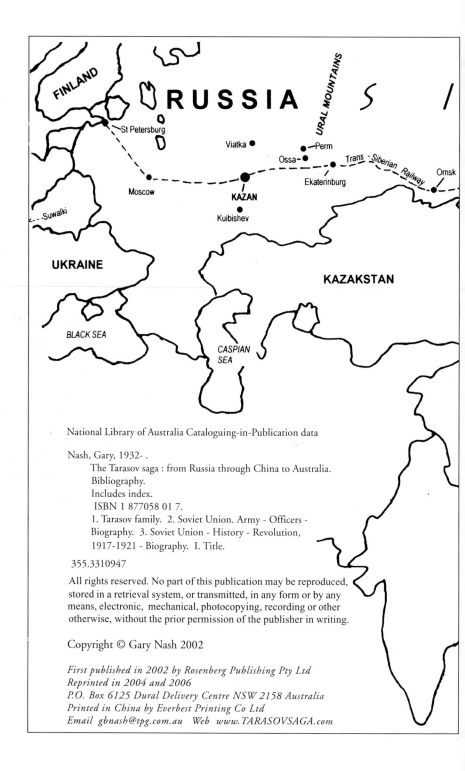

National Library of Australia Cataloguing-in-Publication data

Nash, Gary, 1932- .
    The Tarasov saga : from Russia through China to Australia.
    Bibliography.
    Includes index.
    ISBN 1 877058 01 7.
    1. Tarasov family. 2. Soviet Union. Army - Officers -
    Biography. 3. Soviet Union - History - Revolution,
    1917-1921 - Biography. I. Title.

 355.3310947

First published in 2002 by Rosenberg Publishing Pty Ltd
Reprinted in 2004 and 2006
P.O. Box 6125 Dural Delivery Centre NSW 2158 Australia
Printed in China by Everbest Printing Co Ltd
Email gbnash@tpg.com.au   Web www.TARASOVSAGA.com

FOREWORD

Just imagine if someone came up to you and told you that you and your family were to be deported to Bangladesh in a week's time to start a new life, and that all you could take with you was one suitcase and one hundred dollars.

'Yes, we know you can't speak Bengali, but you'll pick it up.'

And then, after a couple of decades of hard work building up your life there, you would be told to do the same again by moving to Lower Slobovia or somewhere similar.

'Yes, we know you can't speak Lower Slobovian, but ...'

It's hard to imagine, isn't it? But that's exactly what happened to the Tarasovs and to millions of other refugees from last century's wars.

We live now in a wonderful country called Australia. Most of us have a good life. None of us is starving. Most of us own a house. Just about everyone owns a car or two. All of us have personal and political freedom. It is easy to feel that this sort of life is par for the course — that this is the way it's supposed to be — and to forget that it was not always so, especially for those who emigrated here from war-ravaged countries.

It's only when we look back at the deprivations suffered by our parents and their parents that we realise how different their lives were from ours. Most of what we take for granted was impossible for them. Many of what we consider to be the necessities of life were either not available to them, or could only be obtained through sacrifices or extraordinary efforts.

The Tarasovs lost just about everything they owned twice in their lifetime. The first time was when they fled from Russia, and the second was when they fled from China. However, there is a positive side. The tough life, the deprivations — these experiences made our parents and grandparents courageous and resilient. That's what built their character. They had to fight for everything. They learned not to wilt under pressure, not to take anything for granted. They learned to be gutsy.

I have nothing but the highest admiration for the Tarasovs. From the outbreak of World War I nothing was ever proffered to them on a silver platter. But they never complained about their lot. They treated hardship as if it were a normal phase of life, as a stepping stone to a brighter future. They were grateful for the good times when and if they did come, and I am honoured to be a member of this family.

Let me say something about how this book came about. Throughout my life I used to hear my mother and my aunts and uncles talk about the old times, about their life in Russia and China. I always listened with fascination. Grandma Aida had a wonderful memory, and she often told us stories about the early days. She died in 1979 at the age of ninety and many of her memories would have been lost had it not been for my Aunt Jenia, who lived with Aida during the last years of her life and who also had an excellent memory. She was able to recall much of what Aida had told her.

'Someone should write a book about the Tarasovs,' my mother, Nina, often said. But that's as far as it went. However, when I retired in 1990 I decided that it was time for me to do something about it. I informed the tribe that I was planning to write 'the book' and, to my delight, the news was greeted with enthusiasm. As my mother and her four siblings were all alive and living in Sydney, and so was I, there would obviously be no difficulty, I thought, in obtaining all the material I needed.

But such was not the case. All of them loved talking about old times during our warm, cosy family gatherings, but to get them to either write things down or record them on tape was like pulling teeth. All sorts of excuses were given — everything from 'I don't remember' to 'I don't have the time now' to 'Why don't you ask Jenia? Her memory is better than mine.' Finally, and stupidly, I lost patience with the lot of them and gave the project up. Every so often I would raise the subject again, but the earlier enthusiasm had vanished.

An unfortunate event was the catalyst to get things moving again. Nusia, my oldest aunt, contracted cancer and went into hospital for a few weeks. When I visited her, she asked me to bring her an exercise book. 'It's pretty boring in hospital,' she said. 'I think I'll start writing a few things down about my life.' And write she did. Her first contribution was twenty-four foolscap pages of Russian longhand.

Eureka! The belated beginning! I immediately translated it, asked her some questions to fill in the gaps and gave a copy to her three sisters for their comments. The ball started rolling. Every time I received some input, I circulated it to the other members of the family who added further details. And so it went.

The book would have been completed sooner had I not become immersed in other activities. What reinstated it to a higher priority was the death of Nusia in February 1997 and my mother's advancing Alzheimer's disease. I suddenly realised that I was in danger of losing my links to the past. I still had some holes in the book, and it was going to be now or never. By the time I completed it, my uncle Len had died at the age of ninety and my mother had passed away at the age of ninety-two.

I hope that the resulting story will do justice to the Tarasov family and be of interest to those who would like to read about the trials and tribulations of a Russian family during the first half of the twentieth century.

Author's note. The spelling of Chinese names proved to be a bit of a problem. There are two 'official' romanised systems of spelling them. The first, developed in the second half of the nineteenth century by Sir Thomas Francis Wade and subsequently modified by Herbert Allen Giles in 1912, is called the 'Wade–Giles'. The second, called 'Pinyin', was introduced in 1956 and officially adopted by the People's Republic of China in 1979. And then there was the way we spelt the names when we were living in China, which was often different from the other two. For example, 'Tientsin' was our spelling of that city, but in the Wade–Giles system it is 'T'ien-ching' and in the Pinyin system 'Tianjin'. In some cases, the differences are significant — 'Canton', as we knew it, is transformed to 'Kuanghchou' and 'Guangzhou', respectively, and 'Hong Kong' into 'Hsiang-kang' and 'Xianggang'. Very confusing!

So I have decided to use the spellings we, the foreign inhabitants of China, used during the period covered by the book. In deference to scholars among the readers, when the name is first used in the book I have also included the Pinyin version in brackets (when it is different). I have also included this version in the Index.

CONTENTS

In memory of my Grandmother, Aida,
and her tireless determination
to keep her beloved family
together and safe
at all costs

1 RUSSIA 1900–1922

TURBULENT TIMES: 1900–1905

Leonid Alexandrovich [†] Tarasov, my grandfather, whose name graces this narrative, was born on 24 January 1882 in Viatka (now Kirov), a largish town about 800 kilometres northeast of Moscow. Unfortunately, little is known of his parents, except for the fact that his father was a military man, nor is there a surviving record of any siblings. From early childhood, Leonid dreamed of becoming a soldier. After completing his studies at the Alexandrov High School in Viatka, he entered the Military Academy in Kazan, and on completion of his training decided to make the army his lifetime career. Little did he know how turbulent this career was to be.

My grandmother, Aglaida Nikolaevna Kozlova, was born in Kazan on 1 January 1889. Throughout her life she was called Aida. Even though Verdi's famous opera about the Ethiopian princess Aida was premiered seventeen years before her birth, it is unlikely grandmother was named after that heroine. Aglaida is not a common Russian name, but it is certainly typically Russian, and Aida is the normal shortening of it. Moreover, there is no record of Verdi's opera being performed in Kazan before her birth.

Aida was the eldest of five children, four girls and a boy. Regrettably, not much is known about her parents either, except that the family was a happy one. However, while my grandmother had pleasant memories of her childhood, she seemed reluctant to disclose any details. Perhaps the traumatic events that followed were strong enough to obliterate the particulars of her earlier life. Aida was sent to a private school to give her the best possible education and to teach her lady-like manners. From an early age, she was extraordinarily

---

[†] Every Russian name has a 'patronymic' attached, i.e. a name derived from the father's name. In this case, 'Nikolaevna' denotes that her father's name was Nikolai. In the case of Leonid, his patronymic of 'Alexandrovich' denotes that his father's name was Alexander. In addressing a person, the patronymic is dropped only when one is on 'first-name' terms.

Tsar Nicholas II, painted by Serov

beautiful, exuding sultry sensuousness and style. In addition, she was a person of immense resourcefulness, strength and fortitude.

In pre-revolutionary days, Russia had four social classes. The main three were the *working class*, consisting of peasants and labourers; the *middle class* or *bourgeoisie*, consisting of administrative personnel, merchants, clerks, professionals and clergy; and the *aristocracy*, including the nobility (both 'personal' and 'hereditary') and the titulars, such as dukes, princes, barons and counts. Personal nobles were those from lower classes who had been elevated by the Tsar for services to the country — similar to the English non-hereditary peerage of more recent times. Hereditary nobles were normally descendants of earlier elevations, and these persisted through the generations.

The fourth class, the *Cossacks*, was somewhat unique. They were allotted land and a certain degree of autonomy and self-government. For this privilege, each man was required to give twenty years of military service to the Tsar, commencing at the age of eighteen. Their services were mainly used for protection against border incursions and during times of war. At birth, the class of an individual was recorded on the birth certificate and in a special 'Book of Births' so there would be no future doubt as to his or her status. Leonid and Aida both belonged to the hereditary nobility.

Russia was a vast country. In 1900 it covered one-sixth of the land area of the world and its population numbered some 130 million. Fewer than half spoke Russian as their native language. The others were descended from various conquered countries and tribes, bringing with them their own languages.

Although Aida and others of her era steadfastly maintained that life in Russia in those days was wonderful, history clearly discredits that viewpoint. Life may have been fine for a privileged minority, but was certainly not so for the rest. Over 80 percent of the people lived in the countryside. Most were peasants, trying to scrape together a living from a few acres of land. They were highly taxed by the government, whereas the rich paid next to nothing. Many of the peasants lived below subsistence level and most were uneducated.

Although life was not much better for town workers, large numbers of peasants moved to the larger towns to seek a better life. Instead, they found they had to work eleven hours a day, six days a week, for low wages. There were no trade unions, and exploitation of workers by employers was rampant. The working class in the towns was growing faster than any other group, and becoming the most militant.

Double Eagle, symbol of the monarchy

In the Russian autocratic form of government, there were no elections and there was no parliament. The Tsar was responsible to no-one and could do exactly what he liked. He chose ministers to advise him, but was not bound to listen to them and he could dismiss anyone at will. Furthermore, most of his ministers were wealthy landowners who were primarily self-interested. Although most Russians obeyed the Tsar because they believed he was chosen by God, the system was a catastrophe waiting to happen.

The Tsar, Nicholas II, was a member of the Romanov family, which had ruled Russia since 1613. In 1894, on the day after his father Alexander III died, the twenty-six-year-old Nicholas said to his wife: 'What is going to happen to me, and to all of Russia? I am not ready for the role of Tsar. I never wanted to be one. I know nothing of the business of ruling and I have no idea of how to talk to ministers.' He was clearly not suited to the role.

As the people's dissatisfaction could not be vented via the ballot box, it erupted in occasional acts of violence. These were quickly and brutally suppressed by the secret police, the *Okhrana* (meaning 'protection'). Newspapers were censored and anyone who spoke up against authority was beaten or jailed.

The disastrous Russo–Japanese war of 1904–1905 was a catalyst for further unrest among the masses. Relations between Russia and Japan had been severely strained since the Treaty of Peking in 1860, which ceded the coastal strip of Eastern Manchuria from China to Russia. This allowed the Russians to build the city of Vladivostok (Russian for 'Rule the East') and base their Pacific fleet there. On the other hand Japan, with its small size, overflowing population and lack of natural resources, had always eyed China, and particularly Manchuria, with a view to expanding its empire. Thus the Russian presence so close to home was a source of great and escalating annoyance.

In 1898, China granted Russia a lease of the strategic city of Port Arthur (now called Lü-shun), at the tip of the Liao-tung Peninsula in southern Manchuria. This was strategically important for Russia as it allowed her to base her Pacific fleet in an ice-free port. This infuriated the Japanese and, in February 1904, they launched a surprise attack on the Russian fleet, crippling it and occupying Port Arthur.

The news shocked all Russians. How could this insignificant little country have the gall to challenge mighty Russia? 'Let's throw our hats at them! That should be enough to smother them!' was a popular catchcry and troops were immediately dispatched on the long journey to Manchuria to retake Port Arthur. However, without adequate logistical support, troop numbers and leadership, they had little success against the Japanese land forces. In October, with no victory in sight, Tsar Nicholas II dispatched the Russian Baltic fleet to go and finish the job. After a seven-month journey to the other side of the world, the Russians engaged the Japanese in a naval battle, and the Japanese navy sank the whole Russian fleet.

This humiliating defeat was a huge blow to the morale of the Russian people, but it was this conflict that brought Leonid and Aida together.

BIRTH OF THE TARASOV CLAN: 1906–1911

At the beginning of 1905, Sub-Lieutenant Leonid Tarasov was sent to fight the Japanese. A few weeks later, in a battle near Mukden, he was wounded in the shoulder and, after spending some time in a hospital, was sent home to recuperate. In the meantime, Aida was spending her summer school vacation at the country estate of her

Leonid, Kazan, 1905

grandmother, Praskovya. She had been doing this for some years, using the time to undertake additional studies to ensure her success in the next year.

Leonid was a cousin twice removed to Aida, and when Praskovya heard of Leonid's wound she invited him to spend the summer recuperating at her country home. Leonid readily agreed and, to repay her kindness, volunteered to coach Aida in her studies. Love bloomed and they were married the following year. Aida was seventeen and Leonid twenty-four. Their wedding had one casualty. The priest who married them knew they were related but mistakenly thought it was permissible to marry second cousins. For this terrible crime he was threatened with excommunication, then banished to a tiny church in some distant village.

Shortly after the wedding, Leonid was transferred to Suwalki, a small town in Poland near the Belo–Russian border (Poland was, at the time, a part of the Russian Empire). Their first child, Anna, was born there on 12 January 1907. Russian children christened Anna are often called 'Nusia', which is the name by which she was known all her life. As she was only six pounds at birth and the first-born, Aida fussed over her quite a bit.

The family was not wanting. Leonid's salary was reasonable, they were in love and the future looked bright. Happiness brings togetherness, and togetherness has a way of resulting in procreation. The next two children were born in quick succession — Nina fourteen months later on 26 March 1908, and Len (short for Leonid) a year later on 24 March 1909. A few months after Len's birth, Aida became pregnant again. This time, she was less than enthusiastic about the impending event, feeling that a longer break between pregnancies would not have been inappropriate. As abortions were not readily available, she decided to take matters into her own hands. Riding a horse she executed a deliberate, but successful, fall. This gave her a respite for more than five years before the next addition to the clan.

In the meantime Leonid, by now a lieutenant, decided he needed a change of scenery and in May 1910 asked for a transfer to the 23rd Siberian Brigade stationed on the outskirts of Habarovsk in the Far East. On the map, Suwalki is on the extreme left in Poland and Habarovsk on the extreme right in east Siberia. As the crow flies, they are 8000 kilometres apart, and as the train chugs probably closer to 9500 — about the same as the distance from Melbourne to Tokyo, or two and a half times the distance from Sydney to Perth. So it was quite a move.

Leonid went first. Aida followed with her three children — Nusia, aged four and a half; Nina, three; and Len, two — arriving in Habarovsk in early 1911. As no families were allowed on the military base, Leonid rented a pleasant apartment for them in the city. It was too far for him to commute on a daily basis, so he lived on the base and visited them regularly. Observing that the three youngsters were a real handful, Leonid assigned his orderly to help his wife, a thoughtful gesture. The orderly was a hard worker and Aida was pleased to have him. He did all the housework while she looked after the children.

Some time later, Aida's sister Vera came to visit them and ended up staying for over a year. A well-educated, cultured woman, she undertook to get Nusia ready for school, and even taught her to play the piano. In addition, she taught the children some important rules of behaviour and etiquette, for example, always sleeping with their hands on top of their blankets. Vera was not only a great help around the house, but excellent company for Aida.

Life in Habarovsk was fine.

Leonid and Aida, Habarovsk, 1913

Aida and Vera, Habarovsk, 1911

TWO WARS: 1905–1915

However, for the majority of the Russian population life was not at all fine. The Russo–Japanese war of 1905 increased restlessness among the Russian people. Many were forced into the army, food was extremely scarce and living conditions were atrocious. One Sunday a group of militants arranged a peaceful march to the Tsar's Winter Palace to present a petition for political reforms, hoping the Tsar would meet them or at least appear on the balcony. Instead, a hail of bullets greeted them. More than 500 were killed or wounded.

This 'Bloody Sunday' proved to be a historic error on the part of the authorities. As news of the event spread, a wave of violence hit Russia. Peasants attacked the houses of rich landowners. Trade unions were formed. Half a million people were on strike. There was unrest everywhere. Revolution was in the air.

To calm the population, the Tsar issued a manifesto, at the top of which was the formation of a *duma*, or council, to help run the country. Even without the democracy that the people had hoped for, and even though the Tsar could still appoint and sack ministers and pass laws, the measures appeared to be sufficient to quell the unrest. The revolutionary flame was extinguished. It had no leader to keep it alight.

The years between 1906 and 1913 were relatively prosperous. Harvests were good, industry was expanding and there were fewer strikes. Some reforms were introduced, especially in rural areas. Peasants were freed from their debts to the government and allowed to own their own farms. A class of Kulaks (rich peasants) came into being. But in 1914, after a poor harvest, dissatisfaction with the authorities began to grow again and outbreaks of violence became more frequent.

On 28 June 1914, Archduke Franz Ferdinand of Austria was assassinated in Sarajevo. This triggered a series of events that led to Germany declaring war on Russia — the commencement of World War I. The news that Russia was at war seemed to unite the people. Most still believed the Tsar was an emissary of God, that he could do no wrong and that he would win the war for Russia. The military loss to Japan a few years ago was considered to be an aberration. This time, Russia would certainly emerge victorious. Never had the Tsar been so popular as at that moment. However, by Christmas 1914 a million Russian soldiers were dead, wounded or taken prisoner.

On 11 December 1914, amidst these turbulent times, Aida gave birth to a third daughter, Jenia (short for Evgenia). By this time, Leonid had been transferred from Habarovsk to the European front on the other side of the world. Because of the urgency of the transfer, there was no time to arrange to move Aida and the children and they remained in Habarovsk. Fortunately, Leonid had left his orderly behind as Aida's helper. This was useful as she now had three children aged eight, seven and six, as well as the newborn Jenia.

As the mail service during this time was somewhat erratic, Aida constantly worried about her husband. What would happen to her and her family, she wondered, if he were killed? How could she cope with four children and no husband? She prayed fervently for his safe return.

In August 1915, a letter arrived from Leonid. He was in Warsaw recuperating from the effects of a poison gas attack, and the letter instructed her to join him for a few months — and I mean 'instructed': that's the way he communicated with his wife. 'Leave the children with the orderly,' the letter ordered. *'Come alone'*. The last two words were underlined. At the time, Jenia was just nine months old. How could Aida leave her behind at such a tender age? She knew disobeying her husband would be hazardous, and the journey was a long one, but her motherly instincts demanded she take the infant along.

When Leonid saw Jenia in Aida's arms, he was not pleased. Even though he had never seen his new daughter, he was most annoyed that his orders had been disobeyed. He was looking forward to a pleasant time with his wife and was unprepared to take second place to a baby, even though it was his own. The three months Aida spent with her husband were not as pleasant as they could have been and in later years Jenia claimed this incident was the cause of her father's resentment towards her. From that time on, she said, he seemed to

Aida, Vera and Jenia, Habarovsk, 1915

pick on her more than her other siblings,　Leonid , Warsaw, 1915
making her childhood miserable.

At the end of 1915, a month after Aida returned to Habarovsk, she received a letter from Leonid instructing her to enrol Nusia, now nearly nine, into the Marinovsky High School in Kazan. He had decided the war would probably continue for quite a while and that it made no sense for the family to continue to live in Habarovsk. Kazan was, after all, a familiar city to both of them. It was Aida's birthplace and Leonid had done his military training there.

CATASTROPHE IN KAZAN: 1915–1918

Aida had left Kazan when, still in her teens, she had moved to Suwalki with her new husband. Her parents had also left Kazan for some undetermined location, leaving her widowed grandmother Praskovya behind. Why she did not leave Kazan with the rest of the family is not known. In those days it was the accepted practice for the senior female member to stay with the family as the cook and nanny for the grandchildren. Whatever the reason, Praskovya, who was then in her early fifties and a senior citizen by the standards of the day, found herself in a retirement home.

Praskovya was a charming woman with many friends, and this circle of friends did not diminish after she entered the home. If anything, it grew. Apparently one of her many talents was ironing and she was known as the virtuoso of the clothes iron. Her friends used to invite her over for a spot of ironing so they could learn the fine nuances of this chore. In fact Praskovya had never done any ironing before she entered the retirement home, but in the absence of servants she had to learn to do it herself. A new talent had emerged.

Aida had been very close to her grandmother before her marriage and was delighted to find Praskovya still living in Kazan. Knowing her grandmother would have many contacts, she sent her a letter advising her of the family's arrival and asking her to find them a place to live. Praskovya quickly found them a room in a large, two-storey house on the main street, across the street from a church with a tall belfry named *Bogoyavlenskaya* (literally, 'God will appear'). Their room was on the second floor facing the main street. It was quite large, with a small stove in the middle both for cooking

(Left to right) - Nina (7), Nusia (8) and Len (6), Kazan, 1915

and heating. Aida coped surprisingly well in this tight environment, and Praskovya helped whenever she could.

Even though the war was still raging, Leonid was able to pay periodic visits from the front. One of these led to Aida's final pregnancy in early 1916. It was not the greatest of years for either of them, with Aida becoming pregnant again and Leonid suffering concussion and a punctured eardrum from an explosion, followed by a shrapnel wound to his left leg.

When it was time to give birth, Leonid was not around — he had recuperated and was back at the front — and Aida asked Nusia and Nina to walk her to the hospital. She was feeling weak and nauseous, the contractions were becoming more frequent and she was afraid she would not make it to the hospital in time. The fifteen steps leading up to the entrance were especially difficult, and she had to pause to catch her breath.

'I think it will drop out any moment,' she mumbled.

'What will drop out?' the nine-year-old Nusia asked, looking at her anxiously.

There was no answer.

Aida made it to the door and was whisked away by the attendants. Nusia and Nina sat and waited. This was the fifth child, and the slips, as they say, had already been greased. Within an hour, at 10 a.m. on 29 October 1916, the newborn baby's screams were heard. Nadia (short for Nadezhda) had arrived. Her two sisters admired and cuddled the little bundle, kissed their mother and went home.

Although she was just two months short of her twenty-eighth birthday, Aida had now given birth to five children. As she lay in hospital, she pondered the fact that she now had the exact complement of children her own mother had — four girls and a boy. Maybe it's a sign from heaven, she thought. Maybe the Lord is saying 'Enough is enough. You've matched your mother. You can now stop.' Thankfully, Nadia was to be Aida's last child. At the christening, Nusia was the proud godmother. Leonid was still away fighting a war. Soon afterwards, Aida's sister, Antonina (Tonia), came to visit them and stayed for a few months. She loved children and was a great help.

In 1917, while Leonid was still at the front, a terrible accident befell the city of Kazan. Under the city was a huge storehouse of ammunition and explosives. Although the entrances to the complex were outside the town, the network of tunnels spread out underneath most of the city — an unbelievably stupid example of town planning. The existence of the ammunition dump was not common knowledge among the population, but it soon became tragically well known.

Nusia was looking out of the window when she saw huge clouds of black smoke rising on the outskirts of town. As she yelled out to her mother, a huge explosion came from the same direction. The ground shook, the windows rattled and the door to their room flew open. The tall belfry opposite the house began to sway and Aida thought it was about to fall on their house. A moment later another explosion shook the house, followed by yet another. Aida grabbed her handbag, picked up the baby Nadia and yelled to the other four children to follow her.

Rushing out into the street, they began to run in the opposite direction to the black smoke, not quite knowing where they were headed — Aida, with Nadia in her arms, and the four children, hand in hand, trying to keep up with her. The explosions became louder and more frequent. Pandemonium was everywhere. Frightened people ran streaming in all directions. Soon the children began to tire, and as they dropped back a strange woman

Kazan Kremlin, 1912

materialised in front of them and, before they knew it, they were being herded into the cellar of a strange house.

'Sit here. It's safe. You'll be all right,' the woman assured them.

How could they possibly feel safe without mother?

'We want our mother!' they screamed, panic stricken.

'You'll be fine. Just sit here until it's over,' the kind woman was saying.

Her assurances fell on deaf ears. The children continued to scream their heads off, so much so that she had to finally let them go. By that time, Aida realised they were missing and had run back to look for them. Just as she passed the house, they ran out of the cellar and nearly collided with her. Relieved, they clung to her for a moment before re-starting their mad rush.

The explosions continued. The ground was heaving as in a massive earthquake and cracks appeared in the road. Windows shattered, shards of glass flew everywhere. Suddenly, in this melee, they came upon Praskovya.

'Follow me to my home,' she screamed over the noise of the explosions and the crowd. 'It will be safe there.'

The retirement home was some way out of the city and by the time they reached it they were exhausted. Entering Praskovya's tiny room, they slammed the door shut, flopped down in the middle of the floor, regained their breath and waited, not knowing what they were waiting for. Looking around, Aida saw the room had the appearance of a chapel. There were icons in every corner, with burning oil lamps in front of each one.

'Let's pray for it to stop,' Praskovya said, and pray they did, still not knowing what 'it' was.

While they were praying the gardener burst into the room. 'We must all get away from here,' he yelled. 'There's a gas plant around the corner. If the fires get to it we'll all go up with it. Run that way, quick!'

Praskovya remembered she had some friends living in the direction in which he had pointed. It was a fair distance and they had to fight their way through throngs of people, but they finally made it. They were welcomed with open arms and given shelter. By then, it was getting dark and the explosions were becoming less frequent. Soon they stopped completely and the exhausted Tarasovs fell asleep.

In the morning, it was deathly quiet. The previous day seemed like a terrible nightmare. Full of apprehension, they headed home. It was like walking through a war zone. Ruined houses, deep fissures in the roads, rubble everywhere, and the terrible sound of wailing people. Aida had fears the big belfry might have collapsed on their house — after all, it had swayed horribly when the explosions began — and she was immensely relieved to discover the belfry and house still intact.

Later it was discovered that an unnamed hero, a martyr, had saved Kazan from total destruction. This brave man had courageously run back into the tunnels amid the explosions and fires and opened up all the water cocks and valves he could find, thus flooding the underground storage. He died in the process. There is now a memorial to him in the city square.

REVOLUTION! — 1917–1918

At the end of 1916 St Petersburg was hit by a new wave of strikes. It was winter and, because of the war, fuel was scarce, resulting in a breakdown of the transportation system and a shortage of food, milk, candles — just about everything. The situation was getting grimmer by the day.

In April 1917 a quarter of a million workers went on strike. Tempers flared. Troops fired on crowds of demonstrators. The people retaliated by storming the arsenal, setting ablaze the law courts and the *Okhrana* headquarters, and freeing prisoners. Soon the mob was in control of St Petersburg, and the troops, including the Tsar's personal guards, defected and joined them. The ministers were arrested and a Provisional Government was formed under the leadership of Alexander Kerensky. The Tsar was placed under house arrest.

And that's when Lenin appeared on the scene. Arrested in 1895 for publishing a revolutionary newspaper, Lenin had been exiled to Siberia. Released in 1900, he moved to Europe to wait for the right opportunity to return. At the time of the 1917 uprising he was living in Switzerland. With the help of the Germans, who were hoping he would pull Russia out of the war, Lenin was smuggled back into Russia. His revolutionary aims were to overthrow the Provisional Government and the capitalists and to let the peasants share the land. 'Peace, bread and land' was his slogan. But his followers were not well organised and loyal troops easily broke up any demonstrations. A warrant was issued for Lenin's arrest and he fled to Finland. His followers were rounded up and imprisoned. The July uprising had failed.

Conditions in St Petersburg and around the country continued to deteriorate. Russia remained at war and thousands of wounded soldiers and deserters were flocking home. Week by week, food became scarcer — and winter was approaching. Lenin decided to return and, on doing so, recruited followers among soldiers and peasants and made plans to seize power. On 7 November 1917 his followers, having banded into a political party called Bolsheviks (Majorists), attacked key government installations. The remaining loyal troops were routed, the ministers were arrested and Kerensky fled the city.

The Bolshevik revolution had succeeded. The Red flag replaced the tricolour. Lenin was in power. He immediately nationalised large-scale industries, agricultural land, forests and railways ... and he ended Russia's participation in World War I.

In March 1918 Russia signed a humiliating peace treaty with Germany (the Brest-Litovsky Treaty). Besides suffering great human and financial losses, the treaty forced Russia to relinquish considerable territory.

The war had been disastrous for Russia. Despite having a standing army of nearly one and a half million and reserves of three million, Russia had been unprepared for war. The road, rail and distribution infrastructure was inadequate and far inferior to that of its enemies. There was a shortage of just about everything — arms, provisions, food. Morale was low. As casualties mounted, more and more men were called up. By the end of the war, Russia had sent over fifteen million men into action, of whom nearly six million had been killed or wounded.

Leonid fought in the war from its beginning in 1914 until February 1918. He gave his best for his country, serving with valour and distinction. In September 1916 he was promoted to major and in May 1917 to lieutenant colonel. In December, while on two months' leave, he had time to take stock of the political situation. Although the Bolsheviks had gained power, a large opposing faction was unprepared to take their policies lying down. The bourgeoisie, owners of land and industry, organised political and military resistance and a number of prominent generals from the Imperial Army formed contingents of White forces aiming to overthrow the new government and restore the monarchy.

The political scene presented Leonid with a dilemma. Should he return to the front and continue fighting a losing war, or should he join the counter-revolutionaries wanting to return the Tsar to power? On the one hand, he hated the idea of deserting the front and the troops he felt responsible for. On the other hand, being a fervent monarchist he was prepared to risk his life in defence of the monarchy. In the end, he reasoned the war was beyond winning, whereas there was still time to reverse the political situation.

Consequently he requested, and was granted, a discharge from the army and made preparations to join the so-called White Army (as opposed to the communist Reds). Aida begged him to stay with the family in Kazan and leave the fighting to someone else, but he was determined, maintaining it was his duty. There were tearful farewells, none of them knowing whether they would ever see him again. He told his family not to worry, promising to keep in touch. Aida blessed him and the family was left fatherless again.

And that is how Leonid became embroiled in the terrible Civil War that was to split the family and eventually force them all to flee to China.

THE SEARCH FOR HUSBAND AND FATHER: 1919

On joining the White Army in February 1918, Leonid was immediately promoted to colonel and commander of the 1st Kazan Battalion. He was thirty-six. By that time, the Communist Revolution had moved east from St

This photo was sent to Leonid at the front in 1917. This is what Aida wrote on the back of it:

'My dearest, wonderful Lenichka,
Are you well, my precious? How you must be suffering in this terrible war. I would
give anything to be there with you and share in your suffering, and to console you
with my love, my dearest. The situation here is getting worse, but it is nothing
compared with what you must be going through, dear Lenichka. All I pray for is
that I will soon see you again, alive and in full health. I miss you terribly, my
dearest.
I will love you forever.
Yours alone – Aida'

Petersburg to Moscow, which became the site of fierce fighting. After Russia pulled out of the war, returning soldiers boosted both the White and Red Army ranks, depending on their political leanings, and the fighting escalated. The Civil War became vicious and bloody.

It was the innocent village people who suffered most. When troops entered — either White or Red — they would administer what was called 'political justice', shooting some, conscripting others, commandeering horses and wagons and collecting provisions. Often the same villages were later reoccupied by the other side, which would administer its own forms of justice, mostly with vengeance in mind. Many families did not know on which side their husbands, sons and neighbours were fighting.

Initially it was not clear which side was winning, but gradually the Reds began to prevail. Because of the size of the country, it took some time for the Civil War to spread past European Russia. However, the White forces gradually retreated deeper and deeper into the Siberian expanse, being pushed inexorably towards Manchuria and the eastern seaboard. When the Reds occupied Kazan in September 1918, Aida had not heard from Leonid for months. Not only were there no letters, but the monthly transfers of money from his salary had also stopped. Where was he? Was he fighting somewhere in Siberia? Was he still alive? Would she ever see him again?

Life became very difficult. With no money coming in, she took a job as secretary in a government office. Not only was the salary a pittance, but working for the Bolsheviks was a demeaning task. They were a crude and arrogant lot, especially in their dealings with the so-called intelligentsia. For example, her boss would insist she sit on his lap before he signed any papers she brought in. Other officials tried to fondle her at every opportunity. She was considered to be one of 'them', and therefore fair game. For obvious reasons, she hid the fact she was the wife of a White Russian colonel and instructed her children to do likewise. Her friends and neighbours also kept quiet on the subject. Fortunately, Praskovya was able to look after the children while Aida was working.

A year passed with no word from Leonid. While a lesser person would have believed he had been killed, Aida was certain the lack of communication was because Leonid feared that an intercepted letter would imperil her life, and that of their children. But just sitting and waiting was too frustrating and unproductive for Aida to bear, and she determined to search for him.

All she knew was that the White army was somewhere in Siberia. That's all. How she believed she would find him in the midst of a Civil War in a war-torn country the size of Russia remains a mystery. But she was determined to try. Praskovya was very worried about her grand-daughter's determination to rush off into the unknown. She tried to talk Aida out of it, but without success. All she could do was help her pack, give her the few roubles she had saved, bless her and kiss them all goodbye.

Capture of Kazan by the Red Army, 1918

Off they went: a mother with five children aged from three to twelve. Aida had little money, no destination, no friends to stay with and, let's face it, not much prospect of finding her husband. But, where there's hope …

And so began their epic journey across Russia.

To survive, Aida had to sell whatever she had of value, which was not much, just some dresses and a few trinkets. By the time the train brought them to Perm, a largish city just this side of the Ural Mountains, about 500 kilometres from Kazan, they were exhausted and had run out of money and anything to sell. So Aida decided to stay there for a while, get a job and save for the journey ahead.

On the railway station, a woman advised her she would find better prospects in Ossa, a hundred kilometres to the south. More opportunities and fewer Reds, she was told, so the family caught the next train there. The advice was good. Ossa was a pleasant little town, seemingly untouched by the Civil War raging around it. Aida rented a small room and after a few days found a job as a cashier in a cinema. They began to live a very frugal life, saving as much money as possible.

The cinema she worked in employed a blind pianist who provided music for the silent screen action. Yes, a *blind* pianist — a severe mismatch of capabilities to requirements, one would have thought. However, to overcome this drawback the management would hire a young person to sit alongside him and keep him apprised of what was happening on the screen.

That's where Nina and Nusia entered the scene. In the evenings they would take turns to sit next to him and describe the action. They loved it. Going to the cinema was not a normal feature of their previous lives, so this had the hallmarks of a holiday. Not only did they see some fascinating films, but they were even paid for the pleasure. Much later in life Nusia, at the age of ninety, still remembered a film she saw there called *Love Is As Vast As The Sea, Mere Shores Cannot Contain It*. It left a lasting impression on her. 'It was so romantic,' she would say with a deep sigh.

One day Nusia was sitting on a park bench near the cinema when a tall, dark-haired stranger came up to her and introduced himself as Nicholas Kozlov. He said he was her uncle, her mother's brother. After talking with her for a while, he gave her a one-rouble note, telling her he was too busy at work to come and see her mother.

Nusia related this incident to Aida.

'May the Lord be with him,' was her reply.

Apparently her brother was an ardent Communist who had, in earlier days, been involved in political arguments with Leonid so bitter that Nicholas had once even threatened to kill his brother-in-law. This had obviously soured the sister–brother relationship, and one could therefore understand his reluctance to pay Aida a visit — especially as Leonid was now with the White Army, fighting the Bolsheviks.

After a month or so, Aida's sister, Tonia, arrived. I have no idea how she found them. Aida was happy to see her. She now had someone close to talk to and with whom to share experiences. Life became more tolerable, but not for long. Because that is when Jenia disappeared.

Tonia looked after the youngest child, Nadia, while Aida was at work. Nusia, Nina and Len went to school and Jenia, who was five, went to kindergarten. Her mother would take her there in the morning and collect her after work. The kindergarten also served as an orphanage. The orphans lived in, while the other children attended on a daily basis.

One evening when Aida arrived to pick Jenia up, she was nowhere to be found. A search of the orphanage proved fruitless. Aida was beside herself. What could have become of her little daughter?

What had happened was this: it had been a cold winter's day and four or five of the children, including Jenia, were bundled into a sleigh, covered up to their necks with blankets and whisked off to another orphanage in an unknown location. Although the children were not told where they were going, none of them complained. To them it was an exciting outing and they squealed with delight as the countryside whizzed by. The journey took several hours and they stopped on the way to have a meal.

The orphanage, in a remote village, turned out to be just an ordinary house with a few children in it. The reason for the sudden transfer remains unclear, but it seems likely the owners had decided to transform their house into an orphanage. Apparently the government provided subsidies on a 'per orphan' basis, and the owners wanted to stock up quickly to make some easy money. So a deal was struck and the orphans transferred, with Jenia accidentally caught up in the plot. Then again, they may have been kidnapped. Who knows? Those were strange times.

At any rate, a distraught Aida started a frantic search. But she was frustrated at every step by an inefficient and hostile officialdom which was busy protecting its rear. In spite of her determined efforts, it was not until spring, some four months later, that Jenia was located. It was yet another few weeks before she was loaded on to a carriage for the return journey.

When the driver, with Jenia by his side, stopped outside their old address in Ossa, they found Aida's family had moved out and no-one knew where they were. Could they have left town without Jenia? Surely not … They drove to the orphanage, where there was now a new supervisor. A rude and surly woman, she neither knew the family's whereabouts nor exhibited any desire to help. Nor did she want Jenia left with her. 'Don't even think about it,' she cautioned the driver. 'Just take her back where she came from.'

Fortunately, the driver turned out to be a kind man. He could have just dumped her in the street, but instead he wiped away her tears with his sleeve and, taking her little hand in his, said, 'Let's go for a walk to see if anyone recognises you.'

Off they went, walking slowly through the town, with the driver stopping every so often to ask shopkeepers and passers-by if they recognised Jenia. Nobody did. Then Jenia suddenly heard someone scream out her name. She turned around. And there was Nusia waving to her from the front yard of a house. Screams, hugs, tears of joy! She was back home again! As Aida was out, the driver left Jenia in Aunt Tonia's care, but only after obtaining a receipt from her for the returned, and apparently undamaged, merchandise.

Tonia decided to surprise her sister on her return from work, and hid Jenia under the bed. Aida nearly had a fit when the laughing Jenia crawled out and ran to her. The five-year-old did not seem to be fazed by the whole experience. If anything, she appeared to enjoy it. In later years she remembered with pleasure the two journeys, especially the return one, when she was allowed to sit alongside the driver as they sped through beautiful valleys and forests, still covered with a thin layer of snow.

Since arriving in Ossa, Aida had been constantly trying to discover Leonid's whereabouts. There were conflicting rumours about the location of his battalion. This was further complicated by the fact that, in May 1919, the 1st Kazan Battalion was renamed the 49th Kazan Battalion. Aida did not know of this change and all she could discover was that the White forces had been pushed into Siberia and were in full flight.

And at the same time, Leonid of course did not know where Aida and the family were either. To all intents and purposes they were lost to each other in this vast country in the midst of a revolution.

Weeks passed before Aida finally received what she thought was reliable information—that the White Army was now either in Habarovsk or Vladivostok, in eastern Siberia. If that's where the Army is, that's where we should go, she told herself. But that was far, far away and she did not have enough money for the train tickets. To save up, they began to live even more frugally, putting aside every penny they could.

It was nearly a year after their arrival in Ossa that Aida felt she was ready to undertake the journey across Russia. Although her savings were still meagre, she was so keen to start that she was prepared to take a few risks.

'The Lord will look after us,' she maintained, hopefully.

Tonia thought her sister was mad to leave, but Aida was determined to go. Her invitation to her sister to join them was declined and they parted tearfully, knowing they were unlikely to ever see each other again.

Aida decided the first part of her journey would be to Irkutsk in Siberia, a large city 4000 kilometres from Ossa and about halfway to Vladivostok. To economise she took a risk and only bought two tickets for her five children. Whenever the conductor came through on his rounds, Aida would cover the three eldest with a blanket as if they were a pile of luggage and sit little Jenia and Nadia on top. Unbelievably, the subterfuge worked, even though the journey took more than two weeks.

On arrival in Irkutsk their money had just about run out. To continue the journey with a complement of five children was obviously impossible. If Aida were to continue her search, she would have to go alone. That way she could perhaps find her husband before the money ran out. She also felt it would give her more flexibility if something unexpected were to happen.

But with whom could she leave her children? Fortunately, she remembered somebody on the train telling her about an orphanage in the small town of Verhnyi-Udensk (now Ulan-Ude) some 300 kilometres past Irkutsk. But would they take her children? After all, they were not orphans. She tried to think of other alternatives but could not come up with any and decided to give the orphanage a try. They may feel sorry for us, she thought in desperation. After all, my children are well-behaved and shouldn't cause them any trouble.

Not wanting to spend any more of her meagre finances on train tickets to Verhnyi-Udensk, she took another risk. Through an enterprising act of forgery, she changed the destination name on the original tickets to Verhnyi-Udensk. So now they were travelling with three forged tickets for six passengers. And again they got away with it.

By the time they arrived in Verhnyi-Udensk, Aida had sold all she had of value, and had only enough money to buy a ticket for herself for the long journey ahead. All that was left of the food was half a bag of dried bread crusts. But her gamble paid off. The officials in the orphanage took pity on the family and accepted the children, now aged thirteen, twelve, eleven, six and four, on the understanding they would stay for only a brief time. Aida promised that as soon as she found their father she would send the money for their train tickets to rejoin her.

The parting was heart-rending, with the five siblings desperately clinging to their mother, begging her not to leave them, and Aida crying and at the same time trying to console them.

'Don't worry, my pets,' she said. 'It's only for a short time. I'll find Daddy and we'll all be together again.'

She asked them to promise they would look after each other and always stay together. And then she was gone, leaving them the half bag of dried bread crusts.

The children cried and cried. Now they really felt like orphans. The last time she had left any of them was five years ago when she went to Warsaw to visit father with the infant Jenia. But now she had left them, not just for a short visit, but to venture out into the unknown. It was heartbreaking and frightening. The only thing that gave them some degree of consolation was the fact mother had promised they would only be apart for a short time.

This 'short time' turned out to be more than two years.

FIVE LITTLE ORPHANS: 1920–1922

As the orphanage was for girls only, Len was to be transferred to a boys' institution the following day. Allowing him to sleep in the girls' dormitory would have been against the rules, so a cot was set up for him in the hallway. Before going to bed the four sisters came to say goodnight and they all had another good cry.

It was a cold night and Len asked Nusia if he could put her overcoat on top of his blankets. Nusia ran off to get it and the sisters then tucked him in, gave him a kiss and went off to bed.

In the morning, Len was nowhere to be found. He was not in the house or the yard or the street. Missing also was Nusia's overcoat and the half bag of dried bread crusts which their mother had left for them.

Len's disappearance from the orphanage was a terrible shock to the sisters, especially the two eldest, Nusia and Nina. Their mother had specifically asked them to look after the three younger siblings—after all, she had just gone through the trauma of losing Jenia in Ossa and she dreaded the thought of anything like that happening again, especially while she was away. And yet they had lost their brother just one day after she left!

They had no idea what happened to him. Was he kidnapped? Was he lying frozen to death in some snow-covered field? The police were informed and 'missing persons' advertisements were placed in newspapers, with no result. Nusia and Nina felt guilty, miserable and powerless. All they could do was pray every night for his safe return.

The orphanage was a long single-storeyed house on a large plot of land, surrounded by a tall fence. It had four windows looking out on to the street, each with wooden shutters that were closed at night. The entrance hall was spacious, about four metres by four, and its main feature was a large bucket of water and a basin. This was where the orphans washed themselves every morning; there were no other bathing facilities. Once a week, they were all taken to the town's communal bathhouse for a hot scrub.

From the entrance hall, a door led to the manager's room — the girls' nickname for him was *choobastyi*, that is a person with a *choob* (tuft of hair, with the head shaven around it). Another door led to a dining room running the length of the house, with a large table in the middle. From there a door led to the dormitory, which was the same size as the dining room and contained about twenty beds. All the girls were under sixteen. All were orphans except the four Tarasov girls.

There were regular studies, especially in the long winter months, and it was here that Nina received the only lengthy formal schooling she could remember. Over two years of it. All the rest of the time it had been somewhat piecemeal.

The Siberian winters were cold and miserable. As there were not enough warm clothes to go around, outdoor activities were kept to a minimum. Unfortunately, going to the toilet meant going out into the cold, a most unpleasant experience. The outside toilet was behind the kitchen and through a fence. Roofless, it consisted of a long trench with two planks on either side for the feet. Bad enough in summer, it was horrible in winter: there was always snow and ice on the ground and on the planks. As most of the girls lacked proper shoes, they would run out in their socks, which were normally homemade of either thin leather or thick material. Squatting over the hole for any reasonable length of time made the soles of the socks stick to the planks, and they would then have to either tear them off or leave the frozen socks behind and run home barefoot. To avoid this happening the girls learned to lift their feet one after the other, while squatting. Fortunately the girls were not required to go out for the passing of water, as there were large buckets for that purpose inside the building.

Summer was far more pleasant. Study periods were shortened and various outdoor activities organised. A favourite pastime was visiting the nearby woods to collect berries and mushrooms. The children also regularly tended a vegetable garden which they planted on the banks of a nearby stream. Summer was the time for long walks, for running around and for lying on the grass. These were relatively happy days.

All the girls had scheduled domestic duties. After dinner, when everything was cleaned up, the staff organised some interesting and productive activities. A favourite one was the art workshop. Large coloured rolls of used telegraph paper tape would be brought in and the girls would pleat it into various handicraft items, such as Christmas decorations, baskets and flowers, which were sold to help make ends meet.

Often, especially in winter, the girls would sit by the fire and sing — a typically Russian pastime. One of them wrote a poem about life in the orphanage which became such a favourite with the girls that one of them suggested it be sung to the tune of a popular song. From then on, no singing session would pass without it being sung at least once.

Seventy-nine years later Jenia, at the age of eighty-five, was able to recall the exact words of this heart-breaking song:

The candle is burning low, and all the girls should be asleep.
Choopastyi is doing his rounds
Making sure all the girls are sleeping peacefully.
But one girl, with her head bowed on her breast, is sad and cannot sleep.
'Oh, mother, dear mother, why did you bring me into this world?
You have burdened me with a cruel fate.
You have placed me into an orphanage.
I am wearing the orphan's uniform, and obeying their rules.
I am now thin and haggard and working hard,
While you are lying peacefully in your grave,
Not knowing what's happened to me.
I wish you could know how sad my heart is.
There is no-one left to look after me and protect me.'

The kitchen stood in the backyard, about fifteen metres behind the house. There were stories it was haunted. The cook, a crusty old woman who lived in a room adjoining the kitchen, used to tell the children that, during the early days of the Revolution, many Whites were tortured and executed there and their bodies dumped into a large mass grave without any burial service or prayers. 'The souls of the victims are not at peace,' the cook would say. 'Their spirits often roam the orphanage, especially the kitchen. Phantom footsteps, strange shadows, voices …' Every evening, two of the girls would be rostered to kitchen duties and, after cleaning up, would sleep there. Needless to say none of them were enthusiastic about this, but there was no way out of it.

One very hot night, Nina was one of those rostered and she and the other girl decided to sleep on the kitchen porch. The light in the kitchen was on, so they felt reasonably safe. In the middle of the night Nina woke up and, looking up at the open door leading to the kitchen, saw an old man in rags, leaning against the door. She screamed, everyone woke up and the vision disappeared.

When Nina told the cook what she had seen, the old woman assured her there was nothing to worry about.

'He often visits us,' she said.

At the age of eighty-six Nina still had a clear recollection of that frightening apparition.

Eighteen months passed before the children heard from their mother — a joyous letter saying she had found Father in Vladivostok and their brother Len was there with her. Their joy on hearing from mother was eclipsed only by the overwhelming relief they felt on hearing Len was alive. The unjustified load of guilt they had carried on their shoulders for so long was finally lifted.

Aida's letter said Leonid was well and working as a sales clerk in Kunst-Albert. In fact he was still with the White Army, but she was afraid to write this in case the letter was intercepted. She had always instructed her children not to tell anyone their father was an officer in the White Army. Aida concluded the letter by saying she was praying to God to look after her children and she promised to arrange to get them out as soon as possible. In the meantime she would write often.

THE SEARCH FOR MOTHER: 1920

The eleven-year-old Len had not shared his escape plan from the orphanage with any of his sisters because he was afraid they would talk him out of it or, worse still, tell the manager of the orphanage. He had earlier decided there was no way he would allow himself to be separated from both his mother and his sisters. When he had asked the manager whether he could stay with the girls, the manager told him that this was absolutely impossible. 'But don't worry,' he assured him. 'We'll find a nice place for you.'

But where would that be? How far away? Would it be some place like the one Jenia was 'kidnapped' to? And what about mother? Would she be able to survive out in the unknown, all by herself? The possible answers to these questions filled him with fear — and determination. He convinced himself that the only course of action left for him was to catch up with Aida, in spite of the fact she had a head start. After all, he knew she was heading in the direction of Vladivostok, so it shouldn't be difficult to find her, he thought.

By the time he had made up his mind to follow her, night had fallen and, wisely, he decided to leave his escape to the following morning. That night he could not sleep. The excitement and fear of the forthcoming escapade kept him tossing and turning. At first light he put on his clothes and Nusia's heavy overcoat, picked up the half sack of dried bread and crept quietly out of the orphanage. Nobody heard him leave.

The railway station was about a kilometre away and he got there just as the sun was rising. A train was standing at the platform. He tried to sneak on board, but the stationmaster saw him and pulled him off by the scruff of his neck.

'Where the hell do you think you're going?' he demanded.

Len put on a sterling performance, telling him he had missed the earlier train which had taken his mother 'to the East' and that he was desperate to catch up with her. 'I'm alone in the world without my mama,' he said. 'I have to follow her but I don't have any money for a ticket. Please help me, sir! Please help me!'

At first the stationmaster did not believe him, but Len's act finally convinced him.

'Take this little brat on board,' he told the guard, 'but make sure you throw him off at Chita. I don't ever want to see his ugly face again.'

They were not terribly sympathetic to his plight. In those days there were thousands of orphaned and homeless children roaming around, all starving, all looking like little hobos, all pains in the neck.

Chita was 500 kilometres away but with its slow speed and many lengthy stops the train took three days to cover the distance. In Chita Len was duly ejected. He was now on his own. No mother, no sisters, no home, no money, no idea what to do next.

There was not a soul in sight on the snow-covered platform. The place looked deserted, but on opening the door to the large waiting room, Len was surprised to find it packed with refugees, literally hundreds of them, clutching small bundles of possessions, frightened looks on their faces. As he wound his way through this mass of humanity with all its smells and noises he suddenly heard his name called out. He turned and …

Aida was sitting in a corner on the cement floor with her back to the bare wall, waving feebly to him. She looked terrible, white as a sheet, frail, helpless, obviously sick. Len rushed to her and began to stroke her face.

'Mummy, mummy! What's wrong with you?'

It was a great effort for her to speak. When she did it was barely a whisper. Haltingly she related how she had spent the last of her money for a ticket to Vladivostok and how she had been off-loaded in Chita because she did not have a permit to travel any further. Chita, which was by then in Red hands, was the junction of the Trans-Siberian Railway and the Chinese Eastern Railway (CER). Both railways led to Vladivostok, with the Trans-Siberian proceeding through Russian territory and Habarovsk, and the CER going through Manchuria and Harbin. However, while the Trans-Siberian led to the Civil War zone and was off-limits, the CER led to a foreign country. Both routes required a permit and Aida did not have one or any knowledge of how to get one.

After walking around the waiting room to see if she could find someone in authority, she had suddenly felt faint and nauseous. As all the seats were taken, she sat down on the floor in a corner, where she collapsed and lost consciousness. She had no idea how long she had been there.

Fearing she would die without seeing her children ever again, she was overjoyed to see Len and was now hugging and kissing him, tears streaming down her face.

A stranger saw this poignant scene and came up to inquire what was wrong. They told him of their plight, and the man decided to help. On a piece of paper he wrote a few lines describing their situation and how desperately they needed help, and then instructed Len to walk among the crowds in the waiting room, showing them the note. Perhaps a few would donate some money. The paper had a space for them to write their names and the amounts they donated. This was designed to give potential donors a modicum of assurance that Len was not operating some sort of scam. After all, he did look and act like a dirty little beggar.

Even though each donation was small, Len collected quite a bit of money. As a result Aida's spirits brightened. The stranger told her she should see the stationmaster to obtain a permit. With difficulty, she got up and shuffled slowly to the office where, through the combination of her good looks, emotional pleas and a small bribe, she convinced the stationmaster she was going to the front to be reunited with her Bolshevik officer husband whom she had not seen for years. Aida and Len received their permit.

'I think they're fighting somewhere around Habarovsk by now,' the stationmaster volunteered. 'Good luck.'

After boarding the next train, it became obvious Aida was very sick indeed. She could not sit up and she became delirious. A fellow passenger who claimed to be a doctor examined her and diagnosed typhoid fever. He told the guard of the infectious nature of the disease and Aida and Len were unceremoniously ejected at the next station. They had only travelled 200 kilometres or so, and here they were again, dumped into a waiting room — a very sick woman, a boy, no money, no food, no hope.

Len ran around looking for someone to help his mother and finally found an official who had the authority to arrange for her to be taken to the local hospital. Len was then told he would be taken to a children's home, but he yelled and screamed, refusing to be parted from his mother yet again. He got his way and was taken to the hospital, where he was given a bed alongside Aida's and he stayed there for the full two months of her recovery, feeding her, combing her hair, taking out her bedpans and doing all sorts of other chores given to him by an unsympathetic hospital staff. But Len was happy to do whatever they asked, provided he could be with his mother.

As Aida began to recover and get some colour back into her cheeks, her beauty became evident to her doctor, who developed a strong attraction to her. Sensing this, she decided to tell him the truth about her plight. This was quite a risk. He was a Red and he could easily have turned her in to the authorities. Fortunately her intuition had not deserted her. On hearing her story he was deeply moved and assured her he would do everything possible to help her.

When she was fully recovered the doctor gave Aida some money, dressed her in a nurse's uniform and loaded her and Len on to a military Red Cross train headed for the Red forces in Habarovsk. Aida was grateful, but at the same time apprehensive. After all, she did not even know how to bandage a finger, let alone nurse wounded soldiers. The fear her masquerade would be uncovered was constantly with her, but somehow or other everything went well.

Still, she knew they would have to leave the train before it arrived in Habarovsk, so, when the train stopped for a few minutes at a tiny station one night, they slipped off and hid in the waiting room until it departed.

The station was deserted. Not a soul in sight. Not a single light visible anywhere. As there was obviously nothing they could do until morning, they arranged themselves on the waiting room benches and quickly fell asleep.

A kindly voice woke them up.

'What are you doing here, my children?'

An old man dressed in a priest's cassock was standing over them. Aida, who was deeply religious and believed all priests were saints-in-waiting, told him the full story. Father Filoleyev listened with obvious sympathy.

'Come and stay in my rectory,' he said. 'There's room for two more and you can leave when you are ready.'

And there they lived for about four months. To help repay his kindness Aida cooked and did the washing and cleaning for him, while Len did odd jobs such as making candles for the church. The priest told them the headquarters of the White Army was now in Vladivostok and Aida wrote there seeking information about her husband. Soon she received a reply direct from Leonid together with some money for the journey.

It is not clear how Aida and Len managed to get to Vladivostok but in late 1920, seven months after leaving the orphanage at Verhnyi-Udensk, they were reunited with Leonid. They had been separated from him for two and a half years.

Leonid was horrified at his son's appearance and manners. Len was lacking in social graces,

Aida in nurse's uniform, 1920

did not obey any rules, had no respect for the law, and behaved like a little savage — albeit an enterprising little savage. To straighten him out, Len was immediately enrolled as a boarder in the Far Eastern branch of the Omsk Military Academy, where he was only let out to see his family on Sunday afternoons. Indeed, the two and a half years he spent within the strict rigorous military regime of the academy did transform him into a polite well-behaved little soldier.

Len's escape from the orphanage and his search for his mother was, undeniably, a courageous act for a small boy. One should be grateful he did this. His actions probably saved her life. On the other hand, he was unbelievably lucky to have found her at all. He could have been lost forever — and he did cause untold anguish to Nusia and Nina.

THE ORPHAN TRAIN: 1922

In Aida's original letter to her daughters in Verhnyi-Udensk she promised to make urgent arrangements to get them to Vladivostok. She also promised to write regularly and keep them posted on progress. This she did but, mysteriously, none of the letters ever reached her children. So the girls' joy at hearing from their mother was soon replaced by an overwhelming concern at the lack of any further news. Weeks of waiting turned to months, during which Aida was also beside herself with worry. In each of her letters, she had asked them to reply but no replies ever came.

Convinced that something must have happened to her daughters, Aida seriously considered travelling the 4000 kilometres back to the orphanage to pick them up, but Leonid would not let her go.

'It's far too dangerous,' he reasoned. 'There's a war on and the mail system must be in chaos. Write a letter every week and one of them is bound to get through.'

Back at the orphanage, Nina was getting more and more restless. Even though Nusia was the eldest, Nina, with the more assertive and action-oriented personality, had become the leader of the four children. Convinced of the need to do something, she asked the manager if there was any way for them to get to Vladivostok by themselves.

'Sure there is,' he answered. 'All you need is money, which is something neither you nor I have.'

Nina went to the railway station and asked the stationmaster if there was some way they could get on the train without a ticket.

'Not as long as I'm stationmaster,' was his gruff reply.

Then one day the orphanage manager informed Nina that, in a few days, a special train bound for Vladivostok would be coming through Verhnyi-

Udensk, picking up stray orphans along the way. Even though the Tarasovs were not orphans, he knew how anxious they were to leave and told Nina he could probably arrange for them to join the train.

It was a frightening prospect — the long journey, four little girls on a train without their mother — but Nina decided it was worth the risk. It was certainly better than waiting. She told the other three of her plans and they agreed. They trusted Nina and they were desperate to see their mother again.

Nina asked the manager to write and tell their mother they were leaving, asking her to keep an eye out for the train when it arrived in Vladivostok. He did write, but unfortunately he was not able to tell her when it was due to arrive. Nobody seemed to know.

Two days later, the four sisters boarded the 'orphan train'.

Leaving the orphanage was a mixture of both joy and sorrow — joy at the anticipation of seeing their mother again, and sorrow at leaving the people who had given them shelter for over two years and the friends they knew they would never see again. There were tears, hugs, kisses, best wishes.

The orphan train turned out to be a goods train. The wagons had plank beds set up in neat rows, about a foot and a half above the floor. Each had a mattress, a sheet, a pillow and a blanket. There were about 500 children in all, of many races — Russians, Tartars, Armenians, Georgians, Mongols. All orphans. The train was to stop at each station on the Trans-Siberian Railway to pick up new orphans. In addition, the local population was advised in advance of the train's arrival and encouraged to meet it and adopt an orphan or two.

At each stop the children were required to come out of the wagons and show themselves. Some were anxious to be adopted and paraded themselves, hoping to be among the chosen ones. Others stayed in the background, afraid of the uncertainty of it all, terrified of the future. The locals would walk around, peering into the children's eyes, trying to find some spark which would ignite their parental feelings, perhaps someone who reminded them of their dead child, or someone with blonde curls or big dark eyes or a nice smile or whatever. There were many emotional scenes — happiness, when a union was consummated; sadness and even despair when a child was not wanted by anyone, yet again; and tragedy when a brother-and-sister pair was broken up because only one was chosen.

Nina asked an official what they should say to anybody who wanted to adopt them.

'Tell them you're not orphans, but are on the way to meet your parents and therefore not available,' he said.

At one station a woman in black took an immediate liking to the six-year-old Nadia, but Nina gave her the party line.

'We're not orphans. We're not available.'

The woman did not seem to understand this and went on patting and stroking Nadia's head. 'You will never see your mother again,' she murmured to little Nadia. 'She is probably dead. Stay with me. I'll make you happy'.

With tears in her eyes she implored Nina to let Nadia go. She refused. Nadia, on the other hand, did not resist. The little girl was starved for affection and enjoyed this loving attention. That gave the woman renewed hope and she continued to plead with Nina, who had to eventually fetch an official to tell the woman the Tarasov sisters were not orphans. This finally convinced her. Downcast, she gave Nadia one final kiss.

'I will pray to God that you see your mother soon,' were her parting words.

This scene left a deep impression on Nina and she decided that, in future, neither Nadia nor Jenia would be allowed to come out on the platforms. The younger ones were, of course, the most popular and were amongst the first to be adopted. They were the cute, cuddly ones. Nina and Nusia, being thirteen and fourteen, were less desirable and could therefore show their faces with reasonable safety.

As the train rumbled towards Vladivostok the number of children left grew smaller and smaller. Apparently the intake of new orphans was less than the outgoings.

And that is when misfortune struck.

Jenia contracted trachoma, a highly infectious disease of the eyes, and her affliction became quite evident to the train officials. As she obviously needed urgent medical attention, they decided to offload her in the next town, Nicholsk-Ussuriysk (now called Ussuriysk). By that time the only ones remaining on the train were the four Tarasov girls and about eighteen boys in their mid-teens — the rejects, the undesirables. Let's face it, who would want a typically rebellious teenager for a new son?

From previous experience the officials knew that if they offloaded Jenia they would have to offload all four of them. The Tarasov tribe refused to be separated. This gave the train crew the idea of terminating the journey of the orphan train there and then. What was the point of going on to Vladisvostok, they reasoned. Nobody is likely to adopt the teenage boys anyway, and if we go to Vladisvostok they'll probably load us up with more undesirables and we'll have our hands full again on the return trip.

So the girls were offloaded in Nicholsk-Ussuriysk and the train with the teenagers still on board went back to Moscow.

Imagine the girls' anguish. After travelling on the train for over 4000 kilometres, they had been unceremoniously dumped and had no idea how or when they would be able to complete their journey. They would have been even more upset had they known they were only one hundred kilometres short of their destination.

THE RAILWAY TOWN: 1922

Nicholsk-Ussuriysk was mainly populated by railway workers and their families. When the four girls were offloaded, the train officials asked the head of the railway community to take Jenia to the hospital and to house the other three girls with local families. Before leaving, the officials promised to advise Aida of her daughters' whereabouts.

Jenia was taken to the hospital but Nina, who had become the self-appointed head of the family, became concerned at being separated from her, afraid she may never see her sister again. The memories of Jenia's and Len's disappearances were still fresh in her mind. However, the official allayed Nina's fears by producing a hospital document stating that Jenia had been admitted and would be there for at least a month.

After a few hours of waiting on the platform, the frightened, apprehensive and exhausted girls were taken to a large office. There were three couples there, each of whom had been advised that one of the girls was to live with them temporarily and that they were to be sent on to their parents as soon as Jenia was discharged from hospital. The Malov couple took Nusia, the Vassilievs took Nadia, and the Toporkovs took Nina.

As with so many railway towns, all the houses looked the same — single-storeyed with a bedroom, kitchen, dining room, laundry, a small entrance hall and a tiny front garden. But when Nina entered her benefactors' house and was led into the dining room she was amazed to see a table loaded with the sort of foods she had not seen for years — butter, sour cream, lard, sausages.

'Before we start to eat, let's get acquainted,' the man said. 'I'm Alexander Ivanovich and my wife is Evdokia Vassilievna'.

This was quite a mouthful and Nina asked them if she could just call them Uncle and Aunt. They readily agreed and suggested the names of Uncle Shura (a short for Alexander) and Aunt Dusia (a short for Evdokia). (Don't ask me why the Russians are christened with long names which are then immediately replaced by shorter names used for the rest of their lives.)

After the abundant dinner Nina asked Aunt Dusia if they could go and visit Nadia and Nusia to see how they were. This they did. Both were fine, and Nadia was already asleep on the couch.

The next day, after breakfast, Nina and Aunt Dusia caught a bus to the hospital to visit Jenia. Trachoma is a very painful disease. The insides of the eyelids are covered with sores and have to be treated with regular applications of a silver nitrate solution, a very unpleasant process. Although Jenia was in pain, she was relieved to see Nina and hear how she and the other two sisters were faring. Before leaving, Aunt Dusia promised her they would come and visit her every few days.

Aunt Dusia and her husband were warm-hearted, considerate people. They were giving refuge to a child out of the kindness of their hearts. There was nothing in it for them. They were not paid, they could not adopt her and they knew it was only temporary, but they still did everything they could to make the child's stay with them as pleasant as possible. Nina was very grateful and constantly helped Aunt Dusia with the housework and cooking, and also spent many hours telling her about the orphanage, her mother and the orphan train. As promised, they visited Jenia regularly and brought her all sorts of delicacies.

After about a month they were told Jenia was well enough to leave hospital, and the Tarasov children were now ready to re-commence their journey. Officials wrote to Aida in Vladivostok advising her of this. Now it was only a question of receiving a reply and making the travel arrangements. But no reply came. Weeks passed and there was still no word. Aunt Dusia tried to console the girls by saying things took longer in times of revolution. So they waited and waited.

Little did they know their mother was no longer in Vladivostok.

In the meantime, Nusia was living with the Malov family and Nadia with the Vassilievs, while Jenia has moved in with the Toporkovs. The Malovs were not as warm a couple as the Toporkovs, but life was still eminently bearable. Anyway, Nusia consoled herself with the fact this was only temporary.

On the other hand the Vassilievs had developed a very close attachment to the six-year-old Nadia and were treating her like their own child — and Nadia was enjoying this life of relative luxury and revelling in the care, attention and love being showered upon her. What alerted Aunt Dusia to possible problems was the fact that Nadia had begun calling the Vassilievs 'Mama' and 'Papa'. There were also some rumours they were planning to take her away somewhere, maybe even kidnap her, so as not to give her up when the time came.

This information horrified Nina and she, Aunt Dusia and Uncle Shura hatched up a rescue plan. That evening they went to the Vassiliev house and Uncle Shura told them the permit to send the children to their mother had been received (this was, of course, not true) and Nadia and her sisters would be leaving the next morning. He said he had been instructed to get all of the sisters together at their home that night in readiness for the journey.

The Vassilievs were most upset and begged Uncle Shura to let Nadia stay with them for one more night. He refused. They pleaded, but Uncle Shura would not budge — and Nadia was led away. From then on, three of the four girls lived with the Toporkovs, all sleeping on the living-room floor.

During that period there was constant fighting around Nicholsk-Ussuriysk between the Red and White Armies. At first the Whites had the superior forces, but the Reds were reinforced, became better organised and began to dominate. It was interesting to note that most of the population was not really involved in the Civil War, nor did it take sides. They just wanted peace as soon as possible. It did not really matter to them who the winners were as long as they were Russians.

One night, when the town was still occupied by the Whites, the population was awakened by gunfire. Firstly rifle shots, then machine-guns and artillery. The frightened inhabitants spent most of the night lying on the floor of their homes. By morning the fighting had stopped and the word got around that the Reds were about to enter the town. Everyone rushed to the main street to welcome the victorious forces. First one could hear the sounds of a military band, and then the conquering forces came into view, a brass band ahead of the cavalry, followed by the marching troops. Red flags and patriotic banners were everywhere, and even the instruments in the band were decorated with red ribbons. It all looked immensely impressive and triumphant.

The people cheered; bread and salt (a traditional gift of greeting) were offered to the commanding officer; women came out with baskets of fruit and jugs of *kvas* (a drink made from fermented bread); Cavalry officers lifted laughing children up on their horses. There was a real holiday atmosphere. Great fun was had by all.

A few weeks later the whole process was repeated and the situation reversed. Gunfire in the night, fear and trepidation, and in the morning the news that the Whites had retaken the town! Once again brass bands, troops, cavalry, cheers, children on horses, bread and salt, fruit and *kvas*. This time, however, the parade was led by a priest in his white celebratory robes, and the red banners were replaced with the tri-colour white, blue and red flags. But it was fun-time once again. As far as the population was concerned they were all Russian, they were all 'ours' and they were all welcome.

These transitions of power occurred a few times before the final Red takeover.

REUNION: 1922

When Aida received the letter from the orphanage advising her that her children were on the orphan train she was immensely relieved. Luckily, that letter did get through. She was already beginning to lose hope of ever seeing them again. However the stationmaster could not tell her when the train would arrive as it would be stopping at every station, sometimes for days.

She continued to visit the station daily for possible news, but there was none. And then a bombshell! She was informed the train was not coming to Vladivostok. They had got rid of most of the orphans and the train was on its way back to Moscow. Aida was aghast. What has happened to her girls? Where are they? What can she do? Whom can she turn to?

Her anxiety was relieved when, a few days later, she received notification from the officials in Nicholsk-Ussuriysk that the girls had been offloaded there, that Jenia would be in hospital for a while, and that Aida would be advised as soon as they were ready to travel again.

'I'll go to Nicholsk-Ussuriysk and bring them back here,' she told Leonid. But he warned her against this. 'The Reds are close,' he said. 'There's fighting everywhere. If they discover you are the wife of a White colonel they'll rape you and then shoot you. It's safer to let the children come by themselves as soon as Jenia recovers. Let's be patient. It'll be all right.'

Reluctantly, Aida had to agree with the logic. But events overtook them. Nicholsk-Ussuriysk was abandoned by the Whites on 14 October 1922 and it became obvious Vladivostok would fall soon after. It was time for the White forces and their families to either flee the country or face imprisonment or execution. As the writing had been on the wall for some time, preparations for the evacuation had already been made.

The White exodus was via land and sea. By land the Chinese allowed the Whites to enter Manchuria at Hunchun and settle temporarily in Girin (now called Jilin). There were about 7000 of them, with Leonid, Aida and Len in that lot. Those escaping from Nicholsk-Ussuriysk went across the border at Pogranichnaya. The numbers here are not known. Most of these Whites eventually found their way to Harbin, 200 kilometres north.

The sea evacuation was more dramatic. There was only one passenger ship available, the *Laurestan*, and it had left earlier with 400 people who could afford the price of a ticket to Shanghai. The rest, about 9000 of them, were loaded on thirty old navy ships — destroyers, patrol boats, troop carriers, tugs, ice-breakers. Most of the vessels had not been used for years. All were dilapidated, rusted and not seaworthy. The fleet limped along to the Korean port of Genzan (now called Wonsan). As the journey to Shanghai was considerably longer, only the most seaworthy ships went on, carrying some 3000. The rest stayed in Korea for about nine months, aided by the Japanese Red Cross. Most of them eventually moved by land to Harbin.

Vladivostok fell to the Reds on 22 October 1922. The Civil War, which had begun in 1917 and ended in Europe in 1920, had taken another two years to finally end in Siberia. It is estimated some one and a half million refugees fled Russia during the Revolution, the majority to Europe. Most of them felt the Communist experiment would soon fail and they would be able to return home. But this was not to be.

Aida was most upset at the necessity to leave Vladivostok before her children could come, but she had no choice. As soon as they arrived in Girin she remembered she had a girlfriend living in Pogranichnaya, a small town near the Manchurian border some 250 kilometres from Nicholsk-Ussuriysk and, with her husband's blessing, she took a train there. On arrival she promptly sent a letter to the Nicholsk-Ussuriysk officials asking them to write to her in Pogranichnaya as soon as her children were ready to leave. 'And may God

Leonid, Vladivostok, 1921

bless you for all your kindness,' she added. She sent no money for the tickets — she had no money to send — hoping someone, somehow would fund this trip. The fact the officials had already written to Aida was not known to her as she had left Vladivostok before the letter arrived.

But there was a further delay. For unknown reasons the official who received Aida's letter from Pogranichnaya sat on it and did nothing. The Tarasov girls were ready to go but there was no news from their mother. Nina was becoming increasingly worried. Was mother still alive? Will they ever see her again? Finally, in desperation, she asked Aunt Dusia to take her to see the official. When they asked him if there had been a letter from Aida, he suddenly remembered he had filed it somewhere. A quick search uncovered it.

'Now get out and don't bother me again,' yelled the embarrassed official, handing Nina the letter.

When Uncle Shura went to buy the train tickets (with his own money) the stationmaster told him that anyone travelling to Manchuria needed an official permit. But the girls did not have one. After some discussion it was decided Nina and Nusia would go back to ask the official who had mislaid the letter for the permit. Perhaps his cold heart would soften at the sight of two pleading children. At first he said there was no-one in the town with the authority to issue such a permit, but seeing tears welling in their eyes he finally wrote something on a piece of paper, sealed it in an envelope and handed it to them.

The girls were beside themselves with joy. Their long interrupted journey could now be restarted. Uncle Shura sent a letter off to Aida informing her of the impending arrival of her daughters. On the day of departure Aunt Dusia handed them a small red suitcase filled with bread, sausages, butter and fruit. All the families who gave them shelter came to the station to see them off. It was a heart-rending scene.

The train left in the middle of the afternoon and the four girls sat there quietly, daydreaming about their reunion with their mother, occasionally dipping into the red suitcase for one thing or another. Towards evening the conductor and another official came through to check tickets and documents. Nina proudly handed over the tickets and the sealed envelope with the permit. When the conductor opened it he found a handwritten note saying 'These four children are going to Pogranichnaya to meet their mother' — and nothing else. No official rubber stamps, no important signatures.

'Is this all you have?' they asked. 'This is not a permit! You can't go anywhere with this! Whom are you trying to fool? Come on. Start collecting your things. You're getting off at the next station.'

The next station was Grodokova, only one stop short of Pogranichnaya. That really set the brood off. They put on quite a show, crying, screaming, pleading.

'Stop that!' the official yelled. 'It's not going to help. We'll be back in a few minutes. Make sure you're ready to get off.'

When he returned the young Tarasovs were still at it — crying, begging to be allowed to stay on the train until Pogranichnaya. By now they had learned that children's tears and pleadings often melted hearts and this gave them additional incentive to outdo themselves in this endeavour. And it worked! The two officials looked at each other, shrugged their shoulders and walked off. Reprieve!

As the train approached Pogranichnaya, all their little faces were glued to the window. It was now dark. Rain was falling. The train began to slow down and they finally saw the dimly lit platform come into view. This was the moment they had been waiting for. Their eyes desperately searched the platform for their mother. Where was she?

Finally they saw her standing under a lamppost, her head covered by a black scarf and her long black cloak glistening from the rain. She was thin and emaciated. Streaks of rain were running down her face as she anxiously peered into each carriage window. The girls saw her first and began to bang on their window, squealing with delight and yelling 'Mummy, Mummy!' at the top of their voices. Although she could not hear them through the window, she eventually caught sight of the four excited faces and the flailing arms. Rushing over, she pressed her hands against the glass. The train was still moving as she walked alongside of it, her hands caressing the window, tears pouring down her cheeks.

When the train stopped the girls rushed out, crying and laughing, covering their mother's face with kisses, embracing her and burying their faces in her wet cloak. It was the happiest moment of their lives. They were a family again.

Aida took them to her friend's home where dinner was waiting, but the girls were too wound up to eat. They spent the night telling her excitedly about their adventures. They had been separated for over two years. With everything that had happened to them, it was indeed a miracle they were sitting there, in a normal house, all together again.

A week later Aida and her daughters caught the train back to Girin to join Leonid and Len. Shortly afterwards the whole family moved to Harbin to start a new life in a foreign country.

The two years in the orphanage at Verhnyi-Udensk; the 4000 kilometre journey on the orphan train; the stay with the railway families in Nicholsk-Ussuriysk; the final journey without a permit; and the near-ejection at Grodokova — none of these frightening, emotional experiences would be forgotten by the girls. Aida was forever grateful to Aunt Dusia and Uncle Shura. Over the years she sent them many presents in continued recognition of their generosity and kindness to her four 'orphan' daughters.

2 CHINA 1922–1937

HARBIN — 'MOSCOW OF THE ORIENT'

Harbin was, to all intents and purposes, a Russian city. Although it was in Manchuria, its Russian population in 1922 was close to 100,000. It boasted the largest European population of any city in Asia and was by far the largest Russian city outside Russia.

To understand what gave rise to this phenomenon, one has to delve into history. In the seventeenth century, Manchuria was a kingdom separate from China. Its inhabitants, the Manchus, were a militant race long harbouring a desire to conquer China. In 1644 they finally attacked and quickly overwhelmed it. The Manchus maintained a brilliant and powerful government until about 1800, after which they rapidly decayed in energy and ability, thus allowing significant exploitation of the country by foreign governments. The Manchu rule over China was finally overthrown in 1911 when a Chinese republic under Sun Yat-sen was born, with Manchuria as its northernmost province.

In the nineteenth century Manchuria, with its rich natural resources and small population, attracted the expansionary attention of many foreign governments, especially Russia and Japan. Russia yearned for control so as to improve its access to the Pacific Ocean, and Japan saw it as a logical step in the expansion of its tiny empire. Taking advantage of the Manchu rulers' weakened state, Russia bullied China into ceding to it the area between the Ussuri River and the Pacific Ocean, thus giving it an additional 800 kilometres of coastline on the Pacific Ocean. In 1870 the Russians began building Vladivostok and in 1872 the Russian Far Eastern naval base was transferred 1500 kilometres south, from Nikolaevsk to Vladivostok.

In 1897 the Russians scored another political win — a joint venture with China to build a railway across the top of Manchuria. Russia had begun building its Trans-Siberian Railway in 1891. It was to link Moscow with Vladivostok, a distance of 9200 kilometres. But rather than follow the Manchurian–Russian border past Chita, which would have taken the line through Habarovsk, the Russians realised that a line from Chita to Vladivostok through northern Manchuria would be nearly 1000 kilometres shorter, and the terrain would be easier. In addition, it would give Russia some significant political influence in Manchuria. China on the other hand saw this both as an opportunity to open up the sparsely populated region of northern Manchuria and a convenient deterrent to the ever-present threat of Japanese invasion.

The joint venture stipulated the Russians were to provide the rolling stock, all the skilled and some of the unskilled labour. The Chinese were to participate in the funding and the provision of the rest of the unskilled labour. The Russians were granted a ninety-nine-year lease over the line and the properties associated with it, together with the administrative rights to its operation. The line from Chita to Vladivostok was to be 1500 kilometres long and was to be named the Chinese Eastern Railway (CER).

As the line had to cross the Sungari River, a large tributary of the Amur River, the Russians began to look for an appropriate location for such a crossing, preferably halfway along the projected line, at which they would build a town to serve as their administrative headquarters and maintenance centre. As both the Sungari and the Amur rivers were navigable, and the Amur flowed into the Pacific, vital goods and materials could then be transported from Russia to this location, at least in the summer months — in the winter months both rivers were icebound.

In their search, they found a fishing and wheat-marketing village on the banks of the Sungari named Ha-erh-pin, Chinese for 'A Place to Dry Nets'. Re-naming it Harbin (which was easier for the Russians to pronounce), they began the task of transforming it into the CER headquarters. Harbin quickly grew into a major city housing thousands of Russian workers, engineers, administrators and their families. It also attracted a large band of Russian entrepreneurs looking for opportunities in the Far East. The CER project also resulted in an influx of Chinese from northern China, attracted by the earning opportunities of working for the Railway. By 1899 Harbin had a population of over 14,000.

The Boxer Rebellion caused a temporary setback to the development of the project. Boxer revolutionaries tore up railway tracks and pillaged railway stores, threatening the Russian population and causing a mass evacuation of women and children on ships and barges to Habarovsk. Russian warships were sent down the Sungari to Harbin, the revolutionaries were repelled, and the growth of the project and the city was re-commenced.

The CER was completed in 1901. In addition the Russians built a line from Harbin to Port Arthur, a distance of 950 kilometres. It was called the Southern Manchurian Railway (SMR) and was built on the same terms as the CER, except the lease was limited to eighty years. This lease was transferred to Japan after the Russian defeat in the Russo–Japanese war of 1905.

Daniloff's Opera Theatre, Harbin, 1900s

Street scene—all the shop signs are in Russian, Harbin, 1920s

By 1906 the Harbin population had reached 50,000. The Russians had transformed the Place to Dry Nets into a bustling European city of wide streets, imposing buildings and parks. As it grew, this city became known as the 'Moscow of the Orient'. The population prided itself on the fact that the

Trans-Siberian railway and the CER made Harbin closer to Europe than any other city in China. The journey to Paris only took nine days, whereas an ocean journey was more like five weeks.

The street and shop names were in Russian. All the large stores and enterprises were owned and operated by Russians, with only the smaller ones run by the Chinese. The produce sold was exclusively Russian. The Chinese learned to grow vegetables foreign to themselves, such as beetroot, parsley and dill. It was interesting to see how quickly the Chinese learned to speak some Russian. They seemed to be more talented than the Russians in picking up another language. Mind you they had to, as they were the providers of services, food and clothing, and to speak the language of the customer is crucial to the success of a business.

A significant aspect of the original agreement between Russia and China was the granting of extra-territoriality to the Russian population. This meant the Russians were given the right to run the local government administration, have their own police force and law courts and not pay any taxes to the Chinese government. (This right was rescinded in 1917 during the disarray of the Russian Civil War, and was never reinstated.)

Was it any wonder the refugees from the Russian Revolution made tracks for Harbin? It was like a home away from home. In fact, the large influx of White Russian refugees between 1917 and 1922 boosted the Russian population of Harbin to about 150,000, three times that of the Chinese. Harbin had become a small replica of old Russia — on Chinese soil.

A NEW BEGINNING: 1922

When the Tarasov family arrived in Harbin in November 1922 it was like returning to Russia, but without the Civil War. The fact it looked like a Russian town and Russian speech was heard everywhere was a very pleasant surprise. However, the huge influx of refugees did make life difficult, especially with accommodation and jobs. The local population was urged to open its doors, at least temporarily, to the new arrivals and many responded. Thus the Tarasovs were taken in by the Komlev family. Although they only had a smallish apartment — a bedroom, kitchen and verandah — they let the seven Tarasovs stay in the bedroom while papa and mama Komlev and their child moved into the kitchen.

The Komlevs were a wonderfully kind and generous family. Papa Komlev worked for CER as a draughtsman, earning just enough money to feed his own family, but even so they were willing to share what they had with the Tarasovs. In addition, the Harbin population established a communal kitchen for the refugees. Aida went there every day with a small bucket to fetch soup

Theatre and Café 'Decadence', Harbin, 1920s

Railway bridge across the Sungari River, 1930s

for the family. It was not much but it was better than nothing and it helped them survive the initial period.

After a while, Aida began to search for more permanent accommodation and eventually found a tiny house. It was old and rickety and rather depressing, but the rent was cheap. By that time the enterprising Aida was earning some money sewing clothes for retail stores and Leonid found a job in a brass band playing the tuba. Nobody in the family knew he could play the tuba and I'm sure he was no virtuoso, but apparently he played it well enough to get the job. Then again, maybe the orchestra was desperate. After all, there is never a profusion of tuba players. Their total earnings were meagre and their living conditions very basic. But they survived.

Leonid's musical career did not last long. He hated the idea of taking directions from the conductor. He was used to giving orders, not taking them — after all, he used to be an important man, a colonel, and this job was well below his perceived status in life. Regrettably, jobs were scarce and none seemed to match either his skills or his desired status. He had no useful commercial skills and his pride would not allow him to take on menial tasks, such as being a security guard or a taxi driver, even if that were to make the difference between his family eating or starving. This frame of mind eventually caused him to fall into an acute state of depression. He just sat at home in a sulky silence and did nothing to contribute to the welfare of the family. The total responsibility for the family now fell on Aida's shoulders.

This phase probably marked the beginning of the end of Aida's love for her husband. When they first married, she was madly in love with the dashing young officer. Even though she and the children had to constantly move around Russia to follow his military postings, she remained content and loyal. After all, what he was doing was important and she felt it was her duty to support him. Then came the Revolution and they were separated. For over two years she had to fend for herself and take care of the five children. The whole experience made her more self-sufficient and developed her confidence in her own abilities.

When they were finally reunited in Vladivostok, Aida realised more and more that her husband was not particularly interested in the welfare of the children, or her welfare for that matter. He was consumed by his own career and by the Civil War. While Aida had done all the organising and running around to bring the four girls out from the orphanage, Leonid was too busy fighting a war. And when the family arrived in Harbin and he lost his important military status, she discovered him to be a vain, uncaring, demanding and temperamental person — quite removed from the dashing young man she married sixteen years ago.

Aida remained with Leonid for many more years, but she did so out of loyalty to the family, not love for her husband.

Len (aged thirteen) and Jenia (eight) were sent off to school, while Nadia (six) stayed at home. Nusia and Nina, being fifteen and fourteen, were however

Typical Russian businesses—the one on the left is a café, the one on the right a clothes shop advertising dresses, suits, coats and furs—Harbin, 1930s

Harbin railway station, 1920s

candidates for employment, and Aida decided a housekeeping job would be the most appropriate vocation for them. Nina became a live-in nanny for a German family with a four-year-old boy, and Nusia's job was that of a live-in housekeeper and cook for a working Russian couple. Although she had no cooking experience, Aida believed cooking came naturally to women and, with her guidance, her daughter would quickly learn the art.

Nusia left her job after six months because she could not stand the husband. He was never satisfied with anything she did. Aida found her another job, this time as a nanny to a two-year-old girl who was the illegitimate child of Michael Diakonoff, a man in his late thirties, and his young Jewish mistress. During the first year and a half everything was fine, Nusia was happy and so were her employers. But then, suddenly, the situation in the Diakonoff household turned for the worse. He and his mistress began to quarrel incessantly — long, yelling, screaming matches — scaring both the child and Nusia. After enduring this for a further six months, Nusia told her mother she could not take it any more and left their employ. Soon afterwards, Diakonoff and his mistress had a huge row and she left him, taking the child with her.

At the same time, Nina's employers packed up and went to Germany, thus leaving both Nusia and Nina jobless. Moreover their father was still without a job and taking very little interest in finding one. So the breadwinner was Aida. She sewed dresses, took in laundry, worked as a cleaner, did whatever job was available. Nusia and Nina did the housework and much of the cooking, and the younger children went to school. Leonid just moped around the house.

THE LOVELESS MARRIAGE: 1926

Nusia's previous employer Michael Diakonoff had been living in Harbin for many years and was reasonably well off. He was a merchant and an entrepreneur of sorts. Knowing the Tarasovs were going through a rough time, he came one day and told them he had a friend who was looking for an honest man to manage his grocery store, and that Diakonoff could arrange for Leonid to get the job if he wanted it. It was just a small store, but it boasted a significant fringe benefit — an apartment with two rooms and a kitchen at the back of the store.

Although the job sounded too good to be true, Leonid was reluctant to take it on. He had become accustomed to a state of inactivity and, on top of that, he was not at all sure this was his type of job. But Aida persisted and the children all supported her. 'You'll be in charge of an important business,' she insisted. 'Nusia and Nina will be the sales girls and we'll have a nice place to live in. It's a wonderful opportunity!'. Finally he agreed and they promptly moved out of their rickety old house. Leonid managed the stock and did the bookkeeping, and Nina and Nusia became quite good at serving at the counter. Aida stopped working and became a normal housewife. Things started to look up for the Tarasov family.

Michael Diakonoff continued to be kind and generous to the Tarasovs. He often called in, checking on their welfare. Were they happy? Did Leonid like his job? 'Yes of course,' they would reply. 'Thank you for your help and interest.' He even brought small presents for members of the family, continually surprising them by his kind charitable acts.

But Nusia was suspicious. She felt there was something sinister about his constant and unwarranted attention to their family.

'Why is he visiting us all the time? What does he really want?' she would ask her mother.

'Nothing,' Aida would reply. 'He's just a nice man.'

It took nearly a year for Diakonoff's secret agenda to be unveiled.

'I wish to marry your daughter Nusia,' he announced one day when he was alone with Leonid and Aida. 'She will make a good wife and I will make her happy.'

Apparently while she had been looking after his illegitimate daughter, she showed herself to be quiet, meek and unflappable, qualities he obviously valued in a woman.

When Aida informed her daughter of what had transpired, the poor girl was horrified. She did not like him at all — in fact by then she had begun to hate the sight of him. Diakonoff was twenty-two years older than her and only three years younger than her father. Why would she even think for one moment of marrying this 'old man'? But Aida, who had gone through years of extreme poverty, saw this as an opportunity for her daughter to assure herself of a life free of material worries. After all, Diakonoff was rich by their standards, and she spent weeks begging Nusia to grasp this chance for a better life.

Nusia's father, on the other hand, was dead against it, and had he stayed around he probably would have put an end to this courtship. Unfortunately, however, Fate stepped in and took him away from home.

Out of the blue, Leonid received an offer to become the commander of the 105th Regiment of Chang Tso-lin's Chinese Army[†]. Accepting the job meant he had to move to Tsinanfu (now called Jinan), about 400 kilometres south of Tientsin and 1500 from Harbin, but Leonid welcomed the chance to join the military again. He had not been happy in civilian life. The army was

[†] At the time of the fall of the Manchu rule in 1912, Chang Tso-lin was a division commander in Manchuria. By 1918 he became its inspector general and, effectively, its ruler. In 1920 he began to expand his influence into North China and by 1924 he had conquered Peking and established himself as the military dictator of all China. He held that position until 1928 when he was deposed by Chiang Kai-shek.

Nusia and Diakonoff, Harbin, 1927

in his blood and it was the only thing he was good at, the only thing he enjoyed. Of course it meant he would be parted from his family again, but there was nothing new in that state of affairs. But this time he took Len, now seventeen, with him and enrolled him in a military institute there — 'to make a real man out of him'. Before they left he again counselled Nusia against marrying Diakonoff and warned he would not give the union his blessing. However, with Leonid's departure the family's situation became desperate. The store-owner was not prepared to entrust the running of the store to a woman and asked the Tarasovs to move out. As Leonid's military posting had yet to yield any money, Aida started looking for a job. And she became even more insistent with Nusia.

'Look how poor we are, and the future does not look any brighter. Do you really want to have such a miserable life? Accept Diakonoff's offer while he's still keen on you.'

Finally the combination of her mother's constant pleas, the spectre of a continuing life of poverty and the promise of a prosperous existence with Diakonoff was too much for Nusia. Two months after her father left she said 'yes.' No attempt was made to get his blessing. The wedding took place on 1 September 1926 with the reception in Diakonoff's apartment. Nusia was nineteen, Diakonoff was forty-one.

A couple of months after the wedding, Aida received some money and a letter from Leonid instructing her to pack up and move the family to Tientsin. That city was closer to Tsinanfu, and the prospects for jobs and a better life were brighter there than in Harbin. Orders were orders, so Aida, Nina, Jenia and Nadia packed up and left for Tientsin, abandoning the newlywed Nusia.

What irony! Nusia had sacrificed herself, believing her marriage would help the family out of their impoverished state. And now the family had deserted her and she was stuck with an old man she despised.

At the time Nusia had no idea she would be separated from the rest of the Tarasov family for twenty-eight years.

TIENTSIN — 'FORD OF HEAVEN': 1926–1928

The Tarasovs were apprehensive at the thought of leaving Harbin — after all, to them it had been an extension of old Russia. There had been no need for them to learn Chinese and they had felt comfortable and safe, surrounded by a cocoon of Russians. Now they had suddenly been instructed to pull out their roots and move to a real Chinese city to start a new life all over again. The only comforting thought was that Aida's sister Vera was living there. Over the years they had written to each other on an irregular basis and Aida knew Vera liked Tientsin. But that is about all she knew about the place, except that quite a few Russian refugees had already made the same move.

Aida had visions of a large city filled with small Chinese huts such as the ones in the Chinese part of Harbin, with dirt roads, no electricity or water, signs in unintelligible Chinese characters, dirt and filth everywhere. Imagine her surprise when they arrived to find a modern European city with wide paved clean streets, English signs everywhere, white people in the streets and all the trappings of wealth and order. Vera met Aida and her daughters at the station and took them to her apartment, which was quite comfortable and by far the best accommodation the Tarasov family had ever occupied.

Aida was anxious to find out more about Tientsin. Why did it have so many white people? And what were these 'Concessions'? Vera's apartment was on the Italian 'Concession', but most of the Russians were living on the British 'Concession'. What was all that about?

I am not sure how Vera answered those questions, but the historical background goes something like this:

In the seventeenth and eighteenth centuries, during the Manchu rule, most of the Western powers, especially England, France, Spain and Portugal, yearned to have China as an active trading partner. But the trade appeared one-way — the export of Chinese teas and spices to Europe. There was little Chinese demand for Western goods and there were significant limitations placed on foreign trading and religious activities. For example, foreign traders were only allowed to deal with a nominated group of Chinese merchants in Canton, which placed severe restrictions on their activities. In addition, they were only allowed to live in a small defined area of Canton and not permitted to leave its confines without a Chinese guard. And no-one was allowed to teach them the Chinese language.

In 1793, requests that an English envoy be permitted to reside in Peking and that missionaries be allowed to work there were refused. Ch'ien-lung, the Manchu emperor, proclaimed: 'Our dynasty's majestic virtue has penetrated into every country under Heaven, and Kings of all nations have offered their costly tribute by land and sea. We possess all things. I set no value on objects strange and ingenious, and have no use for your country's manufactures. Our goods, however, are absolute necessities to European nations. As to missionaries, the distinction between Chinese and barbarians is most strict and your request that barbarians be given full liberty to disseminate their religion is utterly unreasonable.'

These words, arrogant though they were, clearly manifested the indisputably unique position of the ruler of the Manchu empire and of that vast area's civilisation and self-sufficiency.

In frustration, Britain embarked on an active, covert campaign of smuggling opium into China, usually with the connivance of corrupt Chinese officials. After a while the government became alarmed at the outflow of silver to pay for the imported opium and made a determined effort to abolish the illegal traffic by seizing and destroying the opium in the British warehouses. This led, in 1842, to the First Opium War, which was promptly won by the British, resulting in the Treaty of Nanking. Under the threat of war, similar treaties were signed with France, the United States, Russia and Japan. The treaties included the designation of five ports, including Shanghai, as 'treaty ports' where foreigners could freely reside and carry on trade. Surprisingly there was no mention of any curtailment of the opium trade. Tientsin was not one of the five nominated ports.

In 1857 the Second Opium War broke out, with the British, supported by the French, being victorious yet again. The new peace treaty resulted in Hong Kong being ceded to Great Britain and five additional ports, including Tientsin, added to the previous list of treaty ports. In its weakened state the Manchu government also granted these privileges to Italy, Belgium and Germany. Included in the treaty was the establishment of foreign 'Concessions' in some of the cities. Shanghai and Tientsin were two of them.

These foreign Concessions were extra-territorial — that is they 'belonged' to another country — they were colonies of foreign governments. Each had its own municipal council, court of law and police force. It also boasted its own hospitals, schools, prisons and churches. The foreign government levied taxes and decreed what its citizens could and could not do. The Chinese government had absolutely no jurisdiction over these Concessions, nor did it receive any taxes from the foreigners living there. Garrisons of foreign troops enforced these extra-territorial powers.

The Chinese were most unhappy with this outcome. They felt weak and powerless and dominated by foreign governments. In 1900 this growing anti-foreign feeling gave birth to the formation of the Boxers, a fanatical secret-service society having as its objective the expulsion of all foreigners and the elimination of foreign influence. The Boxers overran the whole of north China, tearing up railway lines, destroying foreign buildings, robbing, looting and killing. To protect their property and quell the uprising, the foreign governments sent in troops. Rashly, the regular Chinese army joined the Boxers and declared war on all the foreign countries. The war ended with the defeat of the Chinese by a coalition of nine foreign governments, which then forced China to pay massive financial reparations for the damage inflicted on their property.

Tientsin was an important industrial centre. Flour milling was the leading industry, handling the vast grain supplies of the northern plains. It was also a major wool and fur exporting centre. Situated on the Hai-Ho River at its junction with the Grand Canal, the Tzu-ya River and the Hsin-k'ai River, it was about a hundred kilometres southeast of Peking. Being sixty kilometres by river from the sea, it was an important terminus in the journey to the capital. That is why it was named Tientsin, Chinese for 'Ford of Heaven'.

After the Second Opium War, Tientsin's foreign population grew vigorously. European merchants flocked in not only because of the business opportunities, but also because of the attraction of living in a Concession owned and governed by their mother country.

Originally, Tientsin had eight such Concessions, and the street names reflected their foreign origin. For example, Edinburgh Road in the British Concession and Rue du Marechal Foch in the French. The architecture, especially of the larger institutions such as banks and municipal offices, was grandiose and mirrored the styles of the mother countries. Each Concession had its business district, its suburbs, its restaurants and its shops. The district outside the Concessions was called Chinatown, where living conditions were Spartan and in sharp contrast to those of the spacious, well-tended quarters of the foreign Concessions.

Originally, foreigners lived in the Concessions governed by their mother countries, but over time the population became more mixed. However, no foreigners lived in Chinatown and the Chinese who lived in the Concessions were generally shopkeepers and tradesmen. English was the common spoken language.

The Russian Concession was on the other side of the river — the 'wrong' side, so to speak, away from all the other major Concessions and the hub of foreign life. There was only one bridge across the river and it was some distance away. As a result, the Russian Concession was sparsely populated and most of the Russians settled down in the British Concession. The main Russian church remained on the Russian side, however, surrounded by a beautiful park known as the Russian Park. To get there one had to take a small ferryboat operated by a couple of Chinese oarsmen, which left when there were sufficient passengers on board.

Important to some later events in our story is the fact that in 1912, to protect America's business interests, the US stationed its 15th Infantry Regiment of about 1000 officers and men in Tientsin.

After World War I, the German and Austrian Concessions were ceded

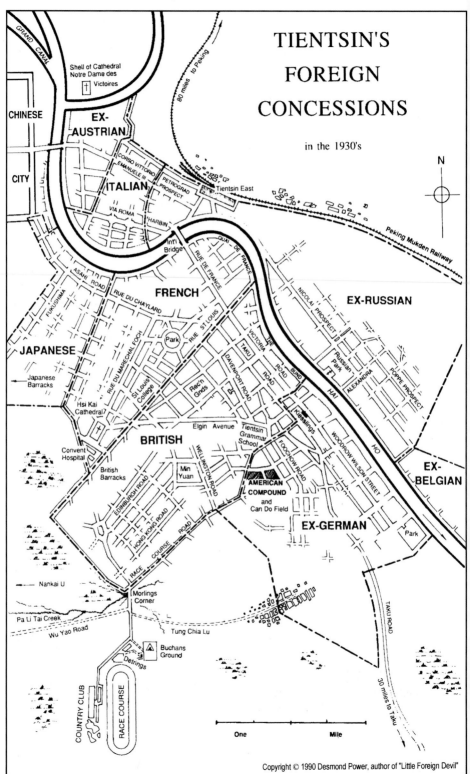

TIENTSIN'S FOREIGN CONCESSIONS

in the 1930's

back to China. The Americans took over the lease of the old German Army barracks for their own regiment and the main street of the old German Concession, previously the Kaiser Wilhemstrasse, became Woodrow Wilson Road. The Russian Concession was ceded back to China in 1923, thus making Russian citizens subject to Chinese jurisdiction. They lost their extra-territorial rights and, from the standpoint of the law and taxes, they began to be treated as if they were Chinese citizens.

With all these Concessions in place, the main street running through Tientsin started off as Woodrow Wilson Road in the old German Concession, became Victoria Road as it passed through the British Concession, Rue de France through the French Concession, Harbin Prospect as it proceeded through the old Russian Concession and finally Via Roma in the Italian Concession.

The British Concession was the biggest. It boasted many banks and business institutions, social and sports clubs, luxurious hotels and apartment blocks, and the Tientsin Grammar School. Its Victoria Park was a popular venue, and overlooking it was a fortress-like structure called Gordon Hall, which housed the British Municipal Council and the British police. Many streets on the British Concession had signs proclaiming 'Do not Expectorate on the Footpath!' I found these signs highly amusing for the use of the word 'expectorate' — it was only in my early teens that I discovered it did not mean 'relieve yourself'. The signs were obviously aimed at the Chinese, for whom spitting was an art form. Yet there was no Chinese translation on the signs

Gordon Hall, home of the British Municipal Council, Tientsin, 1936

and for the few who could read English, 'expectorate' was, no doubt, incomprehensible. The built-in habits of the Chinese population thus remained unaffected.

Both Victoria Park and the park on the French Concession had signs proclaiming, 'NO DOGS OR CHINESE ALLOWED, EXCEPT FOR AMAHS [maid-servants] WITH CHILDREN'. Most of the fancy clubs and all of the foreign swimming pools were also out of bounds to the Chinese — a terrible but accurate picture of the status of the Chinese in their own country.

Vera's apartment was quite luxurious. Nobody seems to remember how she came to Tientsin but she had been there for some time — enough time, it appeared, to have acquired a rich Italian lover whose apartment she lived in. While it was comfortable for the family to stay with her, Aida did not enjoy living in the Italian Concession while the rest of the Russian population lived in the British Concession, some distance away. None of her family could speak either English or Chinese and she was keen to live among her compatriots where Russian was freely spoken.

Through word-of-mouth Aida found a large room on the British Concession in an apartment owned by Gregorii Verzhbitsky, an ex-general of the White Russian Army. The general was married and had two teenage children, a boy and a girl. Living in just the one room was obviously a bit tight for Aida and her three daughters. As there was only one bed, they took turns sleeping on it, two at a time, while the other two slept on the floor. But Aida felt at home — among her own people, so to speak. There was no need for her to learn a foreign language. Russians owned many of the shops on the British Concession and those that were not had staff who could speak Russian.

Leonid, who was still in Tsinanfu, was earning a good salary and sent most of it to Aida, so they were reasonably well off. Jenia and Nadia were sent to St Joseph's College, an English-speaking school run by French Catholic nuns, which they attended on a half-board basis — that is, they were fed a hot lunch every day.

Rickshaw stand, Tientsin, 1930s

Nina became close friends with their landlord's daughter Nadia. As she had never had a close friend, this new experience was most enjoyable. Now eighteen and ready to earn some money to help the family, Nina found a job as a sales girl in a little confectionery shop named Pagoda. As many of the clients spoke

English and she could not, she asked her mother if she could take English lessons. Aida readily agreed, saying she had heard of a nice young man by the name of Vassilii Artemieff who gave private lessons. The man in question was contacted and the weekly lessons began.

Vassilii was twenty-four. Everyone called him Vasia. A slim, good-looking man, he was not only a good teacher but also a real flirt and ladies' man. He took an immediate liking to Nina and did everything possible to make her succumb to his charms. During the lessons he would often hold her hands and look lovingly into her eyes. This amused her younger sisters, who enjoyed spying on them. But for Nina this was the first time a person of the opposite sex had paid any attention to her, and she was a bit overwhelmed and very flattered, even though she did not particularly like Vasia.

Aida and Leonid in his Chinese commander uniform, Tientsin, 1927. *Below,* Len as a cadet in a military college, Tsinanfu, 1927.

After about three months, it was decided Nina now had enough of a grasp of English to do her job and the lessons were terminated. After that, Nina and Vasia went out a few times to the cinema and restaurants, but after a while he realised she was not interested in him and gave up the chase. However, we will hear more of Vasia later…

One day, Nina and her friend Nadia were walking in the old German Concession when they stopped to admire an elaborate exhibit in the window of the Kiessling & Bader confectionary

Kiessling and Bader, Tientsin, 1930s

Kiesslings, inside view at Russian Easter, Tientsin, 1937

shop. It was a large white sugar replica of a Russian cathedral, placed there to celebrate the upcoming Russian Easter. A German called Kiessling had founded the shop in 1906. Originally a bakery, it had gradually expanded to include a restaurant and a confectionary shop. Later he took on a partner —another German, Bader — and the establishment went on to earn a justifiable reputation for the excellence of its products and service. Russian girls staffed the cake and confectionary section and the restaurant waiters were Chinese.

Peering inside, Nina was impressed by what she saw. 'It looks very stylish and professional. I wouldn't mind working there,' she told Nadia.

Nina had always been a girl of action, so the following day she went in to ask for a job. Mr Kiessling himself interviewed her. In halting English she told him the story of how her family had escaped from Russia; about their life in Harbin; how impressed she was with what she saw in the shop; and how much she would like to work there.

'Well, with Easter just a few weeks away, we'll need some additional help,' he said after some thought. 'You can start next Monday at 8 a.m. But you must understand this is only a temporary job. As soon as the Easter rush is over we'll probably have to let you go.'

Nina agreed and on Monday, after being fitted out with a standard white uniform, Mr Kiessling gave her an order book and explained the process of taking orders and preparing invoices. The volume of orders before Easter was huge, not only from Tientsin but also from other cities, and she found herself working every day from 8 a.m. to 10 p.m. As there were no penalty rates in those days, she was rewarded with a small bonus. This was a pleasant surprise. She thought she was just doing her job and did not expect anything extra.

Mr Kiessling was pleased with Nina's performance, recognising in her a keen intelligent girl who was willing to give her best, and after Easter he offered her a full-time position. Nina readily accepted. Her starting salary was $30 a month with full board — breakfast, lunch, afternoon tea and dinner. That was not too bad and on top of all that she was to have one day off a week. A whole day off without work! She had never experienced such a luxury. A day off! How wonderful!

The sales staff consisted of four girls, growing to five or six during the busy holiday periods. After lunch the girls were allowed an hour's rest in a special room upstairs, two at a time. The bosses seemed to be caring people and the rest of the staff were friendly and cheerful.

When Leonid joined Chang Tso-lin's army in 1926 as commander of the 105th Regiment, Chang Tso-lin was effectively the ruler of China. The primary task of the regiment was to subdue or eliminate the various warlords, who shared the same ambition — to depose Chang Tso-lin and become ruler. All were extremely brutal and the battles with them were fierce. In addition, the Chinese Nationalist Party or Kuomintang, under Chiang Kai-shek, was becoming a force to be reckoned with and it too had its eyes on power.

Aida with (l to r) Jenia, Nadia and Nina, Tientsin, 1927

The regiment's main asset was an armoured train, bristling with firepower, which was used to transport the troops to emerging trouble spots. However, these and other measures were still not able to halt the rapid growth of Chiang Kai-shek's forces and in 1928 his Kuomintang troops overran Peking. Chang Tso-lin fled and Chiang Kai-shek took power. And Leonid lost his job.

On returning to Tientsin with his son Len, Leonid again had problems finding a job. Not that jobs were not available. They were. But none were good enough for him. As an ex-colonel, ex-commander, a man used to giving orders, he expected an executive-type position. Unfortunately there were no such jobs available for a man lacking business experience. So once again he became depressed, gave up looking for work and just sat around the house doing nothing and only interrupting his inactivity to reminisce about the good old war days with his landlord, ex-General Verzhbitsky.

Len, who had completed a couple of years of military school in Tsinanfu, became an apprentice electrician, earning just enough to keep himself in pocket money. So the family survived on Nina's salary and on the money Aida earned from her sewing skills.

THE ENTREPRENEUR: 1927–1930

A month after her mother and sisters left Harbin for Tientsin, Nusia fell pregnant. This unwelcome event depressed her even further. It was bad enough losing her beloved family, but now she was facing the ordeal of carrying a child fathered by a man she did not care for. To top it off, the pregnancy made her ill and she hardly left the house, just sat there and felt sorry for herself. This was probably one of the reasons why the birth was two months premature.

Nine and a half months after the wedding, on 18 May 1927, the Diakonoffs' first son Kolia (short for Nicholas) was born, weighing a mere two and a half pounds. When Nusia first saw him she was horrified. He was tiny, frail and shrivelled, like a little old man. He had no fingernails, just little hollows where they should have been. She was even afraid to bathe him in case she broke one of his tiny bones. A live-in nanny was hired, leaving Nusia solely with the task of breast-feeding him when he was nice and clean and wrapped up. Happily, in a couple of months Kolia became more solid in body and began to look like a normal baby.

The Diakonoffs were renting an apartment. It had three rooms, a verandah, an outdoor toilet and a barn. Diakonoff was involved in some business or other — nobody can remember what it was, except that it was quite successful. He must have been an entrepreneurial type because the new business venture he embarked on was quite an enterprising one. Discovering the local council was about to issue tenders for the supply of office furniture, he decided to submit a bid. The fact he had no experience in woodwork or carpentry did not deter him. Sensing this as a great opportunity for long-term business, he was determined to have a piece of it. It was too good a chance to miss.

Surprisingly, Diakonoff won the contract. He hired a carpenter, transformed the barn into a workshop, connected electricity to it, bought some wood-turning lathes, hired six Chinese workers — and the business took off. The carpenter looked after the business

Church and park in winter, Harbin, 1930s

and Diakonoff took on the task of lobbying the decision-makers and greasing the appropriate palms. He was good at this and the business prospered.

The council officials were happy with his products and the word got around. That led to his first order from the Chinese Eastern Railway (CER), the largest organisation in Harbin. And thus began his long and profitable association with CER. Diakonoff established a good relationship with Ivanov, the Russian head of CER, and orders kept pouring in. There was a temporary halt to the order flow in 1929 when China attempted to oust the Soviet Union from its participation in CER. The Chinese arrested the top Russian officials, including Ivanov, and declared an end to the partnership. But the Soviets were not ready to accept this unilateral action and struck back, invading northern Manchuria. After a brief undeclared war, the status quo was restored.

Following the reinstatement of Ivanov, Diakonoff's business flourished so much that the operation had to be expanded. He bought a large block of land in Nahalovka, a Harbin suburb, and built a modern house there with a large woodworking factory. When the house and factory were nearly completed, Nusia's brother Len arrived from Tientsin for a visit. His arrival was most timely. Being an apprentice electrician, he offered to wire up the house and factory. The offer was enthusiastically accepted and the job successfully completed.

The Diakonoff neighbours were a family named Kolbyuk. Their daughter Valya (short for Valentina) was sixteen, a pretty blonde who looked and acted considerably older than her age. Len, who was twenty, took an immediate liking to her and they saw a lot of each other. Nusia even suspected they were intimate, and she was right, because Len later confirmed this. They were obviously a bit ahead of their times.

When the new house and workshop were completed, the local priest blessed the new structures and Diakonoff hosted a big house-warming party. He now employed thirty Chinese workers.

On 12 May 1930 the Diakonoffs' second child Vova (short for Vladimir) was born. He came in at eight and a half pounds, a beautiful strong baby. With a healthy new child and a financially strong business behind them, the future looked bright. Nusia still missed the rest of her family and yearned to be with them, but at least she now had two children she loved and a comfortable life.

TRUE LOVE: 1929

Boris Ivashkoff, Tientsin, 1930

History tends to repeat itself and it nearly did so again in Tientsin. Nina had caught the eye of the Kiesslings accountant, a Finn, who began to court her. Although he had a good job and was well off, he was at least twenty years her senior. She went out with him several times, even though she was not really attracted to him. However, Aida began to exert pressure on her daughter, just as she had done with Nusia. 'He wants to marry you. He'll give you a good life. You'll get to like him eventually,' she told her daughter. 'He's a good catch.'

As far as Aida was concerned, financial security was obviously more important than love. If there was a good chance of marrying for money, as opposed to that tenuous thing called love, it was worth grabbing. Nina did not succumb to Aida's pleas and, fortunately for me, Boris Ivashkoff soon came on the scene.

Aida on a rickshaw, Tientsin, 1930

Boris was a friend of Kostia, the boyfriend of the landlord's daughter, Nadia. He was a handsome man — dark hair combed right back, olive skin and a nice slim figure. Nina liked his looks, but what attracted her most was his bubbling personality. He was a fun person and a good dancer — Nina loved to dance — and he played the guitar and sang with the greatest of feeling. Everyone wanted to be his friend. He was always the life of the party. Nina often saw Boris at parties and at the Russian Club, and she loved his company.

The relationship blossomed on the night Kostia invited Boris, Nina and Nadia to a restaurant for dinner. It was the most romantic place Nina had ever been to — candles, red drapes, soft chairs, a small orchestra playing Russian music. She and Boris danced cheek-to-cheek, sang melancholy songs late into the night and had a great time. And it was that night they fell in love. On the way home, full of this new realisation, they were reluctant to part and went instead to a park where they frolicked on the slides and swings like happy little children.

They became inseparable. Besides going to movies and parties together, Boris would often walk Nina to work in the morning. If she did not see him for a day or two her heart would be filled with longing. Nina took him to meet her parents and they liked him too.

Boris' parents lived in Harbin. He had two sisters, Olga and Lena (diminutive for Helen) and two brothers. His sisters and his elder brother Vassilii lived in Tientsin, while the younger brother Alexander lived in Russia. Olga and Lena were both working and they and Boris regularly sent money to aid their parents in Harbin. Lena, the elder of the two, was a very sweet person, and our lovebirds often went to her tiny flat for dinner.

Boris was in the fur business, travelling into country areas to buy up pelts and then sell them to the trade. His earnings were reasonable, but his travels often kept the couple apart for weeks at a time. Apart from the long absences Nina was very content. Her job was interesting, she was earning a reasonable salary — and she was in love.

It was early 1929.

The Bund, Shanghai, 1889

The Bund, Shanghai, 1935

SHANGHAI — THE 'YELLOW BABYLON'

Len did not like the idea of living with his family. His father Leonid, for whom he had the greatest respect, was constantly depressed and difficult to communicate with. The rest of the family were all females and he had difficulty relating to them. In addition, his mother was full of wise counsel, none of which he felt he needed. So, having heard positive reports about life in Shanghai, he decided to move there, feeling this would give him the chance to start a new independent life. Aida was, of course, against the move — she wanted all the family close to her — but there was no way of stopping the determined Len.

So in 1930, at the age of twenty-one, Len left for Shanghai. What surprised him when he got there was the sheer size of the city. It was at least five times bigger than Tientsin. Its buildings were taller, its streets were busier, its night life more lively, and it had a huge population of Russians.

Let me take this opportunity to dip into some of the history of this unique city.

Shanghai, which in Chinese means 'Above the Sea', is situated on the Whang-Poo River some twenty kilometres from the mouth of the Yangtze River, into which it flows. It is 1200 kilometres south of Tientsin and 2000 kilometres northeast of Hong Kong. When the Treaty of Nanking was signed in 1842 after the First Opium War, Shanghai was included among the five ports opened to foreign residence and trade. The foreigners proceeded to develop it from a small fishing town into China's largest port. In the process it became the most important manufacturing city in China, producing a large proportion of the country's textile, metal, paper and tobacco products.

Two foreign Concessions were established there, the British and the French, named the International Settlement and the French Concession, respectively. The rest of Shanghai was known as the Chinese Municipality, or Chinatown, and remained under the jurisdiction of the Chinese government. As mentioned earlier, the foreign Concessions or Settlements were extra-territorial enclaves, not subject to the laws of China. They had their own infrastructure, they levied their own taxes and their own military garrisons provided them with protection.

Shanghai looked more like a European city than a Chinese one, with wide, paved streets and modern buildings. Especially impressive were the grandiose buildings on the imposing waterfront boulevard called The Bund. These housed banks, hotels, insurance companies, clubs and other business establishments. Everywhere there was a prosperous air of business activity. An infinite variety of cafes, restaurants, cabarets and nightclubs made Shanghai justly famous for its exciting night life. It was the most cosmopolitan city in the Far East, and was often referred to as the 'Paris of the Orient' or the 'Yellow Babylon'.

The earliest recorded Russian presence in Shanghai was the establishment of a Russian Consulate in 1896. At that time, only a handful of Russians lived there — consulate officials, employees of the Sino–Russian Bank and merchants. With the opening of the Trans-Siberian Railway and the CER link to Vladivostok, trade between the two countries boomed and more Russian businesses appeared on the scene. At the start of World War I the Russian population had grown to a few hundred.

In 1922 the defeat of the White Russian forces in Vladivostok led to the retreat of the Whites by land into Manchuria and by sea to Korea. As mentioned earlier, the evacuation by sea was undertaken on thirty dilapidated, rusty, retired old Russian navy ships. The 9000 passengers on board, under the command of Admiral Stark, included soldiers and civilians. Although their destination was Shanghai, it soon became obvious that most of the ships would not be able to complete the 2000 kilometre journey and the admiral decided to head for the Korean port of Genzan (now called Wonsan) where the refugees disembarked.

On reassessing the situation, the admiral determined that only twelve of the thirty ships were seaworthy enough to complete the journey. Only 3000 of the refugees could thus continue. Those who stayed behind were housed in a Japanese Red Cross camp (Korea was then occupied by the Japanese).

The Shanghai-bound fleet was caught in a storm and two of the twelve vessels sank with many casualties. The remaining ten managed to make it to the fort of Wusong at the mouth of the Whang-Poo River some twenty

Genzan Camp, Korea,1923

The dilapidated *'Ohotsk'*, 1923   Brass band on the *'Ohotsk'*, 1923

kilometres from Shanghai, where they
dropped anchor. It was November 1922.

Their arrival was a complete surprise to
the Shanghai authorities, and an unpleasant
one at that. They had no need for 3000
impoverished and ragged refugees. The
foreign residents exhibited the same attitude
and, surprisingly, so did the small group of
Russian residents. There was no compassion
in evidence. To this well-off foreign group
of important government, banking and
business representatives, the unwelcome
influx posed the danger of upsetting the
status quo and undermining the elevated
status of the 'superior' foreigners. The
Chinese authorities instructed the flotilla to
leave forthwith. Admiral Stark acquiesced

General T.L. Gleboff

but not before setting ashore all the refugees, except for the skeleton crew
required to sail the ships out of Chinese waters to Manila in the Philippines,
where the decaying ships were sold for scrap. This group of refugees became
the foundation of the Russian community in Shanghai.

Of the 6000 who were left in Korea, most eventually dispersed into China
and Manchuria, mainly Harbin, except for a group of about 1000 Cossacks
who were determined to get to Shanghai. Selecting the best three ships from
the remaining rustbucket fleet, they patched them up as best they could and,
under the leadership of General Glebov on board the *Ohotsk*, set sail for
Shanghai, arriving at the fort of Wusong on 14 September 1923.

The Shanghai authorities could not believe their eyes. Here were three
more dilapidated ships, laden with beggars under arms. And this time they

Soviet (left) and German Consulates, Shanghai, 1934

were even flying the tri-colour flag of a country that did not exist any more. The general was given forty-eight hours to 'get the hell out of there.' He refused. Instead the flotilla proceeded further upstream, where the Cossacks occupied the Quarantine Station and set up camp.

Protracted discussions ensued but there was no way the Chinese were prepared to relent. The previous year, 3000 Russian refugees had sneaked in and they were not about to let it happen again. As a result, the Cossacks had to stay aboard the ships and in the Quarantine Station for more than three years, under atrocious conditions, with little food, no medicine, and no apparent future. More than forty died from sickness and malnutrition — and all this just a few kilometres from the most prosperous city in China. To buy necessary provisions, General Glebov sold one of the ships to Chang Tso-lin. Another sailed back to Vladivostok with 240 desperate Cossacks on board, who had decided that giving themselves up to the Reds was a better proposition than remaining, without any hope, in limbo.

Bridal procession, Shanghai, 1930s

At the end of 1926, a fortuitous turn of events ended this human tragedy. During the never-ending Chinese civil war, the Kuomintang forces under Chiang Kai-shek captured Hangzhou, 150 kilometres from Shanghai. In the process, they confiscated the British Concession there and arrested the members of the Hangzhou British garrison. It now appeared their next objective would be Shanghai and its lucrative foreign Concessions. To protect their settlements, Britain and France immediately dispatched troops on the long journey to China, but it was obvious they would not arrive in time. So, in desperation, a local Volunteer Corps of foreigners was formed to defend the city. However, this was a hopeless task. They were all amateurs and unlikely to be effective in a serious battle.

And that is when the city administration remembered the existence of the armed Cossacks in the Quarantine Station!

Hasty negotiations took place and a deal was struck allowing the Cossacks entry into the city, provided they helped defend it. The Cossacks quickly formed the Russian Detachment of the Volunteer

Man with a message—the translation is: 'Do not buy Soviet goods. They are soaked with the tears and blood of our brothers and sisters who remain in the land of tyranny and violence. Buying these goods provides them with money to support their murderous rule and their goal of world revolution.'

Corps, and their reputation and presence were sufficient to hold off the Chinese forces until the foreign troops arrived. Some years later one of their original tri-colour flags was presented to the Cossacks by the administration in a ceremony commemorating this assistance. Ironically, it was the same administration that had prohibited the Cossack entry into Shanghai for more than three years.

Originally the Russian refugees had difficulty in finding jobs in Shanghai. Although they were prepared to take on the most menial tasks, these tasks were normally performed by the Chinese who were ready to work for much less money. In addition, the foreign businesses did not wish to hire other whites for menial jobs, fearing it would undermine the status of the foreigners — and that would never do. Again, a fortunate event turned the situation around.

In 1927 the Communists organised a strike against foreign businesses. All Chinese labour was withdrawn, even from such vital services as electricity and water. The strike had the makings of a catastrophe and the Settlement administration felt it had no way out but to surrender to the strikers' demands. But then someone realised there were many Russians still looking for jobs. An offer was made, and these menial jobs were quickly taken up by the desperate Russians. In the process, they showed themselves to be reliable workers and from then on the employment of Russian refugees became an accepted norm. This led to their eventual employment in higher skilled jobs.

In the meantime the migration of Russian refugees into Shanghai continued, especially from Harbin. Two events accelerated this migration. The first, in 1924, was when the Soviets and Chinese decreed that employment in the Chinese Eastern Railway (CER) in Harbin would only be available to the Chinese and to Russians with Soviet passports. Those who refused to take up Soviet citizenship lost their jobs and many of them moved to Shanghai. The second event was the Japanese invasion of Manchuria in 1931 (described later). By 1932, the Russian population of Shanghai had swelled to about 20,000.

BODYGUARDS: 1930

On arrival in Shanghai, Len's first job was with the Shanghai Volunteer Corps. In those days the corps was said to be the most complete and efficient small

army in the world. It included a Russian Detachment, which Len joined. Having studied for two years in the Russian Military Institute in Tsinanfu, it appeared to be the right vocation for him. But after six months he grew to dislike the strict regimentation of the corps and left it. His next job was that of bodyguard.

In those days there were many rich Chinese, some of whom had acquired their riches through shady activities. As banditry was rife, the wealthy Chinese were exposed to kidnapping, extortion and murder from jealous associates or competitors. For protection, many kept an entourage of bodyguards. These were mostly Russians, as the Chinese were reluctant to use their own kind as bodyguards. They felt their compatriots were not trustworthy, whereas the Russians had developed a reputation for reliability and courage.

Len in his bodyguard uniform, 1931

Seeing that there was a shortage of bodyguards in Shanghai, Len wrote to his father in Tientsin asking him if he would be interested in such a job. The idea of being a bodyguard attracted Leonid — after all, it had some military overtones to it — so he decided to give it a go. He did not ask Aida to come with him, nor would she have done so had he asked. She was not prepared to follow him around the world any more.

Under normal circumstances, the impending departure of the head of the family for another city would have been an unhappy event. In this case, however, Leonid's decision to move was accepted without any distress. In fact, if anything there was a sense of relief. Leonid was not really the head of the family any more. He did not have a job and he continued to be sulky, moody, temperamental and remote. He just sat there feeling sorry for himself and believing the world had dealt him a bad hand. The responsibility for looking after the family had long since passed to Aida.

As she had stopped loving her husband a long time ago, his departure was in fact a blessing. They were not living as man and wife any more and she felt his attitude to life had a negative effect on the family. The sooner he left, she thought, the sooner she and her daughters could get on with their lives. The girls too were also delighted at the news of their father's departure. He had always been a tough and cruel disciplinarian. Fear was the governing emotion in their relationship with him. Even now that they were grown up he insisted on controlling their lives — how they dressed, who their friends were, how and where they spent their time.

Good riddance, they all thought.

FEARED, BUT NOT LOVED

Looking back at this state of affairs, one cannot but feel a sense of amazement and sadness. How could Leonid's relationship with his wife and his daughters have deteriorated to such a degree?

Here was a man with a distinguished military career spanning twenty-one years. He fought in two wars and a revolution, became a colonel, was highly respected by his superiors and loved by his men for his decisiveness and courage. Awarded seven medals, one of which was for bravery in action, he had indeed been a fine military man. But his military career was to be both an asset and a liability. On the positive side were the professionalism, integrity, loyalty, pride and prestige that a distinguished military career engenders. But on the other side of the ledger there were two significant drawbacks:

The first was the fact that Leonid's career kept him away from his family and there was little opportunity to bond with his children, who considered him a stranger, an occasional visitor.

Secondly, when he was home Leonid ran his family the same way he ran his troops, treating them as if they were his subordinates. Strict and intolerant, he expected unquestioned obedience from all members including his wife. If they got out of line, swift punishment was meted out in a heartless manner and without the slightest remorse. The children might not have seen much of him but, when they did, they were in mortal fear of him. He was completely intolerant of childplay and pranks, and administered punishment with brutality mixed with a measure of sadism. Patience, love, kindness and consideration — none of these was ever in evidence from him in his family life.

Of the five children, Jenia was the one he seemed to pick on most and he used to thrash her regularly. The thrashing routine was always the same. First he would instruct her to take down the leather belt which was always hanging on the wall in full view, and hand it to him. Then she would be required to take her pants off and lie on the bed with her head buried in a pillow. And then the lashings would commence, with him periodically lifting her head from the pillow to allow her to take a few breaths of air.

This was normally followed by a protracted stay *v oogloo* (standing in the corner and facing it). Often Leonid thrust a book into her hands, demanding she study one of the pages and threatening he would question her later on its contents. There the child would stand, trying to read the page through tear-filled eyes. Once, when she was about five years old, Jenia's father fell asleep during her ordeal in the corner and slept past the time at which the punishment was supposed to end. Although her mother told her she could leave the corner, Jenia was so terrified of her father that she dared not move until he woke up and released her.

Jenia believed her father picked on her because he was paying her back for the time when her mother disobeyed him and taken Jenia with her from Habarovsk to visit him in Warsaw. Her sisters, however, believed it was because she was slow off the mark. For example, she would be in a room with Nadia and Len, arguing and yelling at each other. Leonid would hear this and storm into the room, but while Nadia and Len were alert enough to run out as soon as they heard him coming, Jenia was not and became the sacrificial lamb. And away he would drag her to administer the whipping, with the poor girl often wetting her pants from fright, leaving a trail of liquid on the floor behind her.

As a result, Jenia hated her father all of her life. Although it must be awful to hate your father, this emotion was perhaps understandable in her case.

Nina could only recall one instance when she was whipped. Her father had asked her to go to the shop to buy some *kvas*. Being a typical child, she began to complain, asking 'Why me?' She lost the argument and grudgingly went off to get the *kvas*, but on the way she decided to have her revenge. Instead of going to the shop, she walked around for a while and announced on her return that the shop had run out of the drink. She probably looked guilty or returned too early or both, and Leonid sent Len on the same errand. Len returned with the *kvas* and Nina received a hiding.

Nadia remembered an incident when, at the age of about five, she wet the bed. Her father was most annoyed and told her he would thrash her when he returned from work that evening — he did not have enough time in the morning. Always ready to protect her flock, Aida conspired with Nadia to put her to bed earlier than usual so she would be asleep by the time Leonid came home, thus perhaps avoiding a beating. No such luck. Finding Nadia asleep, he just pulled her out of bed and proceeded with the thrashing.

Nusia did not remember ever being whipped by her father. She didn't know the reason for this immunity but her sisters thought it was because she was always *teeshe vodi, neezhe travi* (a Russian saying, meaning 'quieter than the water, lower than the grass'), never doing anything even remotely risky or aggravating. Under the circumstances she seems to have been eminently prudent.

Aida also had to dance to her husband's tune. For example, he would not allow her to get out of bed at night to tend to a crying child. 'Don't pander to it,' he would say. 'It'll soon stop crying.'

Being of the military, he would get up at 5 a.m. every day, expecting Aida to get up at the same time. Before cooking breakfast, she had to be bathed, made-up and fully dressed, complete with high-heeled shoes. He then expected her to sit at the table with him while he ate. Aida, who liked her sleep, would dutifully sit there, barely able to keep her eyes open. But those were the rules and she had to obey them. This routine was even followed when Leonid was on vacation.

Then, after fleeing to Harbin he was contemptuous of jobs below the perceived eminence of his previous position and remained without work, with Aida carrying the full load. This made him depressed, irritable and moody and an emotional burden to the rest of the family. The two years as a commander in Chang Tso-lin's army was a temporary return to the glory of yesteryear, but after his return to Tientsin he relapsed into his negative, self-pitying frame of mind.

So is it any wonder that, as soon as he left for Shanghai, a sense of overwhelming relief enveloped the family? Suddenly the future looked brighter.

With his impressive military background, Leonid had no difficulty in finding a job as a bodyguard in Shanghai. The work seemed to suit him, for he kept that position for years.

Initially, his son Len was also happy with his bodyguard job. He carried a revolver and a rifle, and the whole idea of being a protector of somebody else's life seemed to give him a sense of power and a feeling of being one of the good guys. But eventually the job got him down. He had to live on the premises and was on call twenty-four hours a day, seven days a week. This left him completely isolated from the Russian community. As well, there had never been any exciting incidents, any shoot-outs. The work became routine and boring.

After about three years, Len hung up his guns, so to speak, and left for another job. His father, however, liked the conditions of his employment and stayed on for many more years.

A TERRIBLE OMEN: 1930

Before Leonid left for Shanghai, Boris Ivashkoff had asked him and Aida for Nina's hand in marriage. Both readily agreed — they liked him. Possible places and dates for the wedding were discussed, but by the time Leonid left no final decision had been made.

Nina had been promoted to head girl in Kiesslings. With this came more money but also more responsibility and longer hours. Nina was a very conscientious young lady, always believing she should give her very best and show the other girls, by example, what hard work and diligence were all about. Often her hours stretched well into the evening and she had little spare time to spend with her beloved Boris. But at least they had Sunday to themselves. Being the head girl, she was able to get the sixteen-year-old Jenia a part-time job at Kiesslings. This helped the family coffers.

Aida went off to visit Nusia in Harbin and stayed there longer than expected. Nina finally had to write to her, urging her to return as soon as possible so the wedding arrangements could be concluded. When Aida returned, she bought a wedding present from Nusia — a bridal veil, garland and two wedding candles. Nina was overjoyed with the gift from her older sister. Trying on the veil made her even more anxious to be joined forever to her beloved Boris.

There were problems deciding on a venue for the wedding reception. The Tarasovs' place was too small and hiring a restaurant or something similar was beyond their means. Fortunately a friend of Aida's, Zoya Arguntiskaya, came to the rescue. Some time earlier Zoya had lost her husband and Aida had been kind to her in her moment of need, consoling her, sewing for her and generally helping her cope with her bereavement. So when Zoya heard about the problem with a reception venue she willingly offered her dining room and the problem was solved.

Nina and Boris, Tientsin, 15 February 1931

Before the wedding, the young couple looked for a room to rent and found one in a house at 8 Tyne Street, owned by the Abalmazov couple. She was a Russian Jew and he a Russified Tartar, both very pleasant people. The house was large — a big living/dining room, a kitchen, and two bedrooms upstairs, one of which was for rent. The husband also insisted on showing them the roof garden which he claimed was a life-saver in summer. He and his wife often slept out there on hot nights.

Nina loved the place, the owners, and especially the roof garden — she hated hot weather. But they were not in a position to rent it until they were married and the wedding date had not been set. As the Abalmazovs had taken a liking to the young couple, they said they were prepared to wait. They did not even ask them for any key money†, informing them they could just start paying when they moved in.

The wedding took place on 16 February 1931. Zoya, Nina and Aida decorated the dining room and cooked a mountain of food. The ceremony was at 4 p.m. It had been snowing from early morning and Nina loved the snow — it added that special aura to the occasion. Only the wedding dress was hired, as she already had the rest, including the bridal veil Nusia had sent her. Boris' sister Lena was the matron of honour.

It was a beautiful ceremony, complete with choir. Russian Orthodox church weddings are lengthy, some ninety minutes, but they are quite spectacular. The celebratory atmosphere; the deep bass voice of the deacon; the joyous singing of the choir; the golden crowns worn by the couple; the sacred walk three times around the *Anoloi* (a table on which the Gospel and crucifix have been placed) — all these add to the atmosphere of this most important of occasions. There were many more people in the church than the invitees, which was normal. Russians can't resist the sight of a wedding car with white ribbons standing outside a church. Curiosity attracts them in droves, to see the couple, to check out the dress, to ogle. Aida did not attend the wedding. According to old Russian beliefs, attendance by mothers is supposed to bring bad luck.

The appearance of a photographer at the end of the ceremony was a surprise to the newlyweds, as they had not arranged for one. It turned out to be Aida's thoughtful wedding present. The resultant six photographs always brought back to Nina the joyous memories of the happiest day of her life.

The Russian tradition was, and still is, that the mother or mothers welcome the newlyweds with bread and salt as they arrive at the reception venue. Boris' mother was in Harbin and could not attend, so Aida had to do the honours. She had baked a round loaf of bread and placed a small saucer of salt on top of it. When the newlyweds arrived, Aida was waiting for them on the porch, holding the plate with the bread and salt.

As Nina and Boris knelt down before her for the official blessing, a terrible thing happened. The plate slipped out of Aida's hands and fell on the floor, where it shattered. What a terrible omen! There was a startled cry from the

† Most of the rental apartments in Tientsin were owned by rich foreigners or Chinese. Before renting them out, they would demand some key money up front. This was normally a significant amount of money, often equivalent to four or five years' rent, and non-refundable — an entrance fee of sorts. The key money did not absolve the tenants from paying rent from day one. However, the tenants had the right to sub-let parts of the apartment and demand further key money if they so desired.

Boris Ivashkoff in his hunting gear, Tientsin, 1931

guests. Aida was aghast. Tears swelled in her eyes. Although the guests quickly recovered and tried to mask the mishap with loud cheers, kisses and good wishes, she remained downcast throughout the celebrations.

The table was laden with food. There were thirty-two guests. Mr Kiessling provided a beautiful two-tiered wedding cake and two large plates of *zakuski* (savouries). There was plenty of vodka and wine, many speeches, and constant cheers of *Gorko!* [†] followed by fervent kisses. Boris made a short but witty speech. A gramophone provided the music for dancing. There were many presents, including some from Nina's father and brother in Shanghai. The party continued well into the night.

Their nuptial night was spent in their room at the Abalmazovs.

THE HAPPY EVENT: 1932

The next day Nina took Boris over to Kiesslings to introduce him to her boss and to thank him for the wedding cake and food he had provided. They all sat down in the restaurant and had a long talk and a few drinks. All the girls came up to congratulate them, as did some of the Chinese employees. Many of the Kiesslings staff had been to the wedding. Nina was happy to show off her new husband and Boris was delighted to see how much the staff admired and respected his wife.

The three-week honeymoon was the first vacation Nina had since she

Boris, Nina and Aida, Tientsin, 1931

[†] 'Gorko' is Russian for 'bitter'. The word is yelled out by guests to encourage a couple to kiss. The kiss allegedly removes any bitter taste from the mouth.

started working at Kiesslings five years before. She and Boris spent their time going out to restaurants, visiting friends and family, taking long walks and just being with each other. It was heaven.

After the honeymoon Boris went back to the fur business, but his long absences were unbearable for Nina and she begged him to find a job in the city. Fortunately his sister, Lena, came to the rescue by talking her boss into giving Boris a job. Although he did not like the idea of an office job — he was used to the great outdoors, to travelling around the country — he accepted the fact that married life demanded a change in his lifestyle. Settling down in his new occupation, he stayed there until the business closed a year later. After that some friends offered him a position as sales-clerk-cum-office-manager in their big dairy shop on Dickenson Road. The idea of being stuck in a shop all day did not appeal to him either, but Nina talked him into it. Although the wages were meagre, between the two of them they earned enough to live reasonably well.

Overall, these were good times. They had many friends and did a lot of socialising. When it was their turn to entertain, the single room they were living in was a bit small so they would take their friends out to restaurants.

In the evenings Boris often spoke of his childhood in Harbin. His parents had been very poor. His father had difficulty in paying for his schooling and his books so, to help fund his education, Boris worked as a dishwasher in a restaurant from 9 p.m. to midnight every night. Although his mother knew this, she kept it from her husband, believing his pride would be hurt. Boris was a good student and completed high school with excellent marks. After working for a few years in Harbin he decided to join his sisters in Tientsin. Boris was a happy positive person, very enterprising and never moody or bossy. Nina, in turn, was a caring loving wife. Together they were deliriously happy.

In September 1931 Nina began to feel unwell. No appetite. Nausea. A check-up at the German hospital revealed that she was pregnant. Nina was overjoyed. Earlier she had convinced herself she was barren. This may appear strange, as only seven months had passed since the wedding, but she was so anxious to fall pregnant that every passing month without conception depressed her more and more. She had always looked forward to being a mother, often dreaming of cooking in the kitchen, with her children frolicking around her. Boris was thrilled with the news and the happy tidings were spread to all their relatives and friends.

The only serious pregnancy craving Nina developed was for *pelmeny* (Russian meat dumplings). As Nina was still working and had no time to make them herself, she often visited her mother to eat this delicacy. Having eaten so many of them, she would later became ill at just the mention of the word *pelmeny*.

As the German hospital was considered to be the best in town, it was the one selected for the impending birth. The female German obstetrician who looked after her showered Nina with useful advice. She felt she was in safe hands.

Easter was on 12 April, and Nina planned to work until then. The volume of orders was huge – *koolichi, paskha,* chocolate eggs. Jenia worked with her as well, learning the job so she could relieve Nina during her absence. Together they worked from early morning to late at night. Nina went on maternity leave on the Saturday before Easter. By that time she had grown to rather grandiose proportions. Mr Kiessling sent her some Easter delicacies and topped it all off with nice bonuses for her and Jenia. The Easter Feast after Saturday night Mass was held at Aida's with both Nina's and Boris' families. It was a joyful event.

On the morning of Sunday, 12 June, Nina began feeling sick. Towards evening the birth pains began and Boris took her to the hospital where the doctor pronounced the birth was imminent and asked Boris to stay with her. He sat there, holding her hand, and they both waited and waited, but the pain soon subsided and Nina fell asleep. Boris did likewise. By morning all signs of an impending birth had disappeared and Boris was sent home. Nina just lay there, bored and disappointed by the lack of any progress.

At about 3 p.m. the nurse suggested she take a quick walk around the ward. She did, and that's when the water burst. The birth occurred at 4 p.m. on Monday 13 June 1932. Boris was summoned by phone and came immediately, full of joy and relief. They were both happy and grateful it had all ended well.

In the evening they brought me in for a feed and my mother had her first opportunity to examine me properly. 'Oh God! Were you ugly!' she used to tell me later. 'Like a monkey — skinny, a long pointed head, terrible skin colour.' She looked at me with great apprehension for a long time, imagining me as a grown man in a business suit, topped by this ugly head. The vision was far from inspirational.

Next morning, my father spent some time with us and the rest of the family soon followed. 'What a lovely boy,' they all said, but I am sure they were just being kind. I could not possibly have improved so quickly. Nina kept quiet, ashamed of herself for having thought of her precious child as ugly. Soon she began to feel like a mother and started to look forward to the breast-feeding periods. As usual the nurses ensured I was clean, sweet-smelling and rosy when I was brought in.

At six weeks I was christened. Both my mother and father liked the name 'Igor', after the valiant twelfth-century Russian prince. The godfather was Abalmazov, our landlord, and the godmother Olga, Boris' sister. The celebrations were at the Abalmazovs. I am told I behaved in an exemplary fashion throughout the festivities.

The Abalmazovs were wonderful landlords. They had become like family and treated Nina and Boris as if they were their own children.

By three months, I was quite cute (so they tell me) — blond, blue-eyed and always smiling. Olga, Lena and my mother's sisters called in often and spoiled me rotten. Nina went back to work and an amah looked after me from 7 a.m. to 5 p.m. six days a week. She in turn was supervised by the Abalmazovs and my grandmother. It appeared I was in safe hands. My mother would have loved to spend more time with me, but she worked full-time, often until 7 or 8 p.m. However, she made sure she devoted all of Sunday to me.

THE INCURABLE ROMANTIC: 1932–1933

In 1932, Aida, Jenia and Nadia moved out of the one room they were renting from the Verzhbitskys into two rooms of a large boarding house. It was a welcome luxury.

Jenia, Tientsin, 1932

Jenia who was then seventeen had grown into an attractive woman, with a slim figure and a sparkling personality. And she had become an incurable romantic, constantly dreaming of being carried away by a knight in shining armour. She was anxious to participate in the social life she had seen Nina enjoy so much, but as she did not have a boyfriend Aida refused to let her go out by herself. Her social life was therefore very limited.

One night, after much pleading, Jenia was allowed to go to a dance at the Russian Club by herself. It was her debut. She was very excited and looking forward to being swept off her feet by some dashing young man. And indeed she did meet a handsome young lad, a sailor called Sergei Soliansky, who fell in love with her at first sight. They danced all night and he would not leave her side. So smitten was he that, when he found out the boarding house where she lived had a vacant room, he arranged to move there with his mother.

Within weeks he proposed marriage. At first Jenia said 'no', but she was so impatient to get married that she soon accepted. Aida was dead against the union and tried hard to talk her out of it, saying Sergei probably had a girl in every port. 'And he's a drunk,' she added. 'And on top of all that he's rude to

Arthur in his US army uniform,
Tientsin, 1932

his mother!' The last accusation was made with great vehemence. In Aida's eyes, rudeness to a mother was absolutely unforgivable.

True, Jenia had seen him inebriated, but to her this was not a cardinal sin. Still, she did become worried by his intense jealousy. Sergei would fly into a rage if she so much as greeted another man in the street. One night, in a drunken rage, he was not only rude to his mother but he actually hit her. That certainly ended the romance and the engagement was promptly broken off. He begged Jenia to reconsider but she stood firm. Shortly after, Sergei and his mother moved out.

A while later Jenia met Arthur Burke, a radio technician with the 15th US Infantry Regiment stationed in Tientsin. A good-looking man, over six feet tall with a nice smile and a cheerful personality, he too fell for her immediately. Although Jenia liked him, she initially rejected his advances because her father Leonid had been dead against foreigners — that is, non-Russians — and this feeling had been bred into all the girls.

Arthur, however, was a determined individual and would not give up. Often he would wait for her outside Kiesslings to walk her home, and he would keep vigil outside the house on weekends, waiting for her to come out so he could walk her to wherever she was going.

The day Aida first met him, Arthur took the opportunity to lay on the charm — and it worked. She admitted to Jenia she liked him and, following this seal of approval, he began to visit Jenia nearly every day.

'Don't mind me. I'll just sit here in the corner and admire you,' he would say if she were busy. That

Russian Club, Tientsin, 1933

was quite all right with Jenia. She loved to be admired.

Arthur was an exceptionally generous man. Not only did he shower Jenia with gifts, but he was also magnanimous to Aida. He bought all sorts of things for Jenia and her family at the army PX— chocolates, coffee, cans of Del Monte fruit salad, nylon stockings, you name it. Aida would often put on a facade of not wanting to accept the gifts, but she always did, delighted by his attention.

One day Arthur asked Jenia if she was going anywhere on Saturday night and Jenia said 'no'. But the next day she was unexpectedly invited to a ball by another suitor and agreed to go, forgetting what she had previously told Arthur. When he dropped in that evening, he found Jenia in her evening gown, waiting for her date. This upset him greatly and he left in a jealous huff.

It was then that Jenia realised she was actually in love with Arthur. They were married on 2 November 1932, six months after they had met and one month short of Jenia's eighteenth birthday. As they could not afford a proper wedding with a reception and guests, they decided to get married in Peking, about one hundred kilometres from Tientsin. This way, all they had to do was buy four train tickets — for themselves, Aida and Arthur's sergeant, the mandatory US Army representative.

After the wedding Jenia wrote to her father in Shanghai asking for his blessing. Leonid replied that he was annoyed he had not been asked earlier, reminded her that foreigners were not to be trusted, and reluctantly gave his blessing.

THE LANDLADY AND THE LOVER: 1933

In the meantime, there were significant changes at Kiesslings. Firstly, Nina was given more responsibilities. Besides managing the girls, she now became the bookkeeper, handling the money, managing the orders and preparing the invoices. That was quite a responsibility for someone with hardly any schooling and whose only training had been on the job. The management obviously had great trust in her abilities and dedication to the job.

The other change involved the two partners, Kiessling and Bader, who decided to sell the business. Bader returned to Germany, while Kiessling retired and continued to live in Tientsin. The business was sold to Tobich, and Austrian and Reichel, a German. As Kiessling & Bader was always referred to as Kiesslings, a deal was struck to retain the name. For that Mr Kiessling was to earn royalties for the rest of his life.

Reichel had already been working in the Kiesslings factory but Tobich was a new arrival from Europe. They were both pleasant men, with Tobich the up-front manager, very people-oriented and a great motivator, while Reichel was the man-behind-the-scenes production manager. Tobich spent a lot of time getting to know his employees and seeking their input. He asked Nina many questions about the other girls and solicited her ideas on improving the business. The previous owners had obviously told him what a treasure Nina was. After getting to know her, he became convinced they were right.

A few months later he took her into his office and they had a long talk. The conversation moved across to her personal life and she told him about their travels across Russia in search of their father, their time in Harbin, her sisters and brother, the fact their father had effectively deserted them, and other personal things. In passing, she mentioned her mother was renting two rooms which she shared with her two daughters.

'Why doesn't she rent a larger apartment?' he asked. 'She could then rent out some of the rooms, perhaps with board, and even make some money on the deal.'

Nina told him they did not have enough money to pay the key money.

'Find the right apartment and we'll lend it to you,' he offered. 'You can pay it back to us through monthly deductions from your salary.'

Nina discussed this with her mother and they decided that they could probably manage a modest re-payment every month. Aida immediately began the search for an apartment with five or six rooms. Within a fortnight she found one in Yang-Ho-Li, a complex of about thirty three-storeyed terrace houses in Davenport Road on the British Concession. The apartment, # 18, was partly furnished and had three large rooms, three small ones, a kitchen in the basement and a terrace off the top floor. It appeared ideal for renting as the rooms were all separate.

Unfortunately, there was only one bathroom, which contained the only toilet in the house, but that would have to do. The key money was very high — $1000 — and this at a time when Nina's salary was $40 a month. But Tobich and Reichel lent her the money and the contract was signed.

Aida hired a Chinese servant to help clean and paint the place. He was called *boika* (Russian/Chinese slang for manservant, derived from the word 'boy'). The three sisters also helped, spurred on by a desire to complete the renovation in time for a New Year's party.

When it was ready Jenia and Arthur moved into one of the large rooms and paid a nominal rent. Nadia moved into one of the small

Aida, Tientsin, 1930

ones and paid no rent— she was eighteen and only earning a few dollars from part-time jobs. Aida moved into the second of the three large rooms and one of the smaller rooms was rented out to a young man. Aida was now a landlady and the *boika* was kept on to help her with running the boarding house.

When Nina received her next pay, she noticed there were no deductions made for the loan. She drew that oversight to Tobich's attention. He ushered her into his office, sat her down and told her there would be no deductions. The 'loan', he said, was a gift from him and Reichel as a token of gratitude for all the contributions she had made to the business over the years. Nina just sat there, stunned. When it all finally sank in, tears rolled down her cheeks and she embraced her benefactor.

Aida met George Chelpanov in 1932 just before she moved to Yang-Ho-Li. Her previous landlord had organised bingo sessions for the tenants and these were often attended by outsiders, including Chelpanov.

A good-looking ex-Cossack officer of thirty-one with a warm gentle personality and a good sense of humour, he took an immediate liking to Aida. Although she was twelve years older than him, she was still a most attractive woman and looked much younger than her age. Though relatively poor, she managed to dress stylishly and had a sultry exotic look about her. And she was very much missing male companionship. Her husband Leonid had been living in Shanghai for nearly four years, seemingly oblivious of her existence, not caring whether she lived or died. She did not know if he would ever return, nor did she care about ever seeing him again. Yet, being a married woman, she had resisted the advances of other men and had lived a celibate existence.

George Chelpanov, Tientsin, 1933

At first she resisted a liaison with Chelpanov, even though she was attracted to him, but eventually she decided to throw caution to the wind and indulge in this unexpected romance. Initially the affair was carried out surreptitiously — she would visit him in his rented attic in a house in Elgin Avenue only five minutes' walk from Yang-Ho-Li — but eventually it became public knowledge and they stopped trying to hide it. A year and a half after they met, Aida moved in with Chelpanov. She had told her daughters she was planning to do so and they had all approved. They wanted her to be happy and they all liked Chelpanov.

It was some time later that Aida discovered Chelpanov's previous long-standing relationship with a widow with two young children. It included some financial support, but the relationship had been terminated as soon as he became serious about Aida. On learning about this, Aida's immediate reaction was one of concern for the other woman and her children — and of personal guilt. She felt responsible for whatever ills befell the poor woman and for years afterwards she included her in her nightly prayers, asking God to protect her from all evil.

Aida's move to Chelpanov's place allowed her to rent out the room she had occupied in Yang-Ho-Li, and soon all of the rooms were rented out, some with board, some without. Aida had become a fully fledged landlady.

The news she was living with Chelpanov finally reached Leonid and her son Len in Shanghai. There is no record of what her husband's reaction was, but one day Len, who had come to Tientsin on business, burst into the Yang-Ho-Li apartment. Only Jenia was home.

'Where's that swine who's wrecked my parents' marriage?' he yelled at her. 'I'm going to kill him!'

'Stop it!' she screamed back. 'Don't you realise what has happened? Father has been away for years. He never writes, he doesn't send any money, he doesn't care about any of us. What do you expect her to do?'

'I don't care. He has defiled the Tarasov name and I'm going to kill him! Tell me where he is!'

Jenia tried to reason with him, but in vain. Finally she told Len that Chelpanov did not live there and that she would never divulge his address. She called Len stupid and told him to leave the house immediately.

MANCHURIA, THE RUSSIANS AND THE JAPANESE: 1917–1932

Although the influx of thousands of White Russian refugees into Harbin between 1917 and 1922 had been a burden to the local Russian population, it also resulted in significant long-term benefits to the city. Many of the Russian refugees were intellectuals — doctors, professors, engineers, tradesmen, businessmen, architects, officers, artists, musicians, writers — and this added a certain 'tone' and 'class' to life there. Over the ensuing years, wonderful schools, theatres, hospitals and cathedrals were built. By 1930 the city boasted an opera company, a symphony orchestra, a ballet troupe, a conservatorium of music, a medical school, a polytechnic institute and a law school. It became a small replica of the civilised aspects of old Russia, on Chinese soil.

The original Chinese Eastern Railway (CER) agreement between Russia and China included the granting of extra-territoriality to the Russian population of Harbin — the right to run the local government administration, have their own police force and courts of law, and not pay any taxes to the Chinese government. Even though this right was rescinded in 1917 during the disarray of the Russian Civil War, the Chinese exerted minimal control over the Russian population, except for the introduction of left-hand drive to make Harbin compatible with the rest of China. Apart from that, life went on as normal.

Kitaiskaya (Chinese) Street, Harbin, 1930s

Railway Union Building, Harbin, 1930s

The gradual migration of the Russians from Harbin to Tientsin and Shanghai began in 1924. That was the year the Soviets and Chinese decreed that employment in the CER in Harbin would only be available to people with Chinese or Soviet passports. Until then the Russian employees had considered themselves just 'Russians'. The Civil War had bypassed them and the majority were not really interested in politics. But the White CER employees now had to make a choice — either get a Soviet passport or become a Chinese citizen. Those who refused were dismissed and many of them migrated south.

The next event to accelerate the exodus was the Japanese invasion of Manchuria in 1931.

Prior to the Russo–Japanese war of 1905, Russia held a twenty-five year lease on the Kwantung peninsula including Port Arthur and Dairen. However, its defeat forced it to relinquish this lease to Japan together with the lease for the Southern Manchurian Railway (SMR). This gave Japan a significant presence in southern Manchuria, and its control of the two key ports in the China Sea and of the SMR allowed it to exert considerable influence over the administration of the railway towns. This control was of growing concern to China and, to reduce the Japanese influence, the Chinese began to build a competing railway in parallel with the SMR. Bad feelings ensued and in 1931, after a bomb attack on the SMR by the Chinese (believed to be a pretext engineered by the Japanese), the Japanese launched a full-scale military operation. They quickly overran Manchuria and declared it an independent state, calling it Manchukuo, with its capital in Chang-chun. The last Manchu emperor, Pu-Yi, was brought out of retirement and installed as the puppet emperor. The Chinese government was too weak to do anything about the occupation and decided to just ignore it.

The Japanese objective was to transform Manchuria into an industrial and military base to facilitate its expansion into Asia, but the presence of the CER organisation and the large population of Russians with Soviet passports in

Harbin were impediments to that objective. The conquerors were not quite ready to confront the Soviet Union, but it frustrated them that they did not have total control over the citizens of Manchuria's largest city. But it did leave them free to do anything they wanted with the White Russians or any of those who had elected to take Chinese citizenship.

However, the Japanese quickly realised that much of the Harbin business infrastructure was in White Russian hands and, if they were to harass them and make their life difficult, they could trigger a mass White exodus which could easily destabilise the region. Reluctantly they decided to leave them alone, but many Russians correctly feared that worse was to come and began migrating south, mainly to Shanghai.

Although Michael Diakonoff had no intention of moving to Soviet Russia, he had taken out a Soviet passport back in the 1920s, believing it would give him more flexibility in his business dealings. To him the passport was just a business convenience. Nusia also obtained one after she married him, but never told her parents. They would have had a fit if they knew their daughter was a Soviet citizen.

Diakonoff's dealings with the CER were progressing nicely and he was making a good living from his woodworking business. The Japanese occupation did not seem to affect him at all. The only minor glitch in the growth of the business was the flood of 1932, which came suddenly and without warning. The whole of Harbin was inundated. The water was a metre deep through their house and all production in the workshop stopped. Although Diakonoff and the workshop manager stayed in the house, Nusia and her two children moved in with the Pavlov family, who lived in New Town above the flood level. Mr Pavlov was the godfather of both Kolia and Vova.

The water stayed around for about a month, becoming heavily polluted with sewage and other waste, producing a serious health hazard. The smell was awful. Considerable damage was done to the workshop and much work had to be undertaken to make it operational again. There was no insurance cover for the significant cost of repairs and replacements and this made a major dent in their savings.

Nusia's first-born, Kolia, was about five when he had a terrible accident. Nusia was about to give him a bath. It was a bitterly cold day and the bathroom was unheated. To keep it warm she filled a large basin with boiling water and placed it in the middle of the bathroom. When Kolia rushed across the damp floor he slipped and fell, plunging his right arm into the boiling water. As he was still fully dressed, Nusia began to desperately peel his clothes off — and the skin from his arm came off with the clothes.

Fortunately the hand healed within a week, leaving no visible scars, all thanks to an ointment prepared by a friend from wax, wood oil and lard.

Flood waters coming in, Uchastkovaya St, Harbin, 1932

Flooded street, Harbin, 1932

Kitaiskaya St in flood, Harbin, 1932

Nusia kept the ointment for years, just in case.

Soon after, Kolia caught a cold and developed a high temperature. Dr Yazkin came to see him and, while he was there, the boy began to convulse, biting his tongue in the process. The doctor examined him further and then broke the news to Nusia that Kolia had a mild form of epilepsy and would require close monitoring from then on.

This disability was to cause him significant distress in his future life.

TO DIE SO YOUNG: 1934

On 26 March 1934, Nina's twenty-sixth birthday, my father's sister Lena threw a party for her. They were all having a good time when, suddenly, Boris' face became ashen and he collapsed with a terrible pain in his chest. Although he recovered within a few minutes and told everyone he was fine, my mother was understandably worried.

The next day she discussed the incident with Lena, who suggested my father go to Tsingtao, about two hours away by train, where there was a first-class German hospital with many excellent specialists. Lena had a friend working in the hospital and she offered to phone her and organise the visit.

Boris did not want to go.

'Don't worry,' he said. 'There's nothing wrong with me. I'm fit as a fiddle.'

Boris Ivashkoff, Tientsin, 1932

But Nina insisted. So I was dropped off at my grandmother's place and Nina, Boris and Lena caught a train to Tsingtao, where Boris was given a battery of tests. The doctors concluded he had suffered a heart attack and decided to keep him in hospital for a week or two for observation. Nina visited him every day.

On the sixth day of his stay, Boris told Nina about the strange events of the previous night. He said he had a vivid dream of falling into a deep chasm — all in slow motion — and seeing his dead mother and father sitting on a ledge, smiling at him as he fell past them. When he awoke he found himself surrounded by the hospital emergency crew. They told him he had been screaming and they were trying to wake him up from his nightmare. What actually happened was his heart had stopped and the hospital crew were working to revive him. Boris did not know this. Not wanting to worry him, they had not told him the truth. It was Lena's friend who worked in the hospital who later told her of the second heart attack.

Another week of tests went by, and by this time Boris was getting very bored. All he wanted to do was to go home and see his infant son again. He was sure there was nothing wrong with his heart. Nina tried to convince him he needed further attention, but she was not game enough to strengthen her argument by telling him about his most recent heart attack, fearing the news might cause another. The doctors were also unable to convince Boris of the need for further examination and treatment, so, resignedly, they prescribed some sedatives and let him go.

On the journey back to Tientsin, the train unexpectedly slowed down and stopped between stations. Looking out of the window, they saw it had stopped opposite a train wreck, which had apparently happened only an hour earlier. It was a terrible sight — bodies everywhere, blood and gore, screams of victims, twisted metal, hissing steam. Boris was about to rush out to help the victims when Nina stopped him, worried about the possible effect of such an action on his health. It was more than two hours before they resumed their journey. All they could do was sit and watch this shocking scene with a mixture of horror and pity. For the next month Boris had terrible nightmares. The awful images of the train wreck preyed on his mind. He became more subdued, less ebullient. Even some of his old humour and optimism deserted him.

On 13 June my second birthday was celebrated. It was a Sunday and both

Mother and Father were home with me. The Abalmazovs threw a big party with all the relatives present and I was showered with gifts. It was also a wonderful day for my parents. The terrible memories of the train wreck had subsided and the health worries of the past few months seemed to have melted away.

The night of Sunday 4 July was very hot and Abalmazov decided to sleep in the roof garden. Boris joined him there. Nina always woke earlier than anyone else to cook breakfast for my father and me before going to work. And that is what she did on that Monday morning. When breakfast was ready she went up to the roof garden to wake Boris. Abalmazov had already risen and was downstairs. Playfully, she gave her husband's bare foot a pull.

Russian church on the Russian Concession, Tientsin, 1927

Oh horror! It was icy cold. She grasped the other one. It too was icy cold. Terror gripped her. She dropped to her knees and shook Boris. There was no response. He just lay there, his wide-open eyes staring vacantly into space. Nina's screams brought the Abalmazovs running up. Their immediate reaction was also to shake Boris and try to wake him. It took a while for them to realise the terrible truth. All they could do then was huddle together, all three of them, and bawl their eyes out.

The doctor said Boris had died from a heart attack during his sleep. From the look on his face, he did not appear to have suffered. He was twenty-nine.

Following Russian tradition, one of the two beds in Nina's room was removed and a large table brought in. It was placed diagonally across the room and Boris was laid out on it with his head in the corner, underneath the holy icon. This way he was looking up at the icon and at God. A candle was lit and placed at his feet.

As he lay there, Nina was told she should go up to the room and sit with him for a while. People assured her it would make it easier for her if she did, but she could not summon the courage to do so. Aida also urged her daughter to go up. 'They'll be taking him away soon,' she said. 'You have to go and see him now.'

Nina does not remember how she got up there. All she remembers is sitting in the room, stroking his feet and talking to her dear 'Borinka'. They had only been married for three years and four and a half months. All her hopes and dreams had been shattered by this tragedy. How could God have been so heartless? How could he have taken away her wonderful beloved husband in the prime of his life?

The funeral was a most tragic affair. The sight of the sobbing twenty-six-year-old mother with her two-year-old child was heart-rending.

After the wake at her mother's place, Nina went home but could not bring herself to go up to their bedroom. That night we all slept on the carpet in the living room — my mother, the Abalmazovs and I. This went on for five days. Try as she would, Mother could not bring herself to go up to the room where she and Boris had spent so many happy days together.

The Abalmazovs realised that Nina could not continue to live at their place. She obviously had to get away from the house where her beloved was taken from her. They soon found a small apartment for her in Tsi-Nan-Li, and even paid the key money.

Nina's wonderful bosses at Kiesslings also responded magnanimously. To help her get over the tragedy, they sent her away for a month to Peitaiho Beach, putting her up at the Peitaiho Beach Hotel, the best place in town, all expenses paid. Every week they sent her parcels of cakes and other goodies, including chocolates and sweets for me. Jenia, Arthur, and the Abalmazovs came to visit and so did a few of the girls from Kiesslings. Nina drowned her sorrow by spending a lot of time with her baby boy.

When she returned to Tientsin and her job, she could not find enough ways to thank her bosses for their supreme kindness. That is why she remained such a hard-working and dedicated employee right to the end. They had been so kind to her and her family she would do anything for them.

What irony! One of the main reasons Nina decided to rent at the Abalmazovs was the roof garden. She loved the idea of sleeping there on hot nights. But that favourite place was exactly where her husband met his fate. Memories of her mother dropping the bread and salt on their wedding day came back to haunt her. The bad omen had come true. No wonder Aida was so upset at the time and cried for days afterwards ... Both Leonid and Len came over from Shanghai to visit and console Nina. She had not seen them for a long time and was happy they came.

Although the Tsi-Nan-Li apartment was comfortable, my mother was worried about living there. Our rooms were on the second floor with the living room opening on to a balcony, and she had visions of me sneaking out, climbing up on the railing and plunging to my death. In addition, Aida was continuously urging her daughter to move to her place in Yang-Ho-Li. One

With the Abalmazovs, Tientsin, 1933

With Nadia outside #18 Yang-Ho-Li,   At my father's grave, Tientsin, 1937
Tientsin, 1936

of her larger rooms had become vacant and she thought it would be ideal for
the two of us.

So, four months after moving to Tsi-Nan-Li, we moved to my grandmother's
place. The Abalmazovs were sorry to see us go — they had paid key money for the
apartment — but they understood the reason and did not object. Fortunately
they were soon able to re-rent the room and recover their investment.

With my grandmother and the *amah* looking after me, and no balconies
within reach, my mother felt much happier. Unfortunately, because she often
worked late into the night, I was normally asleep by the time she came home.
So Sunday remained the only day we could really be together.

My grandmother loved me dearly. Apparently I was an affectionate little boy
and her pet name for me was 'Goolinka'. I don't know where that name came
from. It certainly did not emanate from Igor. Regrettably I grew to hate it. It was
so feminine and babyish. In later days I used to cringe when she called me that in
front of my friends. It always made them smirk and make fun of me.

MORE PROBLEMS IN HARBIN: 1935–1936

A political event dramatically changed the fortunes of the Diakonoff family in Harbin. It concerned the CER. Although the Japanese had been rulers of Manchuria since 1931, the CER remained in Russian hands — its ninety-nine-year lease gave it control until 1996. The fact that Japan did not have any jurisdiction over the main railway line and its administration was a thorn in their sides. But then in 1935, after protracted negotiations, Russia agreed to sell the CER lease to the Japanese. This change had a profound effect on Michael Diakonoff's business. CER was his largest customer, but as soon as the lease was sold to the Japanese, his orders began to dry up. The Japanese believed in doing business with their own kind, eventually cutting Diakonoff out completely.

Blagoveschenskay Church, Harbin, 1930s

He tried to find other customers, but was unable to get enough to replace the CER goose with the golden eggs. With little money coming in, the family had to live on their meagre savings. Diakonoff kept the business going for another year in the hope something would turn up. But nothing did, and he finally had to close it down. The house and the workshop were sold and he rented a smaller house in Chin-he, a downmarket suburb not far from the Sungari River.

However, Diakonoff was not one to sit still. Looking for new business opportunities, he discovered there was a large unsatisfied demand for moulded plastic tops for bottles and jars. So he hired a man who knew something about plastics and bought the appropriate machinery. After a lot of experimentation, they started production and a highly profitable venture appeared to be in the offing. Unfortunately, the Japanese-controlled administration would not grant him a permit to sell the finished products. They seemed to have an aversion for Russian businesses, especially those run by people who had close historical links with the previous Russian administration of CER.

With this venture aborted, the family's financial situation became desperate and they had to move to even cheaper premises, this time to a smaller house on the Buhedu line outside Harbin. And they had to tighten their belts even more.

The entrepreneurial Diakonoff knew Japan was producing many cheap goods which were not available in Harbin, and which he believed would sell like hot cakes. Having talked a friend into becoming his partner, they pooled their meagre savings to go to Japan and buy some of these goods. The trip lasted a month and they returned loaded with dress materials which they thought were particularly good value for money. Unfortunately the Harbin ladies were not enamoured with the materials and the entrepreneurs had great difficulty selling their wares. The business never took off and the two friends eventually quarrelled and parted company.

In 1936, ten years after Nusia's marriage to Diakonoff, Leonid paid his first visit to his daughter in Harbin. Nusia's relationship with her father was a strange one. She says she loved him. After all, he was her father and she believed one must love one's father. But at the same time she had always been frightened of him. Although he never thrashed her — she had been meek, quiet and obedient — she saw the brutal way he had treated her sisters and she hated that. Leonid, on the other hand, always thought of Nusia as a bit of a disappointment. To him, she was colourless and rather dull. But having lived in Shanghai and away from his family for six years, he appeared to enjoy the reunion and his first encounter with his grandsons, Kolia and Vova. The boys were obedient and that made him happy. Leonid liked obedience.

He told them many stories and taught them how to draw. They often played cards, mainly a game called *tetka* (aunty), and he would take books out of

Nusia and her father, Harbin, 1936

the library and read aloud to them in the evenings. His favourite was a book by Krasnov called *From the Double-Headed Eagle to the Red Banner*. It was a sad book and Leonid often had tears in his eyes as he read it. The hero in the book was a man named Sablin. Sixty years later Nusia still remembered the book and the name of the hero.

While living in Shanghai, Leonid had picked up sufficient English to be able to teach it. So he decided during the visit to earn some money giving English lessons. Nusia showed great interest in them and used to sit in and listen intently while he was teaching. Noting this, he asked her whether she would like to take lessons as well and she readily agreed. However, one day, when Nusia was having difficulty understanding something or other, he lost his temper, yelled at her and banged his fist on the table. This frightened the wits out of Nusia. This was the father she remembered and feared. He's got enough patience for other students but not for his own daughter, she thought, and she stopped taking lessons.

Later in life, she regretted this decision. The language would have come in handy during the forty-four years Nusia lived in Australia. When she died in 1998 at the age of ninety, she could not speak a single word of English.

Nadia and Jenia in their Sunday best, Tientsin, 1938

ABANDONED! — 1935–1939

In late 1935 Jenia's American husband Arthur left for San Francisco to renew his passport. All US citizens living overseas had to do so every five years. He told Jenia he would resign from the army and find a job in America. As soon as he was settled, he promised, he would send for her.

After resigning, he discovered that finding a civilian job in the USA was not as easy as he had hoped. America was still suffering from the aftermath of the Great Depression and unemployment was high. Part-time work was all he could find and his income was meagre, just enough to pay the rent on a small room and buy food — certainly not an environment conducive to bringing out a wife.

Arthur and Jenia wrote to each other on a regular basis for about eighteen months, but then his letters suddenly stopped. Jenia became worried. She continued writing to him but there were no replies. After a few months of silence, she sent a letter to 'the house-owner' at his address, inquiring about Arthur's whereabouts, but again there was no reply. She thought of contacting his parents in Canada, but did not know their address. And anyway, he had told her he had run away from home at the age of eleven because his mother used to beat him and he had not been in contact with them since.

Another eighteen months passed and there was still no word from Arthur. It was now three years since he left for America. Had he died? Had he found another woman? Had he forsaken Jenia? Would she ever hear from him again? What was she to do?

Jenia was only twenty-four, attractive, full of life, energy and sex appeal, and very much missing male companionship. There was no shortage of suitors and she did go out with some of them, but no-one was able to erase the memory of Arthur — that is until Volodia Ostrouhoff arrived on the scene.

They met at the 1938–39 New Year's Eve party at the Russian Club. Jenia was with a large group of friends and Volodia had come alone. As he knew some of the people in the group, he joined them — and romance bloomed. The next day he arrived at Jenia's with flowers and chocolates, and the courtship commenced in earnest. He must have been a fast worker for, two weeks later, at the Old Russian New Year's Eve (thirteen days behind the Roman calendar), he proposed. Jenia told him of her situation, that she was married and that she did not know the fate of her husband. Volodia knew all that.

'How long are you going to wait for him?' he inquired.

'I don't know,' was her honest reply.

He asked if he could continue seeing her and she agreed.

Volodia (short for Vladimir) was tall, dark and handsome, with a dash of Georgian blood and a prominent Roman nose. Possessing a good sense of humour and considerable charm, he was always happy and smiling. A persistent suitor, he would come by nearly every day, showering her with gifts. Jenia liked him very much, especially the fact he was always a proper gentleman, never forcing himself on her with kisses or other audacious actions.

Another six months passed and Jenia

Volodia Ostrouhoff, 1940

finally decided there was no point in waiting for Arthur any longer. He had been gone for three and a half years and she had not heard from him for the last two. He must have died, she thought. But before giving up completely she made one final attempt to find him. Through the American consulate she arranged the insertion of a notice in the San Francisco papers seeking information on Arthur's whereabouts. There were no replies. All the signs pointed either to abandonment or death. As an act of finality, she applied for a divorce. It was quickly granted.

Jenia accepted Volodia's proposal of marriage and the wedding date was set for 14 July 1939.

But this was not to be the end of Arthur ...

PEITAIHO BEACH: 1936–1939

In the summer of 1936 Kiesslings opened a branch in the summer resort of Peitaiho Beach and Nina was appointed to run it.

Peitaiho Beach is about 250 kilometres northeast of Tientsin. Its development began in 1895 when the Peking–Mukden railway was built. This line passed through Peitaiho, thirty kilometres inland from Peitaiho Beach. Foreigners were able to own land there as it was included with Chinwangtao as a treaty port. In 1917 a railway line was built from Peitaiho to Peitaiho Beach.

It was a most attractive place. Situated in the Bohai Gulf of the Yellow Sea south of Shanhaiguan where the Great Wall meets the sea, it boasted ten kilometres of magnificent white sandy beaches. The sea was never too rough, there were no unexpected undertows, no sharks and no bluebottles. The water was sparkling clear and bathing an absolute delight. At one end was the Tai-Ho River from which the resort derived its name. Pine-covered hills with the romantic name of Lotus Hills were a short distance inland and, behind them, lakes full of flying game. The roads, though unsealed, were well maintained. No motorised traffic was permitted and transport was by rickshaw, bicycle or donkey.

The resort was not only popular for its beauty but also for its climate, with summers 10°C cooler than Tientsin or Peking, where temperatures of 40°C plus in July and August were not uncommon. The place was very fashionable with the foreign community and many fine villas were built there.

Nina ran the Kiesslings branch at Peitaiho Beach during its operating months, from late May to early September, and this became an annual pilgrimage for her and me.

The standard complement of workers consisted of Nina, a Russian girl and three Chinese men. The girl acted as the salesperson while Nina did all the administrative work and helped behind the counter during the busy hours. In August, when the population reached its peak, another girl would be sent

Nina and two of her Chinese staff at the Kiesslings shop, Peitaiho Beach, 1937

Nina and Murzilka in the simple Kiesslings shop, Peitaiho Beach, 1936

over from Tientsin. The three Chinese were responsible for baking the breads and cakes, making ice-cream, waiting on the tables, tending the garden, meeting the daily train with provisions from the Tientsin factory and other miscellaneous duties.

During the first year of operation Nina was without any sales assistants. All she had were two Chinese, who happened to be very good workers. One she called Murzilka after a Russian children's storybook character, always smiling and full of fun. He was the outdoor waiter and gardener and, over the years, he and I developed a great relationship. The second was a huge bald hulk of a man. His Chinese name was Mongo and since it sounded like the word 'monster' it seemed quite appropriate. He did all the heavy work, such as churning the ice-

With my friend Murzilka, Peitaiho
Beach, 1936

cream by hand and carting coal for the baking ovens.

The Kiesslings property was on the main road, about five minutes' walk from the station and the Main Beach. The shop was quite small — just a single counter, some shelves and a desk. Behind the shop but in the same building were our living quarters, which consisted of one room and a largish covered verandah enclosed by walls of mosquito nets. The verandah served as the living/dining/kitchen area and contained two small primus stoves, two camp beds, a table and some chairs. Adjoining it was a small bedroom with another two beds. At the rear of the house was a garden of about two or three acres, which was set up with tables, chairs and umbrellas, serving as an outdoor cafe. At the back of the garden were the living quarters of the Chinese employees.

The main beach faced east, and the most popular time for swimming was from 9 a.m. to noon. A row of small thatched dressing sheds lined the back of the beach, each owned by a family. There were also one or two communal dressing sheds. At midday the beach would empty, with everyone going off to lunch.

Kiesslings was open seven days a week from 8 a.m. to 6 p.m., with a two hour lunch break from midday. Before making lunch, Nina sometimes rushed off for a quick dip in the sea, as she never had time to do so during the busy morning hours. After lunch we would all have a little snooze. Most of the residents took a midday break for lunch and a nap, and during these hours the streets were largely deserted.

At 4 p.m. the daily train arrived, bringing new arrivals, and the railway station would fill with people, most of them there out of curiosity and to see and be seen. During the peak month of August there were an estimated 10,000 vacationers in Peitaiho.

I really loved our summers there, with its lovely weather, warm water, no school, many friends. I did a lot of fishing, both in the sea and in the river. We went walking, bike riding, hunting, kite flying. It was heaven for me. But it wasn't too much of a holiday for my mother. She rose every day at 6.30 a.m., did a full day's work in the shop and then cooked dinner. After dinner she often spent an hour or two doing the bookkeeping. On top of that, she did most of the housework. But she was happy to do this, as it gave her son an opportunity to spend the summer on the beach. In addition, it offered her family a chance to visit the resort at minimum cost.

As you may have gathered by now, my mother Nina was one of the most unselfish and generous creatures on earth.

Grandpa Leonid giving me a lesson, Peitaiho Beach, 1938

During the summer of 1938 my grandfather, Leonid, came over from Shanghai to spend two months with us in Peitaiho. I had been looking forward to his visit, as I had never seen him before. Although he had come to Tientsin for my father's funeral, I was then only two and could not remember him.

Unfortunately my memories of his visit to Peitaiho are not all that pleasant, the main reason for this being the issue of Russian lessons. Grandfather decided that, at the age of six, my knowledge of the Russian language was wanting and that, out of the kindness of his heart, he would give me daily lessons. His overwhelming generosity did not impress me at all. During my summer

With Grandpa Leonid on Peitaiho Beach, 1938

With Grandpa Leonid on top of Lotus Hills, overlooking Peitaho Beach, 1938

With Nadia and Nina farewelling Leonid at Peitaho Beach station, 1938

vacation, I needed lessons like a hole in the head. But there was no escape. My mother thought it was a good idea, my grandfather thought it was a good idea, so who was I to argue? From then on I had to have a lesson every morning before I was allowed to go to the beach.

My grandfather's favourite pastime appeared to be that of whacking me on the head or forehead with a metal spoon whenever I did something not to his liking. This often happened during the Russian lessons if I was not paying attention or was slow on the uptake. A spoon was always handy, as he liked to sip tea while teaching. The spoon attacks also occurred at table during meals if I did anything to displease him, and this was done in front of others, even those outside the family. I resented this passionately. Firstly, I did not think he had the right to physically abuse me — that was my mother's prerogative. Secondly, doing it in front of others was demeaning. And lastly, it hurt like hell!

But even though my mother wasn't pleased with Leonid's actions, it took her some time to pluck up enough courage to ask him to stop. Past memories were very strong and she obviously still carried some latent fear of him.

Somehow or other, when my grandfather and I were away from the house, the lessons and the infamous spoon, we seemed to get along very well. He taught me how to swim, we went on long walks, and he spent many hours telling me fascinating stories of his military exploits. At the end, I suppose, I was sorry to see him go — and my Russian had improved.

Nina managed to get a job at Kiesslings for her youngest sister Nadia. In fact Nadia was her assistant in Peitaiho from 1937 to 1939, keeping it all in the family, so to speak.

Nadia had become a striking girl. Her looks were different from her sisters. While the others were fair, Nadia was dark haired and olive skinned. Full of fun and energy, she wore her hair short, giving her a tomboyish look. The fact she could never be taken for her father's daughter gave rise to various light-hearted, tongue-in-cheek comments about her possible parentage, to the great distress of Aida, who had absolutely no sense of humour.

Nadia's ardent suitor was Boris Kozlovsky, a young mechanical engineer working for a Ford dealership. He was tall and handsome and, like Volodia,

Nadia at the railway station, 1939

he too sported a grandiose Roman nose. Best of all, he had a sharp wit and a delightful sense of humour. He adored Nadia and it was a good match. Nadia had a strong, assertive and somewhat domineering personality, and in Boris she found a loving, funny, malleable and obedient partner.

In 1938 Boris wrote to her asking if he could spend a few days with her in Peitaiho. She agreed but thought it would be improper for them to stay under the same roof. Besides, her father was then in Peitaiho and there was not enough room for yet another visitor. Alternative accommodation was found and they spent a few wonderful days together, meeting only in the evenings, as she was working during the day. But the evening was the most romantic time anyway.

In those days there was no electricity in Peitaiho, so the streets were unlit at night. A popular pastime was the after-dinner walk. Just about the whole white population would venture out, armed with flashlights or lanterns, to see friends, stop for a talk, exchange gossip. The evening walks were especially popular with young couples. There was even an unpublished rule governing

The lovebirds, Nadia and Boris Kozlovsky, the day before he proposed, Peitaiho Beach, 1938

the use of the well-known private nooks around the beaches. If you occupied one and saw another couple approaching, you blinked your flashlight twice and the interlopers were duty bound to leave and look for another place.

Towards the end of summer the seawater was filled with tiny phosphorescent micro-organisms, about the size of small peas. On a moonless night, they emitted an ethereal light when disturbed. The crest of the waves would be lit up, and as one walked on the wet sand the footprints would light up as well. It was like a fairyland.

And it was in this idyllic setting that Boris proposed to Nadia. They were sitting on a rock and looking out to sea when he popped the question. At first she thought he was joking. After all, she had only known him for a few months. But when she laughed he became visibly upset and she realised he was serious. To calm him down, she accepted. By now she decided she loved him as well.

They were married on 29 January 1939. The reception was at the Tientsin Russian Club. The star attraction, besides the couple, was a six-year-old boy dressed in a white Cossack uniform, who sat on a stool in the middle of the dance floor and played a stirring Russian march on a miniature piano accordion. It brought the house down. I was that boy. It was my very first public performance — and I loved it!

3 THE JAPANESE OCCUPATION 1937–1945

THE INVASION: 1937–1939

In 1937 Japan overran China. Its occupation of Manchuria in 1931 had not satisfied its expansionary ambitions. As the Chinese Army was weak and disorganised, it appeared only a matter of time before Japan would act. All it needed was a plausible excuse to start a war. A minor skirmish between Chinese and Japanese troops near Peking gave it that pretext. This undeclared war and the subsequent occupation were to cost twenty million Chinese lives.

The Chinese Army was no match for the Japanese. Tientsin was captured in July 1937, Shanghai in November, and the Rape of Nanking occurred in December. What happened in Nanking was by far the most cruel and barbaric incident of the occupation. The Japanese killed and raped indiscriminately. Hordes of Chinese were forced to dig trenches, only to be forced into them, doused with gasoline and set alight. Men and women were tied to crossbars and used for bayonet practice. Children were not spared. Neither were the women. The six-week orgy cost some 300,000 Chinese lives.

By the end of 1938 the Chinese Army had retreated to the far west and the war was effectively over. Japan had control of the major cities and the railway lines and had installed a puppet government. The only lingering unpleasantness was the fact that the emerging Communist forces continuously challenged Japan's authority with their guerilla tactics.

The Japanese were ruthless conquerors. They demanded total obedience and respect from the Chinese, under pain of death (literally). But the foreign population remained largely unmolested. At that time there were only three foreign Concessions left in Tientsin — the British, French and Italian — and these were left untouched. The Japanese had enough on their plate without risking the possible wrath of the foreign governments.

But as time went by the presence of these Concessions became more and more of an irritant to the Japanese. Even though they had conquered China, they still had no jurisdiction over the foreigners living in those Concessions, and those foreigners controlled most of the financial and business might of the city.

Gradually the Japanese began making life difficult for the foreigners. Their first major action was the imposition of high taxes on all imports from the West. This was soon followed by the requirement to have special permits to export goods, resulting in massive delays and unbridled palm greasing and corruption.

Two further incidents inflamed the situation. The first occurred when the Japanese asked the British if one of their regiments could take a short cut through the British Concession on their way to the river mouth. The British refused, and not too politely at that. The second was the matter of millions of ounces of silver bullion. Prior to the occupation, the Chinese government had stashed this horde into the vaults of the Bank of China's branch on the French Concession. The Japanese demanded its return, but the French refused point blank.

On 19 June 1939 the Japanese retaliated. They erected barbed wire barricades around the adjoining British and French Concessions, thus isolating them from the rest of the city. All pedestrian and vehicular traffic to and from the Concessions was subjected to intense and delaying search tactics. Many foreigners were subjected to embarrassing body searches, with the Japanese soldiers smirking away as they pawed the most intimate parts of female bodies. There were numerous incidents of citizens being stripped naked in public during these searches. This was, of course, most humiliating, demeaning and distressing to the foreigners — which is exactly the effect the Japanese wanted.

Representations by the citizens to the British and French governments back home had no effect. They were too busy with events in Europe. After all, it was only three months before Britain declared war on Germany.

The barricades remained in place for a year. Eventually, the British and the French capitulated. The silver bullion was released and the Japanese were allowed to march at will through the British Concession. By that time, both Britain and France were embroiled in World War II and the welfare of a few thousand foreigners

in a country on the other side of the world was of minimal concern to their governments. The locals realised they could not rely on any support from their governments and would have to fend for themselves, without any of the special privileges they had enjoyed for so long.

Triumphant march of the Japanese through the British Concession, 1940

Tientsin Russian Volunteer Corps—arrows point to Boris Kozlovsky at left and Volodia Ostrouhoff at right, 1938

PLAYING GOD: 1939

Having finally reconciled herself to the idea that Arthur had disappeared, Jenia was impatiently waiting for the day of her wedding to Volodia. But on the eve of the wedding Fate took a cruel turn. The postman delivered a letter from Arthur!

Jenia was out when it arrived and Aida, recognising Arthur's handwriting, realised the source. It was an awful shock to her. She too had resigned herself to the loss of Arthur and had been delighted with the new happiness her daughter had found with Volodia. And now this! The big question in Aida's mind was: should she give the letter to Jenia or destroy it? Deciding that two heads were better than one, she kept the letter, unopened, to show to Nina when she came home from work. Together, they would determine what to do with it.

When Nina opened the letter, they were stunned by its contents. Arthur was apologising for not writing to his wife for two years. He related a terrible story of woe. Having lost his first job, he was unable to find another. There was no social security and, without money, he could not pay the rent. Becoming a vagrant, he began sleeping on park benches and eating in Red Cross soup kitchens. Six months of this miserable existence had undermined his health. After collapsing in the street he was taken to hospital, where he was diagnosed with tuberculosis. The last eighteen months had been spent in hospital. He said he had not written because he did not want to worry her, thinking he would wait until he was cured. Unfortunately the treatment was not working and he was unlikely to leave the hospital alive. He asked her to reply, care of the County Hospital in San Francisco.

Aida and Nina spent a sleepless night discussing the issues. Showing the letter to Jenia on the eve of her wedding would undoubtedly result in her cancelling it. What then? Would she wait until Arthur died before she married again? Or would she try to borrow some money and embark on a long sea voyage to see him once more before he passed away? And what possible good would that be to anybody? After years of waiting, Jenia was within reach of happiness again. Should this chance be withheld from her? On the other hand, did they have the right to withhold the letter? Did they really have the moral right to play God?

By morning they were agreed on the course of action. They would withhold the letter. Jenia was about to have a chance to be happy again and this unwelcome letter would certainly throw a spanner in the works.

That afternoon, Jenia and Volodia were married.

A few weeks later, another letter from Arthur arrived, and it was again intercepted by Aida. In it Arthur was saying goodbye. He wrote he only had a few days to live, and apologised for all the suffering he had caused his wife.

He said he had always loved her and would go on loving her to his dying day. Aida and Nina had a good cry, but felt their decision to withhold the first letter was now vindicated. Perhaps one day they would show both letters to Jenia. One cannot guess what effect the letters would have had on her life had she seen them.

But that was still not the end of Arthur…

THE BIG FLOOD: 1939

From the beginning of the Japanese occupation, there were skirmishes between the Japanese forces and the Chinese guerilJas — or partisans, as they were called. These skirmishes occurred in rural areas and did not affect city life — at least not until the end of July 1939 when the partisans, for some reason or other, dynamited the four-metre high earthen flood-control wall surrounding Tientsin.

It was the middle of summer. My mother and I were in Peitaiho. Nadia, who was then five months pregnant, was there as well. Boris, her husband of six months, was in Tientsin, working for the Ford dealership and living in Aida's boarding house at #18 Yang-Ho-Li.

It was a Sunday morning when Boris first heard that there was water on the outskirts of town. Curious, he mounted his bike and pedalled south on Taku Road to check it out for himself. Sure enough, a few kilometres on there was water on the road. It was certainly not just a rumour. It will probably reach us in a few days, he thought, and off he pedalled back to see a movie. On the way home from the theatre he was amazed to see water on the road just a block away from Yang-Ho-Li. He and Aida decided it would be prudent to buy some essential provisions, just in case.

But others had the same idea much earlier and all that was left in the shops for any emergencies were candles. Bread was already unavailable. However, there was a flour shop near the Ford dealership, only a few minutes away by bicycle. Boris hurtled off to the French Concession, hoping that the flour was still available. It was and he bought a whole sack of it, placed it on the handlebars and started back. A few blocks from home, the water had risen high enough to make pedalling impossible and he had to wade the rest of the way, shielding the flour from any splashes.

The entrance to the apartment in Yang-Ho-Li was up four steps, and the water was already lapping the second one. By the following morning the water had risen a metre and a half, and there was now about half a metre of water in the entrance hall.

The apartment had two rooms on the same level as the entrance hall. The large room was vacant but a smaller one was rented by Sergei Pootintsev. The door to this room was closed and Boris therefore assumed Sergei was out. Being a thoughtful soul, Boris decided to move the man's possessions to a room on a higher floor. Imagine his surprise when, opening the door, he discovered Sergei sound asleep in the middle of a lake of water. The level was only a few centimetres below his mattress and, floating on the surface like a pair of miniature junks, were his slippers. Boris woke him up and helped the shocked boarder carry his belongings to the second floor of the three-storeyed apartment.

By this time the water in the street was two metres deep. If Boris and Aida were to be mobile, they would obviously need some means of transportation. But where and how were they to find a boat? The wooden front gate was not solid enough to use as a raft and there was no other timber in the house.

One of the boarders, Boris Maksutov, had an idea. He was associated with the Jewish club, Kunst, which was just around the corner and he remembered seeing some wooden boards in the club's backyard. Maybe they were still there. But how was he to get to the club? Swimming did not appeal, so he set off walking across the roofs of the apartments.

One of many homemade craft, Tientsin, 1939

An hour passed and Aida was beginning to worry about her boarder's welfare when they heard his yelling outside: 'Make way for the *Queen Mary!*' And there he was, floating into the alley astride a stack of timber, paddling furiously, a big grin on his face.

With this timber and the wood from the gate, the two Borises were able to fashion a raft which could hold three passengers. They christened it the *Queen Mary.* By the time this craft was launched into the street there was a flotilla of all sorts of handmade craft — enamel baths, tables and the like. One of the most eye-catching was a chair with its legs nailed on top of two horizontal planks. The weight of the passenger caused the planks to sink below the water and it looked as if the chair was floating on the surface.

As our mariners paddled on, they noticed some people were busy fishing out small blocks of wood. At first they could not identify them but then realised they were the paving blocks used in many of the streets. Why were they collecting them, Boris inquired. For firewood, was the reply.

Of course! Two inches thick and heavily coated with bitumen, they would be ideal for stoking the little cooking stove Aida had set up on the third-floor verandah. The Borises joined in the activity and the whole process developed into a furiously competitive game. People frantically paddled backwards and forwards plucking the blocks out of the water. In the excitement, some overbalanced and fell in, but it was great fun.

The hall window on the ground floor now became the entrance to the apartment. The windowsill was just above water level, allowing one to comfortably step out of the *Queen Mary* into the hallway.

Soon, entrepreneurial Chinese hawkers were floating around in homemade craft, selling provisions to the households at a healthy premium.

As soon as the news of the collapse of the floodwall reached them, the Ford dealership management took appropriate precautions, organising the construction of a high brick wall around the property and moving the spare parts up to a higher floor. All other work at the dealership ground to a halt and Boris, who was pining for Nadia, decided to visit her in Peitaiho Beach. As Aida had the situation under control and Chelpanov had moved in to help her, Boris felt he could be spared. He caught what proved to be the last train out of Tientsin, shortly before one of the railway bridges was washed out. Nadia was delighted to see him and my kind-hearted mum let her off earlier each day so they could spend more time together.

Ten days later Boris received an urgent telegram from Ford requesting his immediate return, no reason given. Orders were orders. He had to go. At the station, he was informed the railway line was only open as far as Tan-ku (now called Tanggu), about fifty kilometres short of Tientsin. When Boris asked how he could get from Tan-ku to Tientsin, the railway official just shrugged his shoulders.

At Tan-ku, Boris discovered there was no such thing as a ferry service to Tientsin. However, there were many craft in the harbour and he commenced negotiations to hitch a ride. Most boat owners refused but he was finally able to bribe his way on to a tugboat which was pulling two large barges upriver.

The journey made Boris realise the extent of the devastation. A steep cliff outlined the right bank and indicated the path of the river, but the left bank was nonexistent. The water had spread as far as the eye could see — a huge

Hsi Kai Catholic Cathedral during flood, Tientsin, 1939

The Ford Motor Co about to lift a sunken car for transportation to the workshop—Kailan Mining Administration (KMA) building at right, Tientsin, 1939

muddy lake, with jutting treetops and rooftops. Many of the roofs were covered with people and some with animals, all waiting for the water to subside or for rescue. But there was no-one to help them. The emergency support system was nonexistent.

On arriving in Tientsin, Boris wound his way to the Ford dealership, which was in the French Concession. He was surprised to see the dealership yard filled with cars. Before he left, it had been empty.

'What's going on here?' he asked.

'We've got a fantastic opportunity to make a lot of money,' his boss replied. He then proceeded to tell Boris about this moneymaking scheme. 'We've worked out a way of lifting cars out of the water. What we do is tie two boats together, about three metres apart, place them over the submerged car and lift it up so its wheels are off the ground. Then we paddle like mad and bring the car back here. The owners are prepared to pay big money for the drying and reconditioning work. We're busy as hell! We need every pair of hands we can find.'

Boris worked five sixteen-hour days, sleeping on a camp bed on the premises. On the sixth day he was given a day off and visited the rest of the family in Yang-Ho-Li. To get there he had to rent a makeshift raft, complete

Aida rowing the #18 *Yang-Ho-Li Special*, Tientsin, 1939

with an entrepreneurial Chinese oarsman, an ex-rickshaw owner.

He was appalled by what he saw. The water was still at the level it had been before he left, but now it had turned into a stinking yellow-greenish liquid. Floating in it were dead rats, dogs, cats, pigs — even human corpses. In addition, a number of

Victoria Road in flood, Tientsin, 1939

flour storage facilities had flooded and this gave it a sticky soup-like texture. To try and prevent the spread of disease, the authorities had added some strong chemicals to the water. This potent mixture of chemicals, flour and pollution produced an unbelievable stink. On top of all that, it was now August, the hottest month of the year, and the temperature was over 40°C, with humidity at 100 percent.

When Boris sat down to have a meal with the rest of the family, he could not bring himself to eat — the smell was so terrible. He even had to take a couple of quick trips to the bathroom. The rest were not even conscious of the smell. Their bodies had adjusted to it.

Chelpanov, being an expert carpenter, had constructed a boat — the *# 18 Yang-Ho-Li Special*, he called it. It was one of the most attractive hand-made craft around and was proudly used by all the family. By now, boats had largely replaced rafts and the authorities even developed some special traffic rules, including the banning of motorised craft. Luckily, the electricity supply had only failed for two days, and the water and sewerage services continued uninterrupted.

Most provisions were bought from a flotilla of enterprising hawkers. Aida did the cooking on a small wood-fired stove on the verandah. The hall window was still used as the entrance to the apartment. If a dead animal floated close to the window, it would be casually prodded away with a long stick kept handy for this purpose.

It was interesting to note that there was hardly any whingeing or complaining. People took all these misfortunes and inconveniences in their stride. It'll soon be over, was the general attitude and gradually the water did indeed recede. Six weeks after the start of the flood, it was over.

The authorities instituted a mass inoculation program against typhoid and cholera and covered the streets liberally with lime and carbolic acid. The resulting smell was nearly as bad as the earlier one. The barricades erected by the Japanese had been washed away but were quickly re-erected and stayed up for another year. Overall, the flood and the subsequent clean-up lasted two and a half months, ending in the last week of September, which is when my mother, Aunt Nadia and I returned from Peitaiho Beach. Thankfully, we had missed all of it.

Two months later, on 10 November 1939, exactly nine months and twelve days after their wedding, Nadia gave birth to a healthy son, christened George.

ST LOUIS COLLEGE: 1937–1941

In 1937, at the age of five, I was sent to the Russian School, a combined primary/secondary school. Here all the teaching was done in Russian and all the students wore uniforms, with the boys in 'toy soldier' gear. As my mother did not have enough money to buy me a uniform, she and Aida sewed one up for me. The only item they could not make was the smart military cap. That had to be bought. Whenever a photo opportunity came up and I was in my uniform, I would go into salute mode.

After a year in the Russian School, my father's sister Lena talked my mother into moving me to the Tientsin Grammar School so I could learn English. She believed I had to be brought up understanding a universal language. Russian, she thought, would be picked up automatically through family interaction, but English would be essential for any future career. She was right, of course. The Tientsin Grammar School was a coeducational institution run by the British. It was more expensive than the Russian School and Lena offered to help pay the fees. By that time she was married to a rich Englishman called Howell and was well off.

As my mother was still working six-day weeks and generally came home late, I did not see anywhere near enough of her. My upbringing was therefore largely in the hands of my grandmother and whichever of Nina's sisters was then living with her. As I was not their child, they were reluctant to punish me if I misbehaved and I was apparently gradually

Jenia with me in my saluting pose, Tientsin, 1937

getting out of hand. What I needed, my mother decided, was an environment with more discipline than I was getting at home.

And that's why I became a boarder at the St Louis College for boys, a Catholic school run by Marist Brothers. It was much more expensive than Tientsin Grammar, but Lena came to the rescue again, paying the extra cost. I was eight years old.

Although the teaching language of St Louis College was English, none of the Brothers had it as their first language. The closest was Brother Aloysius, an Irishman; the rest were German, French, Spanish — you name it — anything but English. Each spoke the language well, but each had a pronounced accent, the end result being that the students developed peculiar and unique accents. Children are particularly susceptible to outside influence, and they mimic whatever accent they like most. So no two students leaving the college ever sounded the same, and to this day these individual accents have largely remained with them. Even now, no-one is able to guess my parentage. I've been taken for Irish, Canadian, American, Scottish, but never Russian.

The only foreign language taught was French, not Chinese. Isn't that amazing? Here we were, living in China, surrounded by Chinese and likely to be here for the rest of our lives, but they thought it was more important for us to learn French than Chinese.

The college had seven classes and they were, for reasons unknown, listed in descending order — class 7 for beginners and class 1 for seniors.

Class 7 was run by Brother Francis, a strict colourless young German.

Class 6 by Brother Otto, another German — a real sadist, who loved to inflict bodily pain and operated some sort of annoying hand-held clicking device to attract the students' attention.

Class 5 was run by Brother Konrad, yet another German, who was the most popular Brother in the College. Always cheerful, he had a great sense of humour and was a fantastic goalkeeper in soccer. His nickname was Jim-Boom. It was most entertaining to see him dive for the ball while dressed in the mandatory full black Marist tunic.

Class 4 was run by the Irish Brother Aloysius, also a decent chap with a sly sense of humour.

Class 3 was the domain of Brother Nestor, an ugly and humourless Frenchman with a long, curly, smelly beard.

Class 2 was run by Brother Vincent, a Spaniard — strict, but charismatic, so it was difficult to hate him too much.

And Class 1, the senior class, was run by two Brothers — the Spanish Brother Claude, an excellent teacher with a dry sense of humour, who used to address us as 'diluted asses' (not smart enough to qualify as 'regular asses') and the rotund Brother Charles, another German. Brother Charles was a paedophile. He loved fondling and kissing some of the younger students.

Charles

Otto

Aloysius

Francis

George

Vincent

Nestor

Jules-
Raphael

Eight of the Brothers of St Louis College

Brother Konrad as goalkeeper, Tientsin, 1942

St Louis College, Tientsin, 1940

Being in charge of the stationery store, he would entice his victims there, hiding behind the shelves to do his bit. A despicable character, but a good teacher.

There were also stories of Brother Otto's paedophilic activities. He used to practice them in the attic, and only with the boarders. His favourite pastime was to spank a boy's bare bottom, ever so gently, so lovingly — ugh! A fellow boarder, who was a close school friend of mine, told me tearfully of being molested by Brother Otto, and I myself saw Brother Charles in action.

Why did the victims not report these acts? Possibly because they were afraid of retribution, maybe because they were afraid nobody would believe them, or maybe they obtained favours from the Brothers in return. Who knows?

The playground activities were supervised by old Brother George, a Frenchman. We called him *Koziol* (Russian for 'goat') because he wore a goatee beard. He was the most ancient of the Brothers, probably in his seventies at the time, but he had a keen eye for mischief, of which there was a lot, and powerful lungs for the incessant whistle blowing he engaged in.

The big chief was the director, Brother Jules-Raphael, another Frenchman. We glimpsed him very rarely — he was the man you saw before you were expelled from college. Otherwise he maintained a low profile. All I remember of him was his sizeable, red nose.

Our school day began at 6.30 a.m. — ablutions, prayers in the chapel (mandatory, whatever religion you were), breakfast, homework, and then classes at 9 a.m. Each class began with a recitation of three Hail Marys. The school day ended at 4 p.m. and was followed by recreation, homework, dinner, homework again, chapel, ablutions and bed at 9.30 p.m. The dormitory slept about fifty boarders. School was on for six days a week, with Wednesday and

Saturday afternoons off. Wednesday afternoons were normally devoted to sport.

Boarders were not permitted to visit home during the week, even during the half days off. Exceptions were only granted to those who attended music lessons or other events of an educational nature. On Sunday we had to attend morning Mass, Catholic of course, before being allowed to go home at about 10 a.m. And we had to be back by 6 p.m. So we were, in effect, given only eight hours of freedom a week.

I was a somewhat skinny and fragile boy — not sickly, just rather delicate. When I joined the college I was, at eight, the youngest boarder in the school. The Brothers, I think, took pity on me and treated me kindly. Most of the other boarders were the real ruffians of the school — those whose parents desperately wanted them out of their sight and in a corrective institution — whereas I was there because my mother worked long hours and couldn't look after me, though perhaps there was the little matter of my getting a bit out of hand.

Mother visited me at least once a week. She would bring soap, toothpaste and other provisions, and re-make my bed (she claimed the bottoms of the sheets were always black because I did not wash my feet thoroughly enough). In addition, she used to review my scholastic progress with the Brothers and, most important of all, regularly brought me a box of cakes and other delicacies, courtesy of Kiesslings. The wiser senior students monitored my mother's visiting schedule, and would then fight their way to sit at the table with me to share in the spoils. We had tables of eight in the dining room, so I would not often get more than one-eighth of the booty — share and share alike, was the motto –

– but what I lost in cakes I more than gained in popularity.

Class 5 soccer team—I am standing on extreme right, Tientsin, 1942

The grounds of the school were clay. There were no lawns. Half the area was devoted to a two-thirds size soccer field and the other half was used for other sports, mainly softball and volleyball. There was also a shed which was open on one side and used as a handball court. I played all the sports except volleyball but was not really good at any of them. However, my favourite was soccer.

I loved the position of goalkeeper – – not the ideal position for a short guy like me, who could only reach the crossbar in his last two years of school, and that only after a mighty leap. But goalkeeper I had to be, as I was a great fan of a local Italian soccer team whose goalkeeper was a handsome acrobatic player named Dalducca. He would dive bravely and spectacularly for the ball, bringing gasps of delight from the onlookers. I was determined to be as skilful and popular as he, and had dreams of spectacular diving saves in important matches, accompanied by the squeals of female fans.

Every lunchtime, there was a half-hour soccer match, the odd-numbered classes against the even-numbered, with just about all the students participating. Only the real sissies abstained. It was one hell of a mess on the field, but great fun. I was always the goalkeeper, and a rather bad one at that, but I compensated for this lack of prowess by performing my duties with great gusto and getting much grimier than anyone else on the field. In fact I did not have much competition for the position of goalie. Nobody else wanted it — it was too dirty a job.

Mother hated the idea of my playing soccer for two reasons: firstly she considered it dangerous, especially in my heroic position as goalie; and secondly she was sick and tired of having my shoes mended. Although I had proper soccer boots, I only wore them for the rare big matches, not for the daily lunchtime games.

Handball was another sport I liked. As regulation handballs were too expensive, we used worn tennis balls. As they were much heavier, they had to

Bro Konrad in the College yard, Tientsin, 1942. Note the paper-plastered windowpanes to protect from shattered glass during air raids. The handball court is in the background.

be hit with a clenched fist rather than an open palm. This bashing played havoc with my hands. They would swell up and the skin would crack across the knuckles, especially in winter. My mother did not think much of this sport either. It would ruin my hands and affect my future virtuosic piano career, she thought.

Another pastime which made a mess of my hands was marbles. I was a marble fanatic for a couple of years, and the continuous rubbing of the knuckles on the ground would chafe them to the bone. Mum devised a special pad which I used to tie across my knuckles to protect them. It was crude but effective. Several other students adopted Mum's invention.

The Marist Brothers were fervent believers in the adage of 'spare the rod and spoil the child'. Their rod was a thin bamboo stick, which they used frequently to dispense public floggings. Perhaps 'floggings' is too strong a word, but they were certainly painful. For minor misdemeanours, the punishment was a whack across an outstretched palm. More serious violations resulted in multiple strikes. If you pulled your hand away at the last moment you were given an additional penalty strike.

For the most serious misdemeanours, the target area became the backside. The victim would be required to bend down to make the skin in the target area nice and tight. The bamboo rod would then descend and hit the rear with a vicious whack, accompanied by sympathetic groans from the rest of the class. I remember one victim attempting to lessen the pain by surreptitiously stuffing an exercise book into his pants. Unfortunately the sound of the stick hitting the exercise book was markedly different to that of an unprotected rear and the Brother uncovered the subterfuge. The result was a doubling of the number of strokes.

MY WORLD OF MUSIC: 1939

I have loved music for as long as I can remember. At home we had a gramophone and quite a few records, mainly of the Russian crooner Leschenko, and I played them at every opportunity. I knew all the melodies and even the words. My dream was to be able, some day, to either sing or play an instrument.

At about the age of seven, a year before I became a boarder in St Louis College, my mother decided I should take piano lessons. We did not have a piano, but Mother believed that was unimportant. The selected piano teacher was a middle-aged lady by the name of Madam Hohlachkin, and I had two lessons a week with her.

Madam Hohlachkin was undoubtedly the worst thing that could have happened to me from a musical standpoint. She was a horrible person — domineering, temperamental, impatient — and she completely lacked the ability and/or desire to motivate her students. Because I did not have a piano at home, I was not progressing terribly fast and she made my life a misery. Whenever I did anything wrong, which was often, she would tell me my head was filled with cabbage instead of brains. Her favourite punishment was to make me stay back after the lesson and stand in a corner, a typically Russian punishment. To make matters worse, she did this to me while she was giving her next lesson, inflicting upon me the humiliation of a public chastisement. In addition, she would tell the new student what an absolute idiot I was. I hated her for this and I hated the idea of being taught by her.

After a year of this torment I had become a boarder in St Louis College and had a piano to practise on. However, my heart was not into practising. I knew that, however much work I did and however well I played, she would find fault with me. Why bother? Why am I doing this? I asked myself. Why am I subjecting myself to this torture, when I could just stay back and play sport instead?

Brilliant! And that is exactly what I began to do. I must have skipped about eight lessons in a row before my mother found out. It could have gone on forever, except that my mother sometimes picked me up at the studio in the Kiesslings car to give me a lift back to the college. Arriving at the studio one day, she was informed that I had not been around for weeks. The jig was up! Mother went to the college and asked Brother Director for permission to take me home for an hour or so 'to have a little chat' with her son. I braced myself for a well-deserved hiding, but she sat down with me and quietly asked what was up. She knew I loved music and was very keen to learn the piano.

'Something must be very wrong. What is it?' she asked me.

I burst out crying and poured out the whole sad story to her.

'Do you still want to take piano lessons?' she asked.

'Yes I do,' I cried, ' but not with that horrible woman.'

'All right,' she said. 'I'll find you another teacher.'

And find me another one she did. His name was Nikolai Sajin and he had the reputation of being the best piano teacher in the Far East. Back in Russia he had been a pupil of Alexander Scriabin and he now had a successful studio with many talented pupils. Mother went to see him and told him the whole story. He listened patiently but then said: 'I'm sorry, but I can't take him. I have too many students as it is. Besides, once a child loses his interest in music it's very difficult to rekindle it.'

Mother begged him to take me, assuring him I still loved music and would be a keen dedicated student — and, of course, that I had great talent. He finally relented. To make sure my interest was rekindled as quickly as possible, he went easy on the dull exercises and scales and, instead, gave me attractive little pieces to study. As a result, I practised a lot and began to look forward to each lesson. Sajin's key strength was his ability to make the study of music interesting for the younger pupil. This he did by inventing little stories for each work I was required to study, something that would give my impressionable young mind a visual image of what the music was supposed to represent.

I remember well the story he spun for Rachmaninov's famous Prelude in C sharp minor, the one with the tolling bells. 'A beautiful young girl falls into a coma. Her family thinks she is dead, and buries her. She wakes up and starts screaming, tearing at the coffin lid — but to no avail. Gradually she runs out of energy and air, and dies.'

Fifty years later, I related this story before performing the work at a concert in Australia. A woman came up to me at interval to tell me she had been moved to tears by my performance, even though she had heard the piece dozens of times before.

I don't think it was just the quality of the performance which brought out the tears ...

LIFE IN THE 'YELLOW BABYLON': 1930–1940

Between 1930 and 1937 Shanghai was an important centre of commerce. Business boomed and the future looked very bright. Somehow or other, the city had been insulated from the post-Depression gloom of the rest of the world.

This was also the period that saw the greatest growth of Shanghai's Russian population. After the Japanese occupation of Manchuria in 1931, life in Harbin had become increasingly difficult for the White refugees. Moreover, the Harbin

Cathay Theatre on Avenue Joffre, Shanghai, 1934

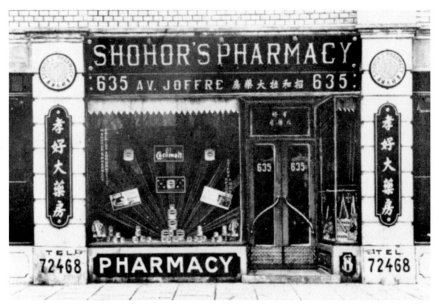

Russian pharmacy on Avenue Joffre, 1930s

Nanking Theatre, showing the Johnny Weismuller film 'Tarzan and His Mate', 1934

climate did not help things, with the temperature ranging from 30°C in summer to -40°C in winter. As a result, the exodus of Whites to the warmer and more hospitable environments of Peking, Tientsin and Shanghai accelerated. Most settled in Shanghai, whose White Russian population in the late 1930s grew to over 40,000.

Over the years, the Russians had developed an enviable reputation among the foreigners and now occupied important positions in both the commercial and business worlds. They had entered the successful middle class. Although stateless, they enjoyed total personal freedom. Avenue Joffre on the French Concession became the centre of the Russian community, so much so that there were more Russians in that part of the city than Chinese. The avenue was gradually transformed from a colourless residential street into a bustling, chic thoroughfare, full of elegant Russian shops and restaurants. The surrounding area boasted Russian churches, cathedrals and schools. The Russian Regiment of the Shanghai Volunteer Corps numbered 900 and was highly regarded.

Shanghai's cultural life was lively and energetic. Theatre, ballet, opera, art and concerts were in profusion. Russian musicians dominated the Shanghai Philharmonic Orchestra. Many celebrities visited the city, including film stars, musicians and singers. The famous Russian basso Feodor Shaliapin came, and so did the crooner Vertinsky and the renowned pianist Arthur Rubinstein. In those days the 'Yellow Babylon' was a great place to live.

Valya Kolbyuk, Len's first wife, 1938

After leaving his employment as a bodyguard, Len worked in a variety of jobs, including office work with the Shanghai Municipal Council. But he seemed to have difficulty in finding jobs that satisfied him. Fortunately there were plenty of employment opportunities.

Len had developed into a good-looking charismatic fellow with a nice sense of humour and a positive attitude. In his spare time he had taken up gymnastics, which had given him a good, strong body. All these physical assets made him attractive to women. And he, in turn, developed a great appetite for the opposite sex.

And it was this appetite which was to undermine many of his future relationships.

His first victim was Valya Kolbyuk.

Len displaying his gymnastic
prowess, 1933

Valya was the Harbin girl with whom Len
had a short affair when he visited his sister
Nusia in 1929. At that time he was twenty
and she was sixteen. Valya was infatuated
with him — he was her first love. She wrote
to him regularly over the years, first in
Tientsin, then Shanghai, and Len replied
occasionally. As far as she was concerned,
he was the man she would wait for till the
end of time.

In 1937 Valya moved from Harbin to
Tientsin and immediately looked up the
Tarasov family. A friendship developed with
the Tarasov sisters, eventually leading to Nina
hiring her for Kiesslings. When Len heard
Valya was in Tientsin, he came for a visit. The
romance re-ignited and he proposed to her.
She readily accepted and they were married
in Shanghai in early 1938.

Valya was a strikingly beautiful girl and they made a handsome couple.
But the marriage did not last long. Even though he had a lovely partner, Len
could not keep himself from eating forbidden fruit. When Valya realised this,
she too began dabbling in extra-marital activities. As Len worked night shifts
in Jessfield Park, tending the animals in the small zoo, Valya had ample
opportunity to do her dabbling.

After returning from work one morning and discovering some incriminating
evidence, Len slapped Valya around a bit. Terrified, she confessed her infidelity
and told him everything about her lover, including his name and address. Len
ordered her to pack her things and be out of the house by the time he returned.
He then ran to her lover's house and knocked on the door. A German opened
it, immediately recognising the wronged husband. Realising the game was

The Russian Regiment of the Shanghai Volunteer corps on parade, 1933

up, he began to cower and beg forgiveness. Len, who had earlier been as mad as a hornet and ready to kill the man, suddenly found himself cool, calm and collected.

'I know you've been screwing my wife,' he said, with great composure, 'but you'll be relieved to know I'm not here to beat the daylights out of you – – although, of course, you deserve it. Instead, I'm here to tell you that you are welcome to her, body and soul. I've thrown her out of the house and she's now all yours! Enjoy each other!'

With that, he turned on his heels and walked away. They were divorced soon after.

The Japanese had conquered China and Shanghai in 1937. Although there was some resistance put up by the Chinese army, it was quickly overpowered. In the process, the Japanese bombed parts of Shanghai, taking great care not to damage the foreign Concessions and provoke the ire of Britain and France. Most of the bomb damage was in the district known as Hongkew, one of the Chinese residential areas, which became something of a ghost district.

During 1938 and 1939, Shanghai witnessed the arrival of thousands of Jews from Europe, mostly escapees from the Nazi regime in Germany and Austria. They had arrived in Shanghai by default. Having tried and failed to obtain visas to 'civilised' countries such as America, Britain and Spain, they had discovered that China had no entry restrictions. Thus Shanghai suddenly became a most desirable destination, with 20,000 arriving there during those two years.

Unfortunately, due to the phenomenal growth of Shanghai over the years, there was little accommodation for the newcomers in the foreign Concessions and the Japanese decided they should all be relegated to a new area. The area they selected for the Jews was the bombed-out district of Hongkew. The Japanese reasoned the Jews were probably loaded with money and would have the means to rebuild the area.

Not all of them, of course, were loaded, but overall they did have sufficient funds and determination to rebuild the district and transform it into a microcosm of Europe. This Jewish ghetto eventually boasted synagogues, kosher food shops, fine restaurants and, of course, entrepreneurial business establishments. Over the years, the Jewish cultural life became second only to the Russians.

WE WANT YOU TO BE A SPY! — 1939

The Japanese were responsible for Jenia's and Volodia's move from Tientsin to Shanghai.

After their marriage in July 1939, the couple were very happy. The fact that they were not well off was, of course, a disappointment to Aida who was still living in hope of a rich son-in-law. But with Volodia working for the Tientsin Chinese Police and Jenia at Kiesslings, there was at least enough income to lead a modest life.

Volodia was talented at languages. Besides Russian he could speak Ukranian, French, English, Chinese and Japanese. Ukrainian was his native language (he was born in the Ukraine from a Russian father and a Ukrainian mother); French and English he learned in school; and Chinese and Japanese were picked up in the process of his business dealings.

When the Japanese authorities realised he was multilingual, they tried to recruit him to spy on the Soviets. Volodia refused. But they would not take no for an answer and continued to pressure him. Volodia kept refusing. Finally they resorted to threats: 'Is your wife healthy? Do you want her to remain healthy?'

Volodia decided it would be wise for them to move to Shanghai. As it was too dangerous for him to apply for a visa — the Japanese would certainly find out he wanted to skip town — he decided to move without official permission. In this he was aided by his friends in the Chinese Police, who were prepared to do anything to spite the Japanese invaders. It was a risky proposition, but it came off, and he and Jenia arrived in Shanghai without incident.

They were hoping to stay for a while with Len, but he had moved to a small rented room and there was not enough room for them. Fortunately Len's landlords let the Ostrouhoffs occupy another room on credit until Volodia could find a job.

And that is when Arthur came back into Jenia's life.

Eight months after their wedding, another letter from him arrived at Jenia's Tientsin address. Once again it ended up in Aida's hands. She was amazed to receive it. After all, months earlier he had written to say he had only a few days left to live. In the new letter, Arthur wrote he had experienced a miraculous cure and was now feeling much better and hoping to soon leave the hospital. He was asking Jenia to begin the process of obtaining a visa to join him in America — not knowing, of course, she had married Volodia.

Aida and Nina decided it was time they stopped playing God. Jenia should be told about this letter and also the earlier two. They dispatched all three to Len and asked him to pass them on to her, using the appropriate discretion. The letters were a terrible shock to Jenia. She cried her heart out. Although Volodia was terribly distressed, he was also most understanding, even offering to have their marriage annulled so she could go to America to join Arthur.

'If you choose to go to him, remember I love you and I'll always be here for you if something happens to him,' he assured her.

Just before this, Jenia had received a letter from Volodia's father in Harbin, whom she had never met. The letter contained a train ticket for her to come and visit him so they could get acquainted. This, she thought, was a great opportunity for her to get away and think the whole mess through.

After staying with her father-in-law for a month, Jenia came to the conclusion that her love for Arthur had dimmed and the love of her life was now Volodia. She wrote to Arthur telling him how much she had suffered during the period of his silence, and that she had married another man whom she loved very much and with whom she planned to stay for the rest of her life.

A few weeks later Arthur replied to say his health had again turned for the worse and his days were numbered. He begged forgiveness for the hurt he had caused her, and told her he always loved her. Wishing her happiness in her marriage and her future life, he said goodbye.

That was his last letter.

PEITAIHO BEACH HAPPENINGS: 1940

In the early days of our summers in Peitaiho, when I was still a little kid, my mother Nina used to hire a nanny or an amah to look after me for the summer. One year she hired a Russian nanny who was much older than the ones I was used to — at least sixty — a small ugly unpleasant woman, whom I disliked intensely.

One evening she decided to go to the toilet, which was in the back of the garden, a fair way from the house. As it was dark and there was no moon, she thought she could save herself a long walk by relieving herself in the bushes.

In those days, stray dogs were making a nuisance of themselves, often sneaking into the

Nina and the lovely Diana, Peitaiho Beach, 1940

garden at night for food scraps. Mongo the 'Monster' was intent on keeping them out. As the nanny crouched down in the dark to do her thing, she must have made some sort of canine noise. The vigilant Mongo heard it, picked up a heavy wooden yoke and threw it with great force in the direction of the noise. His aim was true. The yoke hit the nanny on the head and nearly tore her ear off. She came running into the house, her pants around her ankles, blood streaming from her ear.

'He's killed me, he's killed me!' she was screaming.

Mother rushed her to hospital, where the ear was sewed back on. But the excitement was all too much for her and she caught the next train back to Tientsin. Mongo had the fright of his life, but secretly I congratulated him. Good riddance!

My mother would take at least one salesgirl with her to Peitaiho. Until 1939 it was Nadia, but in 1940 she brought in the lovely Diana. She was about twenty-two and the prettiest girl I had ever seen. Although I was only eight, this did not stop me from having a crush on her. My childish adoration must have been obvious to her but, in spite of that, she became my willing guardian and friend. We played cards together, went to the beach, rode donkeys. She would come with me for my daily one-hour piano practice in the nearby church, even though it was during her lunch break. She was a real friend and I have the fondest memories of this lovely girl.

One evening my mother and Diana went out for an evening walk, the well-established after-dinner practice. As they passed a rowdy group of four or five men, one of them ran up to my mother and proceeded to cover her hands with kisses.

'Nina my dear Nina, it's me, Vasia. I haven't seen you for ages! Where have you been?'

At first Nina was confused and could not work out who this strange young man was.

'I'm Vasia. Remember? Vasia Artemieff. I was your English teacher about twelve years ago, when you first came to Tientsin.'

'Oh yes, I do remember you,' she said, recalling his amorous pursuit and

Nina, Queen of the Beach, Peitaiho Beach, 1938

her rejection of his approaches. She had not seen him since then.

The three of them sat down on a park bench and talked about old times. Vasia seemed overjoyed by this reacquaintance and followed up this encounter by coming to see her every evening for the rest of his two-week vacation. He appeared so enamoured of Nina that Diana decided it would be prudent for her not to accompany them for their evening strolls.

After leaving Peitaiho, Vasia bombarded my mother with love letters. His interest in her was understandable. She was, at the age of thirty-two, an attractive, mature woman. In fact, just two years earlier she had won the Peitaiho 'Queen of the Beach' contest.

When Mother returned to Tientsin, they started to go out regularly and the courtship took off in all seriousness.

MY NAKED AUNT: 1941

Lena, my father's sister, was married to an Englishman twenty-six years her senior. I did not know his first name as I used to call him Mister Howell. He was sixty-five at the time, while Lena was thirty-nine. He was quite rich and they lived in a beautiful apartment in Victoria Park Mansions, overlooking Victoria Park — five huge rooms, two bathrooms, a large kitchen and an enclosed verandah. There was beautiful furniture and expensive carpets everywhere, and a full-sized German Ibach concert grand piano in the living room, one of the few grands in Tientsin. I don't know why they bought it, as Lena was not much of a pianist.

Lena, Boris Ivashkoff's sister,
Tientsin, 1936

As a boarder I was allowed to use the school piano for practice, but naturally I preferred Lena's grand. The school piano was an ordinary instrument housed in a tiny bare room, whereas Lena's concert grand was a superb instrument occupying pride of place in a beautifully furnished large living room. I loved playing it, with the lid opened of course. I am sure there was not another music student in Tientsin who had access to such a fine instrument.

Sajin's studio was only two minutes' walk from Lena's apartment, and I would practise on the grand before or after the Wednesday and Saturday lessons. Lena gave me the key to her apartment so I could get in if she were out, thus giving rise to a memorable incident.

One afternoon, I go to the apartment to practise, letting myself in with my key. To be on the safe side, I decide to check to see if there is anyone at home. I walk into the bedroom and, lo and behold, find Lena and Howell both asleep in the big double bed, their bodies covered by a large white sheet. Being a considerate boy, I decide to wait until they got up, lest my music disturbs them. I pick up a magazine and sit down in an armchair in the corner of the bedroom to await their awakening.

Suddenly, Lena stirs and gets out of bed to go to the bathroom — and she is stark naked! She does not see me. I am glued to my seat, speechless, looking at my first naked woman ever, the words of greeting stuck in my mouth. After taking a few steps, she senses a foreign presence, sees me and screams. I am spluttering apologies, she is yelling at me to get the hell out of there. Mr Howell wakes up, and jumps out of bed — and he's naked too. And he starts yelling. I rush out in a panic. Bedlam!

When she gets dressed Lena tells me, in no uncertain terms, that I must be the biggest idiot in the world. I readily agree and promise never to do anything so stupid again. Reluctantly she allows me to keep the key to the apartment.

THE SOOTHSAYER: 1941

In 1941, when Nina had her annual leave, she went to visit Jenia and Volodia in Shanghai. Earlier she had written to Jenia about Vasia, and also about Ahonin, a Romanian who was another one of her suitors. Ahonin was the financial manager at Kiesslings. He was about ten years older than Nina and very well off.

To Jenia she had written that both of them were anxious to marry her, and that she herself wanted to re-marry — not only was she lonely, but she also believed a stepfather would be good for me — but she could not decide which man she should choose. Although she did not love them, she did like both of them. Her mother was dead against Vasia, believing him to be a philanderer and a drunkard, whereas she thought Ahonin was a good catch because he was rich. However, Nina preferred Vasia.

In reply, Jenia suggested that one way to resolve the issue would be to visit the Shanghai clairvoyant, Buchbinder, who had an awesome reputation for accurate predictions. Deciding she had nothing to lose, Nina asked her to set up an appointment.

Nina was ushered into a darkened room, so dim that she could just make out the shape of Buchbinder seated behind a large desk. Sitting down, she looked around. When her eyes adjusted to the darkness, she realised all the walls of the room were covered with eerie paintings of the devil and hideous

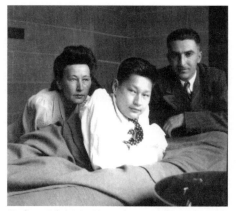

(Left to right) Mrs Zung, her paraplegic son and Volodia Ostrouhoff, Tientsin, 1943

Beelzebub masks. She was taken aback. Her expectation had been that a clairvoyant would be in touch with the good spirits, not the devil. This was hideous. She got up to leave, but his reassuring voice stopped her.

'Don't worry. This is all for show,' he said quietly. 'Just ignore it and let's talk about what brings you here.'

Sitting back down, she studied him carefully. He appeared to be about thirty-five, clean-shaven, with no distinguishing characteristics except for his piercing eyes. They were striking. She felt as if they were digging right into her soul and that he knew all her inner secrets. This would have normally made her uncomfortable, except the eyes were also kind and sympathetic. For a while they just sat there quietly, looking at each other, and she then noticed a large crystal ball on the desk in front of him. It seemed to be emitting a faint pulsating light.

'What would you like to know?' Buchbinder asked her.

Nina composed herself and told him she was there to find out about her marriage prospects. He nodded, took a cane, asked her to hold one end of it and then placed the other end on the crystal ball. After looking into it intently for what seemed to be an eternity, he spoke. This is the essence of what he said:

'You have suddenly and tragically lost a very close member of your family. There are now two men in your life. One is of your nationality and the other is not. You will soon be together with the one who is of your nationality. In the not too distant future, you will leave this country and go overseas. You will never be rich, but you will have a comfortable life.'

Before Nina left for Shanghai, Jenia had written that Buchbinder was also capable of forecasting a person's future from a photograph. A friend of Jenia's, Mrs Zung, heard Nina was going to see Buchbinder and asked her to show him her son's photo. The boy, aged about twelve, had fallen down the stairs when he was a toddler, damaging his spine and becoming a paraplegic.

'Please find out if he will ever walk again,' she asked Nina.

Nina took the photo out and showed it to Buchbinder.

He studied it for a while, his left hand on the crystal ball, and then said: 'This boy had a terrible accident and cannot walk. He will never be able to walk. When he turns fifteen, he will die under the knife.'

Nina was horrified. 'Should I tell her this?' she asked.

'That's up to you,' he said. 'However there is nothing she can do to alter the future.'

My mother then showed him a photo of me.

'I feel you are worried about this boy's health. Why?' he asked.

'Because his father died young from heart failure,' she replied.

'Stop worrying. This child was born under a lucky star,' he assured her. 'He is very fortunate. Don't worry about the heart problems. Many illnesses are not hereditary and this one has not been passed on to him. He will have a long happy life and you will get much pleasure out of him.'

Well, Buchbinder was right on all counts.

Nina did marry Vasia, left China and was never rich.

At the age of fifteen, the Zung boy did die from a failed operation on his spine. Mrs Zung had not been told of the prophecy, only that she should go on taking good care of him.

And I have had a charmed life. Hopefully, it will be also be a long one.

ARMBANDS FOR THE ENEMY: 1942–1943

Following Japan's Pearl Harbor attack on 8 December 1941, the Allies declared war on Japan and conditions in China deteriorated significantly. Business slumped, unemployment reached new heights and there were shortages of just about everything. As Britain was now at war with the Japanese, the British Concession in Tientsin was confiscated and, in a mock pompous ceremony, the Japanese handed it back to the Chinese. All associated Concession privileges were removed.

The citizens of Britain, USA, Holland and Belgium were branded as the enemy and required to wear bright red armbands at all times. These were about ten centimetres wide and inscribed with a large black Chinese character denoting the nationality of the wearer. The penalty for failing to wear them was a public beating. The French did not have to wear armbands. After their capitulation to the Germans in 1940 and the establishment of the collaborative Vichy government, the French were considered by the Japanese as neutrals.

The purpose of the armbands was twofold. Firstly, they indicated to the Japanese which members of the white population they could easily and rightfully bully. The second and more onerous objective was to show the Chinese that their 'foreign exploiters' had now been subjugated. The 'ill-gotten territory' of these 'greedy foreigners' had now been returned to their rightful owners, the Chinese, by the 'magnanimous' and 'heroic' Japanese conquerors.

Secretly, the Japanese were hoping the Chinese would take this opportunity to ill-treat the banded ones — spit on them, jostle them, refuse to serve them in the shops, maybe even beat them up. But nothing like that ever happened. What the Japanese failed to realise was that the Chinese harboured their strongest hatred for the Japanese themselves. By definition, an enemy of the Japanese thus became an ally of the Chinese. Their greatest desire was to rid their country of the Japanese. When that was done, they would turn their focus on evicting the 'foreign white devils'.

As for the stateless White Russians who had no passports, they were not at war with anyone and were left alone. Life seemed to go on as usual for them, although times were pretty tough.

The well-publicised Japanese atrocities were not aimed at the whites, although at all times one had to be very respectful to the occupying forces. The Chinese, however, were in mortal fear of them, as the Japanese considered them to be the scum of the earth and treated them as such.

As Kiesslings was a firm owned by allies of the Japanese, the business went on operating and Nina's job with it. Interestingly, citizens of the warring European nations — for example, the Germans and the British, or the Germans and the Russians — lived happily together in spite of the fierce war raging between their countries back home. There was very little animosity evident. The war was half a world away and the residents tended to disassociate themselves from it. They continued to be civil to each other, just as they had been in the old days. Kiesslings went on hiring Russian girls, and the Russian staff bore no resentment to their bosses.

Even in St Louis College, which was highly multinational, there were few quarrels between students of warring nations — except for the students in Class 5, which was run by Brother Konrad, a super-patriotic German who had been the most popular Brother among the students.

It all started when Brother Konrad began to precede each morning class, immediately after the three Hail Marys, with a recitation of the latest German short-wave radio news regarding the successes of the Nazi forces on the European front. He was especially vociferous about General Paulus' successful march on Stalingrad. This of course irritated the Russians who sat together at the back of the class — the 'Blockheads from Kamchatka', as Brother Konrad called them. Supporting the Brother were the fascist Italian students, the French (supporters of the Vichy government) and the Portuguese. On the side of the Russians were the Jews, the neutral Chinese, the anti-fascist Italians and the Greeks. There were no Germans in the class, as most of them attended the German school.

Every morning the Portuguese Simois Brothers would enter the class, click their heels and yell out 'Heil Hitler!' Brother Konrad would nod with pleasure and reply 'Sieg Heil!' The 'Blockheads from Kamchatka' would hiss. And so it went. There were even claims of favouritism for the German supporters — better marks, fewer reprimands — and prejudice against the Russian group.

One day in early February 1943, the Simois brothers entered the class with their customary 'Heil Hitler!' greeting. To everybody's surprise, Brother Konrad retorted with 'Sit down and shut up, you blockheads!'

What caused this change of attitude? The answer became obvious at the next recess when one of the seniors broke the news that a BBC broadcast the previous night had announced General Paulus' surrender to the Russians. The remnants of the German 4th and 6th Armies — 91,000 frozen, starving men and twenty-four generals — had surrendered with him. The siege of Stalingrad was over. It was the beginning of the end for Nazi Germany.

Brother Konrad never mentioned the war again.

MALARIA! — 1942

Back in Shanghai, Uncle Len had married again. His new wife Galya (short for Galina) Koulli was an attractive girl with an infectious laugh, eleven years his junior. She had been a friend of his first wife Valya and in better times the three of them had seen a lot of each other. Len gravitated to Galya on the rebound, so to speak, and they were married in December 1940, in spite of the strong objections of Galya's mother, Katya Grachova, a highly intelligent lady with a degree from Moscow University. In Len she saw a philanderer and a no-hoper, incapable of supporting her daughter and any children coming from the marriage. But Galya was in love and there was no stopping her.

Len grew to hate his mother-in-law. He felt she was always poisoning Galya's mind against him, and he was jealous of their close relationship. Maybe he also felt inferior to her because of her academic qualifications. Whatever the reasons, the hatred on both sides was deep and obvious. And, true to form, it did not take Len long to get back to his philandering ways. Galya should have listened to her mother. Len was not suited to married life.

During the summer of 1942 Jenia, who was also living in Shanghai, contracted malaria. She was very ill and needed a lot of care. Unfortunately Volodia could not afford to pay for a hospital stay or a live-in nurse, and medicines were expensive and hard to obtain. He was then working for the Russian Regiment of the Shanghai Volunteer Corps (a quasi-military police force) and living in their barracks. Although it was called a 'volunteer' corps, most of the members were full-time employees. Volodia's working shifts only allowed him to be home every second day from 9 p.m. to 6 a.m. When he was home, he would care for Jenia, but between his visits she was all alone.

As her condition began to deteriorate, the doctor told Volodia that Jenia would die unless she had full-time care. Her only relative in Shanghai was her brother Len, but both he and Galya were working and not in a position to provide this help. Volodia had no choice but to send Jenia off to her mother in Tientsin.

The Ostrouhoffs were desperately short of money. Volodia's Volunteer

Corps salary was paltry and the rent was high. There was little money left for food and absolutely none for clothes. What had saved them from starvation was the monthly ration of nine kilograms of flour which the corps provided. There was no money left for a train ticket to Tientsin, so Jenia wrote to Nina asking for help, and Nina immediately sent her the money for the journey.

With the war on, one needed a visa to travel between cities. To obtain a visa, one had to go through a long and cumbersome bureaucratic procedure, requiring visits to many offices in various parts of the city. As Volodia was working during the day, he asked for time off but it was refused. His only remaining alternative was to resign from his position. The resignation was a bitter one. The head of the corps vowed he would never allow Volodia back into the corps. Regrettably, Volodia had no choice but to accept the consequences. Jenia needed a visa and this was the only way he could get enough time to obtain one. With her gone, he was sure he could find other employment.

After Jenia was examined by Dr Nathing in Tientsin, he told Aida, in confidence, that her daughter's condition was very serious. Besides the malaria, she had some unusual problem with her stomach which prevented her from keeping any food down. He gave her some injections to stop the malaria shakes, but had no diagnosis for the stomach problems.

It was summer and Nina was in Peitaiho Beach running the Kiesslings branch. When she heard of Jenia's condition she told Aida to put her on the next train to Peitaiho. 'The sea air will be good for her and I'll nurse her back to health,' she promised.

My aunt Jenia was as skinny as a rake when she arrived, and Nina began to fatten her up, forcing her to eat a lot of cream, butter and other 'healthy' foods. And sure enough, after a month or so she was back on her feet and her stomach problems had disappeared. Returning to Tientsin, Jenia was still weak and Mrs Zung invited her to stay with her. Mrs Zung was a Russian woman, married to a rich Chinese businessman; they had a huge house and — would you believe it? — their own private fleet of rickshaws!

Meanwhile, Volodia had no luck finding another job in Shanghai. Unable to pay rent or even feed himself, he moved in with some friends. The future looked very bleak. There was now no thought of Jenia coming back to join him. Instead she wrote to him, asking him to move to Tientsin, and Mrs Zung sent him the money for the journey.

When he arrived, he was a shadow of his former self. His loss of weight made his aquiline nose appear even more prominent. In addition, he was downcast and fretting at the thought of not being able to provide for himself and his wife. He looked tired, drawn and wrung out. Mrs Zung came to the rescue by kindly insisting he stay with her for a month so she could fatten him up.

PARALYSED! — 1942–1944

Shortly after Jenia left Peitaiho Beach, Nina received a letter from her father, Leonid asking her if he could spend some of his vacation time with her. Nina had not seen her father for four years and was happy to have him visit, even though she had just spent a month looking after the sick Jenia. However, memories of my grandfather's earlier visit were still fresh in my mind and I did not look forward to his visit, seeing myself subjected once again to his Russian lessons and his spoon attacks. Fortunately these did not eventuate – – perhaps because I was now four years older, or perhaps because he had become less demanding and aggressive. Anyway, it was a welcome change and we got along quite well.

Some six weeks after his arrival, grandfather had a stroke and became partly paralysed, losing his speech and the ability to move his legs. My mother's workload increased out of sight. Besides running the shop, she now had to look after a bed-ridden father. He would lie in the small room and thump his walking stick on the floor whenever he needed something, and Mum would immediately come running in from the shop to tend to his needs. It was an excruciatingly difficult time for her.

She looked after him for a few weeks but his condition did not improve and she had no alternative but to send him to a hospital in Tientsin. Jenia was asked to meet him at the station and check him into the Russian Hospital on the German Concession, which she did, even though she was not yet in full health herself.

One day, on the way to hospital, Jenia called in to see her old friends at Kiesslings and Mr Tobich invited her into his office. She still looked very thin and fragile and he showed great concern for her condition. When she informed him her father was in hospital, Tobich told her to call in daily on the way there to pick up some provisions for him. From then on, Jenia would pick up a thermos flask of hot soup and a carton of ice-cream, courtesy of that extraordinary human being, Tobich.

After a few weeks Leonid was released from hospital and moved into Yang-Ho-Li, occupying the room on the top floor of Aida's boarding house. He was still bed-ridden. Even though she was then living with Chelpanov, she came in daily to cook for him and bathe him, and Jenia and Nina also helped when she was not there. Towards the end, Aida even hired a full-time nurse to look after him. She spent a large amount of time and money looking after a husband who had completely ignored her welfare since he left for Shanghai twelve years earlier, from whom she was now separated and for whom she had no love left. This was an incredible act of compassion. Leonid's condition never improved and he died in 1944, two years after his stroke, at the age of sixty-two. Sadly, ex-Colonel Leonid Alexandrovich Tarasov was not mourned by anyone.

AN UNWANTED PREGNANCY: 1942–1943

In late 1942, the Ostrouhoffs were still living with their benefactor, Mrs Zung, and Volodia, who had by then recovered and put on some weight, began to look for work.   But it was not easy to come by.

Nina was able to get Jenia a job back in Kiesslings in their branch on the French Concession, and that at least brought in some money.

But then, Jenia fell pregnant. The news devastated her. The timing was extraordinarily inopportune: there was a war on; there were shortages everywhere; they were extremely poor; and the future was uncertain. Bringing another human being into this chaotic world, she thought, would be unfair to both child and parents. An abortion was seriously considered, but Jenia did want a baby — it was just the timing that was wrong — so the idea of terminating the pregnancy was soon dropped. I'll work up to the end if necessary, she thought, and perhaps we'll be able to save up a bit of money.

But that was not to be. Within a few weeks Jenia found she could not tolerate the smell of the confectionary and she had no alternative but to leave work.

Volodia could not find a regular job and began dabbling in the black market, buying hard-to-get items and re-selling them at a profit. This brought in a reasonable amount of money, but the income stream had peaks and troughs. During peaks, Jenia and Volodia were pretty good at spending their money. During one of the peaks he even bought his father a small goat farm in Peitaiho. Regrettably they were not good in the saving-for-the-future department, so they relied heavily on help from their extended family during the inevitable troughs.

Jenia, Volodia and little George, Tientsin, 1944

Aunt Jenia was well pregnant when she visited us in Peitaiho in the summer of 1943. She and I got along very well. Jenia was a warm, affectionate person and a marvellous storyteller, especially in recalling movies she had seen. We often went to the beach in the afternoon and she would relate the story of a movie in the most colourful detail. To me, it was as good as seeing the movie itself, maybe even better. The story took just about as long as the movie. She remembered the most amazing details and related them with extraordinary vividness. I loved every minute of it. During the few weeks she spent with us, I carried on as if it was my job to protect my aunt from all harm. It was a very warm relationship between the eleven-year-old boy and the pregnant Jenia.

On 27 September 1943, Jenia and Volodia's son George was born. Soon after, Volodia found a job with UNRRA [†] and they had a constant, though small, income. Jenia loved her husband dearly and felt he was a wonderful, sensitive and caring partner. They were very happy together.

THE SECRET WEDDING: 1943

My mother's suitor, Vasia Artemieff, was six years older than she was. He had a good job with the Italian Municipal Council and lived with his mother on the Italian Concession in one of the council's apartments, which they shared with another council employee.

Vasia was a real ladies' man — a touchy-feely sort of individual who could not keep his hands off attractive women. Correction, off any women. Not that he was offensive, but he did like to stroke and kiss their hands and generally act like a stricken puppy. Some women liked it, others did not. Regrettably, my mother belonged to the former category.

Vasia's mother, Elena, Tientsin, 1946

Vasia's mother, Elena Alexandrovna, had a severely bowed back. A bad fall in her youth had damaged her spine and she was told she would have to wear a special corset for the rest of her life. The corset was duly made, but after bringing it home she placed it in a drawer and never used it. Besides her hunched back, she also sported a hooked nose, which made her look quite unattractive. Sit her on a broomstick and she could easily have passed for a witch. But her looks belied her character. Elena was a kind, quiet and warm person. Her daughter had died giving birth, leaving him as her only offspring, and she doted on him.

I did not like Vasia. There was something about his style that grated on

[†] United Nations Relief and Rehabilitation Administration — a body formed in November 1943 with the purpose of assisting war-ravaged nations with relief supplies and providing camps, personnel and food for the repatriation and care of millions of displaced persons. Although the United Nations Organisation, as we now know it, was only formed in 1945, the term 'United Nations' was used during the war to signify the Allied countries.

me, and I am sure I displayed my aversion to him via my body language. His favourite trick was to tickle my ribs, which would break me out into peals of involuntary laughter and he thought I was enjoying his 'playfulness', which I certainly was not. I hated it.

He courted my mother Nina with great determination and she finally succumbed to his efforts. Before accepting his proposal of marriage, she asked me for my approval. She knew I did not like Vasia, but she asked me anyway. I told her it would be okay with me if it made her happy.

While my feeling for Vasia was one of dislike, my grandmother Aida hated him with a passion for two reasons. Firstly, she believed he was intent on eroding the relationship between my mother and me. He was intensely jealous of the attention Mother paid to me, believing he, instead, should be the centre of her life. Aida thought this was a despicable attitude. The second reason was that she considered him to be an alcoholic. He did drink a lot and was often inebriated, but at that stage he was not really an alcoholic. That was to happen later. But probably, with her sixth sense, Aida knew what the future held in store for her daughter, and she was right.

Aida was never one to hide her feelings. Her intense hatred was quite evident to Vasia through her manner, speech and body language. That is the way she always was. Vasia tried to win her over with presents and flattery, but it had absolutely no effect on her. She knew he was the wrong man for her darling daughter and there was no way she was going to change her mind.

As they were unlikely to obtain Aida's blessing, and Leonid was in the last stages of his paralytic illness and incommunicado, Nina and Vasia decided to have a secret wedding. This they did on 18 November 1943. There were no invitations sent out, no guests, no reception. Just the two of them in a simple church ceremony, followed by a quiet drink back at Vasia's place. Aida, Jenia and I were informed of the wedding after the event.

My mother became Nina Artemieff. I remained Igor Ivashkoff.

LIFE IN HARBIN: 1942–1944

Nadia, Aida's youngest daughter, had married Boris Kozlovsky in Tientsin in 1939. Soon after, she

Nina and Vasia wedding photo, Tientsin, 1943

gave birth to a son, George. Boris had a good job with the Ford dealership and they lived a comfortable life … But not for very long.

Shortly after the start of the Pacific war in 1941, the Japanese closed down the Ford dealership. Boris could not find another job and things began to look grim. But a letter from his father in Harbin gave him fresh hope. In it, his father, an ex-officer in the White Russian army, urged him to move his family to Harbin. 'Work is plentiful here,' the letter said, 'and your sister will be delighted to see you again.' In desperation, they moved. It was June 1942. Their son George was not quite three.

When the Kozlovskys first arrived in Harbin they stayed with Boris' sister, Natasha. In 1936 she had married a Japanese man by the name of Matsuda, who was attached to the Japanese War Ministry and spoke fluent Russian. A lanky unattractive man, he had managed, somehow or other, to snare the pretty Natasha. Nobody understood what she saw in him but she claimed she had married for love. Before the wedding, he took up the Russian Orthodox religion and was baptised with the Russian name of Anatoly.

Matsuda turned out to be a caring husband, a loving father to their two daughters, Irina and Marina, and a happy, kind person. Photography was his main hobby and his daughters were his favourite subjects. They lived in a large house with all sorts of modern conveniences, obviously not short of money.

Being a mechanical engineer, Boris was soon able to find employment with a large Japanese timber company called Kondo. However, as many of the White refugees from the Revolution were university graduates, Harbin had an oversupply of engineers. Consequently his salary was pitifully low, in fact half that of a mechanic. After a month he realised he could not make ends meet —

Matsuda with daughter Irina, Harbin, 1940

Natasha with her two daughters, Marina (left) and Irina, Harbin, 1942

The Kozlovsky family—Nadia, Boris and little George, Tientsin, 1941

the money was only sufficient to feed their son, and no more — and he began to look for other means of earning money.

As petrol was scarce during the war, Boris and an acquaintance saw an opportunity to start a business converting petrol-driven engines to gas-driven. This called for the installation of special coke-burning converters to produce the necessary gas. These were normally mounted at the back of the vehicle and looked like miniature furnaces — crude but effective. The entrepreneurs identified a source for the converters and began production in a rented garage. The work was backbreaking and dirty, the hours long, and the conditions not enhanced by the severe winter weather. The garage was unheated and the temperature often dropped to -40°C. In such cold weather, if you touched a metal part with your bare hand, your skin stuck to it. To make matters worse, the two partners did not get along well. And to cap it all off, it was barely profitable. After a few months, the business was closed down and Boris was out again looking for a job.

This time he was luckier. Through some friends he was offered the position of manager of a large workshop employing about thirty mechanics, welders and fabricators. The salary was reasonable, but there was still only enough money to feed the family and pay the rent. Nothing for clothes or small luxuries.

After living with Natasha's family for a few weeks, the Kozlovskys had found some rental accommodation and moved out. The house they moved to had a kitchen and three rooms, of which they rented two, with the owners living in the third. Boris' father decided to join them, so the family was now four in number. As the back door was used as the main entrance, the owners allowed them to use the front lobby for additional living space.

The accommodation was very basic. There was no bathroom. The toilet was in an outside shed, just a hole in the ground. Although there was a well in the backyard, it was not deep enough to provide clean water. Every morning a Chinaman would deliver two buckets of water, which was kept in a tank in the kitchen alongside a portable copper basin. A large coal-fired cooking stove was the only source of heat in the entire house. As there was a shortage of coal, they had to be very economical with its use, especially in winter. Boris often brought coal from work, furtively carrying the lumps in the pockets of his trousers and coat. On winter mornings there was often a layer of ice on the water in the kitchen tank. After lighting the stove, everyone would sit there in their coats and gloves, waiting for it to heat up. When the daily coal ration was used up, the stove remained cold for the rest of the day and night.

The authorities forbade the use of any electrical appliances or heaters — the city had a shortage of electrical power — but Boris brought home a small 500-watt hotplate which he found in a junk pile at work. Surreptitiously, they would switch it on every morning in their bedroom. It was a godsend, for it not only provided warmth but allowed them to boil some water for a cup of tea. They made sure neither the owners nor the neighbours were aware of this risky practice. Had the authorities found out, they would have been jailed. It soon became obvious why the front door was not used in winter. It faced the prevailing winds and was covered in snow and ice. There was no way one could pry it open until spring.

The adults occasionally went to the public bathhouse to have a proper wash, or sometimes to Natasha's, but little George was bathed in the copper basin in the kitchen. Nadia then used the water to wash their clothes, which would be hung out to dry in the yard. In winter they would, of course, be brought in frozen stiff. This was a blessing in disguise as, when thawed, they would be damp and ideal for ironing with the coal-fired iron.

The summer months were more pleasant. Boris and his neighbour, another engineer, constructed a shower in the backyard, supplied by an overhead tank warmed by the sun. The last user of the shower had the responsibility of refilling the tank, carting buckets of water from the water pump a block away. The system worked well.

RATIONING: 1942–1944

Nadia's household chores included cooking, doing all the laundry, ironing and constant clothes mending, as they had no money for new clothes. And, of course, there were the interminable hours spent in long queues to buy the necessities of life. Nadia often took young George with her so they could take up places in two queues at the same time.

During the war a ration card system was introduced. When the Japanese first took over Manchuria in 1931, renaming it Manchukuo, they proclaimed it to be a separate country consisting of five primary national groups — Japanese, Chinese, Russian, Manchurian and Korean. In line with these categories, five different types of ration cards were issued. The Russians were given cards for bread, the Japanese for rice, and the others for maize. The daily bread ration was one small white loaf per child and one small brown loaf per adult, except on Sundays when the adults were issued with white bread as well.

Ration cards for products such as sugar, salt and cooking oil were issued less often. Towards the end of the war, these products were practically unobtainable. Meat was allocated only to the Japanese, with just the bones handed to the rest. Towards the end of the war even that practice was curtailed.

Liquor was rationed as well. The Russians were allowed one bottle of vodka per month. As Boris' father was considered to be a member of a different family, the Kozlovskys were able to get two bottles. Costing seventy-five cents each via the ration card, they were promptly sold on the black market for $11. The proceeds went to buy food to supplement the rations, such as sugar for little George.

There were strict controls in place to enforce the ration rules, with plainclothes police constantly examining people's bags and parcels to guard against violations. However, in times of shortages there is always a black market, and Harbin was no exception. If you had the money, you could buy just about anything. But the Chinese black-marketeers had certain rules. They were prepared to do business with the Russians and other nationalities, but not with the Japanese, whom they detested. The Japanese knew this and it made them even more determined to stamp out this illegal trade.

A few doors from Nadia's house, there was a shop selling black-market meat, and she went there on special occasions. She was adept at stretching this rare carnivorous pleasure by using a lot of sauces, vegetables and the like. Once, when she was in the shop, the lookout — every black-market shop had one — spied a plainclothes inspector approaching the shop and sounded the alarm. Before she knew it, the shopkeeper opened a trapdoor and pushed Nadia into it. And there she stayed, in complete darkness, visualising the opening of the trapdoor by an armed Japanese, being carted off to jail, never seeing her family again ... Eventually the danger passed and she was let out.

George with his grandfather, Harbin, 1942

The Kozlovskys were better off than most. Boris' father worked as a teacher of English in the Japanese War Ministry and this entitled him to a ration card for products from the ministry's food shop, where he was occasionally able to buy small issues of items that were not even available on the black market, such as eggs, flour, Japanese sweets and the like. But the Russians who worked in the ministry soon killed the goose that laid the golden eggs. They began selling these prized items to others for inflated prices and, stupidly, often did so right outside the ministry's shop. It was soon obvious that the privilege was being abused and the range of items available to the Russians was severely curtailed.

Boris' factory was on the outskirts of town, and Chinese farmers often brought produce to sell there, illegally — rice, corn, wheat, beans. Boris bought some, storing it during the day in his desk drawer and then filling his pockets with the goodies for the journey home. It was too dangerous to carry them in a bag. Bags were the black-market inspectors' favourite targets.

Thank God for men's pockets. These were tough times and Boris' pockets saw a lot of action — from various farm produce in summer to lumps of coal in winter.

THE CIVIL DEFENCE CORPS: 1942–1944

Nadia had another onerous duty. She was the family's representative in the *Tonari-gumi*, as the Japanese called it — the Civilian Defence Corps. The main function of this Corps was to fight fires during and after enemy air raids, if they ever happened.

For defence purposes, the city was organised into sectors. The smallest entity was a sector of ten houses, called a Level 1 sector, complete with a Level 1 leader. Ten Level 1 sectors formed a Level 2 sector of a hundred houses with a Level 2 leader. The Level 1 leaders all took their directions from their Level 2 leaders. And so it went up the line. Instructions would be passed down through this chain of command. The Level 2 leaders and those above them were all Japanese. The Level 1s were Russian.

The corps members were primarily women, as it was assumed the men would probably be at work during the raids. All were issued with uniforms — rubber shoes, trousers, a coil of rope attached to the belt, a shirt, gloves and a headscarf.

There were regular drills for the corps members, organised by the sector leader at deliberately unpredictable and inconvenient times. To start the drill, he would come running to each of the ten houses under his control, knock on the doors or windows and order his members to be at a certain place in five minutes. Attendance was mandatory. Nadia would immediately put on her uniform and rush over.

The drills commenced with a lecture, after which the leader would inform the group of an imaginary bomb which had just landed on one of the ten houses, say house #7. Off they would run, carrying ladders, buckets and other paraphernalia. The leader then planted a small incendiary device somewhere in the yard or on the roof, and the team would spring into action. Some rushed to the well to get water, others shovelled sand onto the fire, some just ran around looking busy. And so it went until the leader was satisfied the 'crisis' was over. Before dispersing, they all went back to his home for a debriefing. This whole process normally lasted about an hour and a half.

Which brings us to an interesting incident one Easter Sunday morning.

Nadia in her Civil Defence Corps uniform, Harbin, 1943

The Kozlovskys had been to the Easter midnight Mass the night before, followed by a small traditional celebration at home. They had fallen into bed at about 3 a.m., looking forward to a long sleep, perhaps even until midday. Nadia was very tired, as she had spent all Saturday cleaning out their rooms for the holy feast, washing floors, windows and curtains, and changing the bed linen.

Suddenly at 7 a.m. they were woken up by a loud knock on the window and the unwelcome voice of the sector leader. 'Up you get! At my house in five minutes! On the double!'

Nadia could not believe her ears. A drill on Easter Sunday! This is a sacrilege, she thought. God will punish him for this. But orders were to be obeyed, and she donned her uniform and rushed out. The others remained in their beds, feeling sorry for Nadia but thankful it wasn't one of them.

A few minutes later Boris was alerted by the sound of approaching voices. He looked out of the window and — oh, horror! — the whole bunch of them were on the way to their place. Guess where the leader decided to plant the incendiary device? Yes, right in the middle of their entrance hall!

The well-drilled Civil Defence team went into immediate action. Buckets of water were poured, loads of sand furiously shovelled — the complete catastrophe! When the drill was over and the fire extinguished, they complimented each other on a job well done and ran away, leaving the Kozlovskys in a state of shock. When Nadia returned from the debriefing, it was noted she was not in the best of moods.

Every 1st, 10th and 20th of the month was declared a Civil Defence day for the entire population. Everyone had to wear special fire-retarding uniforms all day, both at home and at work. The uniforms were similar to those worn by Nadia, including the coil of rope, but the men wore rubber boots instead of shoes and a cap with a shroud instead of a scarf. During these days, sirens were sounded at irregular intervals and all traffic ground to a halt — cars, buses, trams, bicycles. Everyone — drivers, passengers, pedestrians, shopkeepers, workers — was required to lie flat on the ground until the all-clear was sounded.

While on the subject of sirens, a special one would go off every day at midday. Once again, all traffic, work and conversation came to a halt and everyone was required to face east and observe a minute's silence to commemorate the slain Japanese war heroes. The penalty for disobeying this law was jail.

EPILEPSY! — 1938–1944

Nadia's eldest sister Nusia was still living in Harbin and the Kozlovskys saw the Diakonoff family often. By 1942 Nusia had three sons. The two eldest, Kolia and Vova, aged fifteen and twelve, had been boarders at the Lyceum of St Nicholas for four years. Misha (short for Michael) was only five at the time.

Kolia was a poor student, not very bright and highly strung. In addition, he was rather sickly and spent a lot of time away from school. Although he studied hard, there were few tangible results. When asked a question in class or sitting for an exam, he became completely dumbstruck, his brain emptying itself of all pertinent information.

On the other hand, Vova was an excellent student. In fact, during the four years they were in school together Kolia only completed two classes and Vova overtook him, finishing one class ahead.

The school had the following system for boarders: if a student's mark for the week was 3 or above (out of 5), he was allowed to go home for the weekend; with a mark of 2 or less he was denied that privilege. Even if his parents came to visit on the weekend, he was not allowed to see them.

Every Saturday morning, all the boarders used to line up in the schoolyard and the headmaster would yell out: 'All those with twos, one step forward.' And out they would step, with Kolia more often that not in that group. The rest were free to go home, while the failures marched back into class. The teachers gave them special tasks, and if need be the students were kept up all night until they got the right answers.

It was not uncommon for Kolia to miss out on weekend leave for four or five weeks in a row.

Kolia and Vova did not get along. They were always fighting. Vova was jealous of Kolia, annoyed that he seemed to be the favourite son. He was the one for whom his parents bought new clothes and shoes, whereas Vova wore Kolia's hand-me-downs. Moreover, Vova considered Kolia a sissy, a coward and useless at just about everything, whereas he was a good student and a hard worker. Yet for reasons he could not comprehend, Kolia was the favoured child.

Once, during a fight, Kolia fired his

Diakonov family, Harbin, Easter 1940

air gun at Vova, with the pellet just missing his eye. The relationship between the two of them was close to hatred.

Diakonoff's business was not going at all well, and he became increasingly concerned about the future. The boarding school fees were such a drain on his meagre finances that he decided he could not afford to go on paying them. As Vova was doing well in his studies, he enrolled him into another school close by. But to Kolia, he said: 'Listen, son. I don't know whether you are lazy or just plain stupid, but what I do know is that I am wasting my money sending you to school. I think I'll just buy you a shovel so that you can collect shit for a living!' With those inspirational words, Kolia's scholastic career was abruptly terminated. This was 1944. He was seventeen.

Diakonoff had some contacts in Churin's, the largest Russian department store in Harbin, and he decided to try to get Kolia a job there. After some investigation he came to the conclusion the fur department offered the best long-term prospects for his son. Diakonoff was impressed at the fur expert's ability to blow on a fur and immediately establish what animal it came from, how old the animal was, its source and its quality. It looked very professional and interesting. It could be the right job for Kolia, he thought. It doesn't appear to be too difficult. He will train as an apprentice furrier for three months, at the end of which he should be able to classify furs. His career will then take off and, before long, he will become a qualified furrier.

Unfortunately Kolia did not show any talent for this work. After a few months, there was no visible progress, on top of which he seemed unable to work under pressure. When asked a question, he would become tongue-tied. All he could manage was the job of a sales clerk in the fur department, and even there his performance was marginal.

The crunch came when Kolia had an epileptic fit at work. This was the first since his original mild attack at the age of five. It frightened the daylights out of the customers and his fellow workers. The situation was exacerbated by the fact that, in those days, Russians thought epilepsy was contagious and could be caught just by witnessing a fit! This made Kolia's job at Churin's precarious. After a few more fits he was summarily fired. He had been employed for less than a year.

Kolia's fits occurred at irregular intervals, sometimes once or twice a day, sometimes several days apart. Often he could feel one coming and would lie down until it passed. But sometimes they caught him unawares. If the family saw him having a fit, they would rush over to place something between his teeth to stop him biting his tongue. This was not an easy task, as epileptics have prodigious strength when they are convulsing.

Their doctor called the illness *ispugan* (meaning 'the effects of a fright'). 'Medical science has no cure for it,' he said, 'but I have heard there are some Mongolian medicine women who can cure illnesses through magic spells.

Churin's Department Store, Harbin, 1930s

Why don't you see if you can find one? Maybe one of them can help him. Let's face it, there's nothing more I can do.'

Nusia began asking everyone and anyone if they knew where she could find such a 'medicine woman'. Finally her search was rewarded and a scrawny old Mongolian woman came to their house. After examining Kolia, she took three pieces of charcoal, placed them on a plate in front of a holy icon and poured some water over them. Then she filled her mouth with this liquid and sprayed Kolia's face.

'Do not wipe it off. Let it dry,' she instructed. 'And I'll be back tomorrow.'

For the next two days she returned to repeat the ritual. On her last visit she gave Nusia further instructions. 'Go and buy a black chicken, pluck it, de-gut it, boil it and then feed it to him. He must eat it all and he must drink all the water it was boiled in. If it takes more than one day to do this, so be it. But he must consume it all.'

Nusia did as she was told. Kolia ate the entire chicken and drank the murky soup. Miraculously, his epileptic fits vanished, never to return.

This was the first of several strange Mongolian cures to be experienced by the Diakonoff family.

Vova's new school was quite a distance from home, so Diakonoff gave him a rouble every week for the tram fare. Seeing that he was never given any pocket money, he began to walk to and from school, an hour each way, spending the saved rouble on the sort of things children like to buy. After a year or so, his school marks began to deteriorate, partly because he was tired from his daily hikes and partly because he was bored with school and wanted to get a job and some proper spending money. His ambition was to become an auto mechanic.

When he first broached the subject of leaving school with his father, there were objections. But Diakonoff finally relented — the family could use the additional money, he thought — and Vova was allowed to leave school and get a job in a garage.

Kolia was still without work. After being fired from Churin's, he seemed to lack both talent and desire for work. While employed by Churin's, he used to spend most of his small salary on girls. He loved parties, restaurants and dates, and contributed nothing to the family income, but his parents let him get away with it. After all, he was their backward, sickly first-born.

Despite now being jobless, his appetite for girls and the good life had not abated. His solution to his financial crisis was to fund this appetite by selling some of his clothes. One winter's day, he left home in his fur coat and came back without it. 'I must have left it somewhere,' was his lame excuse.

When that money ran out Kolia sold more of his clothes.

It did not take long for his parents to realise what was happening. Diakonoff was most upset with this new development. He was only employed part-time, Nusia was not working and Vova was only earning a tiny salary as an apprentice auto mechanic. In the meantime, Kolia was selling his clothes to live a carefree useless life.

We can't go on like this, he thought. I'll have to do something about it.

Vova, Harbin, 1945

SIMPLE PLEASURES: 1943–1944

Many of the White Russian refugees who fled to Harbin during the 1917–1922 period were well-educated 'intelligentsia' and there was also an abundance of artistic talent. Even during the difficult war years there was always some cultural event or other being staged, such as operettas, concerts, ballets, art exhibitions and poetry readings. All the performers and organisers were volunteers, and entrance fees for the events were kept low so that most of the population could attend and forget, for a few hours, the miseries of exile and war.

Another popular form of entertainment was the house party. In those difficult times, it seemed people yearned to socialise as much as possible. These house parties were the essence of simplicity. The guests would bring their own food and liquor. The music normally came from an old acoustical gramophone, often with a pillow shoved down the horn so as not to alert the authorities. Towards the end of the evening old

Harbin Polytechnic Institute, 1930s

Russian songs would be sung — about nature, about love, about Mother Russia, all in a minor key, all sad, all nostalgic. Most of the Whites originally believed their stay in China would only be temporary; that the Russians would eventually overthrow the Communist government and they would all return home. Eventually, they realised that China would be their home for the foreseeable future. This gave their singing an added degree of poignancy.

The Kozlovskys often visited the Diakonoffs. The visits were especially nice in winter — after all, the Diakonoff house was better heated than theirs. One evening, they were chatting away when the subject of *pelmeny*, the Russian dumplings, came up. They had not eaten any for what seemed to be years, and suddenly found themselves overcome by an uncontrollable desire to have some, and have them there and then.

A couple of minor problems stood in the way. There was no flour for the dough and no meat for the filling. But there was no stopping them. Nadia remembered she had some flour back home, and Boris was dispatched to get it. Although it was a two-hour return journey by bus, tram and foot, the thought of steaming bowls of *pelmeny* was sufficient incentive for him. In the meantime Diakonoff was sent out on a search for meat.

Boris returned first, closely followed by Diakonoff lugging a steaming hunk of freshly slaughtered pig meat. Although they knew it was dangerous to eat freshly butchered pork it was too late to succumb to such fears. The urge was too great. Feverish work was commenced and by midnight they were sitting at the table gorging themselves on this delicacy. What joy, what excitement! And all this over a simple Russian peasant dish.

One Christmas the Kozlovskys received a parcel from Tientsin from little

George's godmother, Zoya Walters. In it were three tins — one contained Del Monte coffee, another fifty Camel cigarettes and the third some porridge for her godson. Coffee could not be found anywhere in Harbin, and the rationed cigarettes (ten per day per smoker) were absolutely awful. Once, when Boris' cigarette went out he poked it to try to find out why — and some sand poured out. Another time, he discovered some rubber wire insulation in the filling. The Camels tasted sublime.

This simple parcel made this Christmas a memorable one.

THE ART OF BRIBERY: 1944–1945

Towards the end of 1944, conditions in Harbin became desperate. There was hardly any food, the Japanese were becoming increasingly belligerent, and another miserable winter was about to arrive. From Aida's letters, it appeared the situation in Tientsin was better and jobs for engineers were plentiful, so the Kozlovskys decided it was time to go back.

Boris applied for a Tientsin visa but was told he had to first produce evidence that there was a job waiting for him there. So a letter was dispatched to Aida, asking for her assistance in the matter. Sure enough, within a couple of weeks she obtained a job offer for him from the Tientsin North China Alcohol Factory. How she did this, God only knows.

Armed with this offer, Boris went back to the visa office. The Japanese official cross-examined him for a long time and asked him, among other things, whether he owned a bicycle. Boris was surprised at the question but answered he did not. He wished he had — it was a long hike from home to work. For some reason or other, the Japanese appeared to be very disappointed by the reply. Boris was told the visa process would take about a week or two, and he would be informed by letter when it was ready.

Preparations were commenced in readiness for their expected departure. Furniture and other non-portable goods were offered to friends, and notice was given to their landlord. As Boris' father decided to stay in Harbin, alternative accommodation was found for him. And Boris left his job.

And that's when the visa refusal arrived.

Luckily, a friend gave Boris a part-time job, thus keeping his family one step away from starvation.

Boris decided to appeal to Natasha's husband Matsuda for help. They knew he was attached to the War Ministry and that he was an important man in the Japanese military establishment. They even believed he was a spy as he had, on several occasions, made unsuccessful attempts to recruit Boris to do some spying against the Russians. After hearing of Boris' visa problem, Matsuda told him to apply again and then leave things to him.

So Boris went back to the visa office, filled out a new application and handed it to the same official who had asked him about the bicycle. The surly Japanese took it without saying a word. This time the Kozlovskys were confident of success. Matsuda would make it happen. He was an important man. By this time bereft of furniture, Boris and Nadia were sleeping on the floor and eating off it as well. But they consoled themselves with the thought that this would soon be over.

Two weeks later, the official letter arrived. Trembling hands opened it. It was another refusal! Matsuda was obviously not that important. In desperation, Boris went to see the official to seek an explanation, but without warning the Japanese turned belligerent and began to yell, threatening Boris with jail.

Boris told the sad story to one of his friends. 'You mean you did not offer him a bribe?' the friend asked. 'Why do you think he asked you if you had a bicycle? You think he was interested in your mode of transport? Wake up, my friend!'

Boris suddenly got the message! But how does one give a bribe? He did not own a bicycle. So what should he offer instead? What are the rules of bribery? And anyway, is the official the right man? If not, who is? He began to ask around, and finally his sister Natasha came to his aid. She knew someone who knew someone who knew a Jewish businessman by the name of Mordohovich who had some connections in high places. A meeting was arranged and Boris told him the whole sorry tale.

'I know the Japanese general in charge of all these departments,' Mordohovich said. 'If he gives the word, it will be done. Unfortunately, like all of them, he's corrupt. Just the other day he was telling me he needs a good pair of leather riding boots. On the black market they cost $700. If you get me the money I'll buy the boots, invite him for a cup of tea, present them to him and describe your predicament. I think there's a fair chance your problems will disappear.'

But where was Boris going to get $700? That was two and a half times his monthly salary when he was working full time. There was no alternative but to send another letter to Aida asking her for the loan of this sum — 'to help oil the wheels of George's baby carriage', the letter said, a euphemism in case the letter was opened by censors.

Aida, who could apparently move mountains, came up with the money and it was duly delivered to Mordohovich. As promised, this was soon followed by a visa approval. When Boris went to pick up the visas, the same Japanese official was sitting in the same office. This time he just pushed the visas across his desk without even looking up or uttering a word. The delighted Boris snatched them up and rushed out of the building while the going was good.

Aida had sent more than the required money and, together with Boris' last pay cheque, the Kozlovskys had some spare cash, so they decided to splurge it on a first-class train ticket to Tientsin. Why not? After all, they had suffered three years of deprivation.

The departure date of 20 November happened to be a Civil Defence Day, which meant everyone had to wear a special uniform. It did not matter whether you were on the way to the station to catch a train out of Harbin. If you were seen without the proper uniform, you were in danger of being arrested.

The Kozlovskys must have been quite a sight when they entered the carriage and sat down among the first class transit passengers. Nadia looked particularly stunning. She was decked in dark baggy trousers, rubber shoes, a khaki shirt, a blue scarf on her head, a coil of rope tied to her belt — and a silver fox fur around her neck. This fur was one they had brought with them from Tientsin. They were concerned about packing it into a suitcase in case a customs search uncovered it and mistakenly took it for black-market goods. The safest place for it, they reasoned, was around Nadia's neck.

MY STEP-GRANDFATHER: 1942–1944

My grandmother Aida had been living with George Chelpanov since 1934. He had lodgings in a terrace house on Elgin Ave about two blocks from Yang-Ho-Li, where he occupied an attic on the third floor with a window overlooking the small park opposite the Empire Theatre. A steep staircase led up to the attic. The communal bathroom was on the floor below. There was no kitchen, but I seem to remember a small sink and a portable electric hotplate in the room. It was a largish room, with the ceiling following the rake of the roof. I remember it as being very cosy.

Visiting my grandmother on Wednesday afternoons after my piano lessons I remember with the greatest of pleasure. She would give me a few coins and I would go to the deli in Dickenson Road to buy some fresh bread and Russian *chainaya kolbasa* (a garlicky sausage). We would then have tea with lots of Carnation milk, which I loved, and thick slices of sausage on buttered fresh bread.

George Chelpanov — I called him Uncle George — and I got along famously. He was a wonderful man and he loved children. Being very handy with his hands, especially in woodworking, he showed great patience in teaching me how to use a fret saw. I even produced some picture frames, which were then displayed with great pride in our home.

But most of all, I enjoyed our Sunday fishing expeditions to the lakes. Uncle George was an avid fisherman and I often went to their place on Saturday night to sleep over, in readiness for an early rise the next morning, as George maintained the fish were at their hungriest just as dawn was about to break. The fish in question were golden carp and the lakes were full of them. We would select a spot, fix the rods and throw in the lines just as the first chink of light appeared over the horizon. For bait we used dough rolled into small balls, suspended on a hook below a float.

'Fishing for carp is an art form,' Uncle George used to say, and he was right. They were the smartest fish in the world and very suspicious. Rather than just grab the bait, they would slowly suck it into their mouths — no swallowing — and then gently rise in the water, checking for suspicious signs. This would cause the float to flop down into a horizontal position. The slightest move or sound would scare them away. After the appropriate wait, with the float lying flat, one gave a mighty heave and, hopefully, the bait would then be deep enough in the carp's mouth for the hook to catch.

We would spend all day out by the lakes, doing battle with the fish. For food, grandmother would normally give us a slab of cooked meat, some tomatoes, a few garlic cloves and a thermos flask of tea. Of course, Uncle George also took along a small flask of vodka, an essential ingredient for a fishing trip.

They were wonderful times, and Uncle George and I developed a close, warm relationship.

One day an awful thing happened to him. He went to the toilet, strained himself and burst his intestines. (Later, Aida, in typical Russian-wife fashion, was to claim this happened because his intestines had become dangerously thin due to his excessive intake of vodka over the years.) Anyhow, whatever the reason, they burst and he was carted off to hospital. When the medicos opened him up and saw the mess inside, they all thought he was beyond help. They debated whether they should just close him up and let him die, or have a go anyway, just for the practice. Fortunately they did the right thing and, to everybody's surprise, he survived, but only just.

Regrettably, another misfortune befell Uncle George a week later. He was still in hospital, on a very strict diet, when a nurse walked past him with a tray of *piroshki*, which are small Russian pies of minced meat in deep-fried dough. The aroma whetted George's appetite and, jokingly, he asked her if he could have a couple. Without bothering to check if he was on a diet, the stupid nurse gave him two. Deciding the nurse knew best, a surprised Uncle George devoured them — and his intestines burst again. Back on the operating table he went and this time they were sure he would leave this world. But he survived yet again.

And right to the end of his life, he maintained it was his vodka-drinking history that saved him from certain death.

LEARNING RUSSIAN: 1943

I suppose I was about eleven when my mother decided my Russian speaking and writing skills left much to be desired. A year in the Russian Primary

School at the age of five and a few dozen lessons from my grandfather was all the Russian education I had been subjected to. Of course, I spoke the language fluently, but that was because I had a Russian family and Russian friends. But my writing skills were poor and Mum thought it was time for me to get up to speed on my native language.

The teacher selected was a nice old lady whose name I cannot remember. She was a good teacher and able to ignite my interest in lessons which I had initially thought would be a waste of my valuable time. And in the process she introduced me to Russian literature. Keeping me away from the heavies — Turgenev, Dostoevsky, Leo Tolstoy and the like — she pointed me in the direction of Pushkin, Lermontov, Chekhov, Gogol and Alexei Tolstoy. I devoured the books she lent me and we would then discuss them during the lessons. I found these books much more interesting than the Shakespeare we learnt at the College.

It is interesting to note that, although we lived in China and were likely to go on living there for the rest of our lives, most of us 'foreigners' could not really speak Chinese and, most peculiar of all, we did not even think it was necessary to learn the language. Sure, we all picked up enough Chinese to give instructions to shopkeepers and rickshaw operators, but none of us were fluent in it. There was no need to be, we thought. We 'foreigners' lived and moved within the 'foreign' communities and Concessions without mixing with the Chinese. All our friends were 'foreigners', my schoolmates were 'foreigners' — there were very few Chinese students in the college — and most of the Chinese shopkeepers spoke either Russian or English anyway. So why bother? 'Do you really need to know Chinese to call a rickshaw?' Even our college thought it was more useful to teach us French as a second language.

There is no doubt that we thought of ourselves as the important people and the Chinese as second-class citizens. I hate to admit this, but we were racists and we acted as supremacists, and I am thoroughly ashamed of this now.

THE PERILOUS GAMBLE: 1943

Towards the end of 1943 the Japanese decided to move the 'enemy' nationals into various internment camps around China. The Tientsin enemies were to be taken to a camp in Weihsien.

Their departure was carefully choreographed by the Japanese for maximum propaganda effect. The Chinese population was informed in advance that their 'foreign enemies and exploiters' were to be moved to prison camps, and that, on a certain day and time, they were welcome to come and watch this happy event.

Thousands of Chinese and Russians congregated on the main street to watch the exodus. The footpaths were thronged with on-lookers, while hundreds of Japanese soldiers with bayonets on the ready lined both sides of the street. Then, from the distance, a truck filled with Japanese gendarmes appeared, moving slowly. Behind them walked hundreds of the 'enemy' foreigners, carrying whatever they could of their remaining possessions, all heading to the railway station. Surprisingly, they did not look downcast or terrified. To the surprise of the Japanese, the on-lookers started waving to the prisoners and yelling 'Goodbye!' and 'Look after yourselves!' both in Chinese and various foreign languages. A prisoner yelled out 'Don't worry about us, we'll be back soon!' Some Chinese even tried to shake the hands of the departing, only to be brutally admonished by Japanese rifle butts.

This proved to be a propaganda fiasco for the Japanese. They had expected the Chinese to be hostile and antagonistic to the foreigners, but they had not allowed for the fact that many Chinese had worked for the foreigners and were now without jobs and, more importantly, that they hated the Japanese much more than they hated the foreigners. After this, all t departures of prisoners were done secretly in the middle of the night.

Before leaving, the 'enemy' foreigners had all their possessions confiscated, including their businesses and real estate. And that's when my mother Nina took the greatest risk of her life.

Lena, my father's sister, was married to an Englishman and had become a British subject … and by definition an enemy of the Japanese. However, she had elected not to change her maiden name of Ivashkoff to Howell and many of their possessions, including the apartment, were shown in her name —

which was the same surname as Nina's (this was a few months before she married Vasia Artemieff). And that is what gave Lena the idea of hatching a plot to save her possessions.

'Listen, Nina,' she said. 'The apartment is in my name, Ivashkoff, which is the same as yours. So how would they know it's not your apartment? The Japanese will leave you alone — you're stateless and not their enemy — and you can then live in my apartment until the war is over. What do you think of that?'

Nina was not too happy with the idea. She asked a lot of 'what if?' questions, but Lena had answers for all of them. She had thought it all through. Reluctantly, Nina agreed to the deception. It was a huge risk to take. I suppose she went along with it because she felt she owed a great debt to Lena for all the financial assistance she had provided for my education.

Lena immediately set about training my mother to forge her signature, which Nina picked up very quickly. When the Japanese officials came to do an inventory of the goods to be confiscated, Lena told them the prearranged story and Nina nodded in agreement. They must have both lied convincingly, because Lena and her husband were carted off to the internment camp and Nina moved quietly into the apartment.

But that was not the end of the saga. A few weeks later the Japanese officials returned to interrogate Nina further. They asked to see the documents of sale for the apartment and asked Nina to sign a blank piece of paper so they could verify the signature. They also asked her to show them where Lena and Howell had been sleeping. Nina's knees were shaking as she pointed to a bedroom, the one decorated in Chinese style, which contained many valuable artefacts. The officials examined the room and then went into a huddle, while casting suspicious glances in Nina's direction. She was terrified, fearing her story was not holding together. After what appeared to be an eternity, the officials announced they would return in a week.

It was an agonisingly long week of waiting. Nina's friends and relatives were no help. They just kept telling her how dangerous this deception was, and how she could even be shot if the truth were uncovered. But Nina had promised Lena to do her best to save her possessions, and she was determined to go through with it. Anyway, it was now too late to back out. The deception had already begun.

When the officials returned, they proceeded to seal the room where the Howells were supposed to have slept. They then instructed Nina to vacate the apartment within three weeks, removing all the remaining possessions. This was a strange decision. It seemed they were not quite sure whether Nina's story was true or not, and had come up with this compromise. After they left, she collapsed with relief on the sofa. The perilous gamble had worked and the remaining furniture, grand piano and chests of goods were moved to Vasia's place on the Italian Concession.

With Lena's departure, her contributions to my schooling stopped and my mother could not afford to have me continue as a boarder. At the age of eleven I became a normal day student, living at home — at last.

I had been a boarder for over four years, and I must say the memories are not unpleasant. Apart from the fact that I would have liked to have gone home on Saturday afternoons instead of Sundays at 10 a.m., I did not feel in any way underprivileged. And there was certainly discipline in the college — not harsh, but quite strict and generally fair.

INTERNMENT CAMPS: 1943–1945

The internment camp to which the Howells were sent was at Weihsien, a small city on the Shantung Peninsula, 500 kilometres from Tientsin. Situated in the compound of the former Presbyterian mission, it was about three kilometres from the city proper. The old gate to the former mission was graced with Chinese hieroglyphics proclaiming 'Courtyard of the Happy Way'. Fortunately, most of

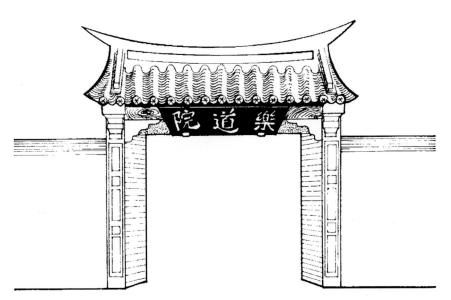

Courtyard of the Happy Way, 1943

the inmates could not read Chinese or they might have been lulled into a false sense of wellbeing. It was definitely not going to be a happy time.

The camp housed 1800 people — Americans, British, Belgians, Dutch — all the nationalities that were then at war with Japan. The inmates hailed from Tientsin, Peking and Tsingtao. All were housed in dormitories of ten to thirty for the singles, and in rows of three-by-four-metre rooms for families of up to four. A separate isolated compound housed a group of Italians, whom the Japanese considered traitors after the downfall of Mussolini and were determined to treat worse than the rest.

The buildings were in a terrible state of disrepair, with leaking roofs, cracks in the walls and broken windows. There were no private facilities. The toilet consisted of four blocks of five toilets each, Chinese squat-style, which worked out to be one cubicle for every ninety inmates. As the flushing systems did not work, each user had to bring his or her own supply of water in a can. Because the water supply was generally limited and had to be pumped by hand from a single well, the inmates brought their slop water for this task. There was no toilet paper or cleaning material or disinfectant available.

Washing facilities were primitive, consisting of four washrooms with faucets supplying a trickle of water into cement troughs. Food came from communal kitchens run by the inmates. The raw material was of dreadful quality — rotten vegetables, smelly meat — and there were no refrigeration facilities. Outbreaks of diarrhoea and dysentery were common.

In winter the temperature often fell below freezing point and there were

Weihsien—electrified barbed wire, guard tower and section of the hospital wing.

even occasional snowfalls. But heating facilities were practically nonexistent. There were tiny stoves in each dormitory and some in the mess halls, but they were largely inadequate. To make things worse, there was no kindling wood or paper available to start the fires, and hardly any coal to stoke them.

The Japanese supplied the kitchen with daily rations of flour for bread. Apparently they were of the opinion that Westerners all ate a loaf of bread a day, and the flour ration was accordingly generous. The Japanese were, of course, not informed of their miscalculation and a bit of good, old-fashioned ingenuity came to the fore. All eighteen hundred loaves were baked daily and the unused loaves were split down the middle to dry in the sun. The dried loaves were then used to fuel the stoves. When the Japanese inquired about the rows of loaves in the sun, they were told they were being toasted 'for the children'.

Although nowhere near as bad as a Japanese prisoner-of-war camp, the internment camp was pretty awful nevertheless. But Weihsien was less onerous than some of the other internment camps, especially one of the Shanghai Camps, Pootung, which had been set up in a condemned tobacco warehouse and was ruled by a despotic commandant.

Compared to the Japanese commandant of the Pootung internment camp, the Weihsien commandant was quite humane. He even allowed the inmates to receive food parcels. More often than not, these parcels arrived intact with only a few items pilfered by the Japanese. Luckily, their taste in food was quite different to that of the Westerners, and not much was stolen.

Lena used to write to Nina, asking her to send food parcels. 'Sell whatever you have to,' she would write, attaching a list all the items she needed. Nina sold two of Lena's carpets and two of her three fur coats. She had to. She could not afford the provisions from her own salary. However, Lena's beloved furniture remained intact and so did the rest of the goods in her chests.

Mr Howell, who was much older than Lena, died in the Camp in 1944 after a long illness.

Towards the end of the war, the food in the camp deteriorated both in quantity and quality. Representations to the commandant were rebuffed with the statement that the inmates still had better conditions than the besieged citizens on the Japanese mainland.

As mentioned earlier, during 1938 and '39 some 20,000 European Jews, mainly from Germany and Austria, had sought refuge in Shanghai. The Japanese established a ghetto for them in the Hongkew area and most lived there without being bothered by the authorities. Over the years, many of them moved out of the ghetto and established residences and businesses in other districts, including the old foreign Concessions.

In 1942, the Japanese made the following proclamation: 'Since Germany has deprived the Jewish people overseas of their nationality, German Jews will hereafter be treated as de-nationalised Jews. Those who are or will be made use of on our part will be treated in a friendly manner. The rest of them will be placed under strict surveillance so that any hostile activity may be eliminated or suppressed.'

So they too, like the White Russians, became stateless.

At the end of 1943, when the enemy aliens were sent to internment camps, Shanghai was visited by Germany's infamous 'Butcher of Warsaw', Colonel Josef Meisinger, who insisted the Japanese apply Hitler's 'Final Solution' to all the Shanghai Jews. The Japanese rejected this demand, but it was not because they were fond of the Jews or had any moral scruples. The likely reason was that the execution of 20,000 people would have taken considerable planning and effort, and would have been rather messy. Anyway, the Jews were not in their way and they did not cause any trouble. Besides which, the Japanese had no great love for the Nazis.

However, they did agree to a compromise — they would transform the Jewish ghetto in Hongkew into a prison of sorts. Surrounding it with barbed wire, they instructed all the European Jews living outside the area to move to the ghetto and posted guards at all entry and exit points. From then on, the inmates were required to obtain exit passes if they wanted to venture out, specifying where in Shanghai they could go and when they were to return. Violations of these rules were punishable by beatings or incarceration.

Apart from that, their life was allowed to go on as before. The Chinese still sold them the necessary provisions, the Jewish shops and businesses in the ghetto still operated, and the only serious inconvenience was the curtailment of their freedom to move outside the ghetto.

4   AFTER THE WAR
1945–1949

END OF THE WAR: 1945–1946

On 6 August 1945, an atom bomb devastated Hiroshima. On 9 August, another one demolished Nagasaki. And on 10 August, Japan surrendered.

American troops entered the Weihsien camp on 17 August and the liberation process commenced. It took some time for the Americans to liberate the main cities in China and make them safe, so it was not until 22 October that the Tientsin contingent was finally airlifted back to its city — more than two years after the initial formation of the camp.

Homecoming was not a pleasant experience. Most found their houses and apartments empty — no furniture, no fittings, no clothes or any other possessions. The Japanese had cleaned out their homes and the Chinese had pilfered whatever was left. In addition, many found their previous jobs had been filled or the companies they had worked for had ceased to be.

The future for foreigners did not look at all bright. There were few opportunities left. The foreign Concessions had been abolished. Industries were shrinking. Unemployment was high. All this resulted in a massive exodus of foreigners to their mother countries. The same happened in Shanghai. In addition, of course, the Japanese, Germans and Austrians were deported *en masse* back to their countries, so the foreign population was dwindling at an alarming pace.

The Chinese, however, welcomed this exodus as a cleansing of their country from foreign domination. They were finally winning jurisdiction over their own land. The only foreigners who did not leave were the stateless Russians. They had nowhere to go…

For Lena, the perilous gamble had paid off. Nina returned all her possessions including the furniture and the grand piano. Lena had only lost the contents of the sealed room and the few items Nina had to sell to pay for the parcels. Unfortunately the relationship between them deteriorated when Lena began

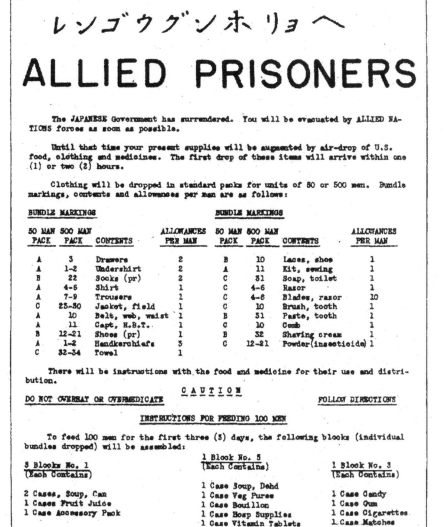

Leaflet dropped from the air on Weihsien, August 1945

to voice her unhappiness with Nina's choice of the items she had sold.

'How could you have possibly sold that fur coat? It was my favourite. You should have sold the other one.'

The complaints were petty and unreasonable, and Nina was deeply hurt by them. The camp experience and the death of her husband seemed to have affected Lena's perception of things, and as a result their friendship could not be rekindled.

For me, the big loss was the beautiful grand piano. I had had it as my very own for over two years.

Soon after, Lena sold all her possessions and migrated to Canada.

At the end of the war the Kiesslings firm was expropriated by the Chinese government and Tobich and Reichel were deported to their mother countries. Their employees, both Chinese and Russian, were sorry to see them go and gave them a big farewell party. They had been good employers and were well liked. Many of the staff even went to the railway station to see them off. The firm continued to operate under the Kiesslings name, and Nina and the Russian salesgirls kept their jobs. The new Chinese bosses were kind and polite to the staff, and life at Kiesslings went on with little change.

When the American forces entered Tientsin in late 1945 everyone was delighted to see them. As for the US soldiers, they had fought a terrible war and were very happy to have won it and to have come to a civilised town like Tientsin. Having been away from their families for so long, they yearned for family life and were anxious to make friends with the white population. They had no great love for the Chinese. To them, they looked too much like their hated enemies, the Japanese.

At that time we were still living on the Italian Concession in Vasia's apartment, and the Kozlovskys, having returned from Harbin, were living with Jenia and Volodia in Aida's boarding house. All of us made friends among the American military and often invited them to family dinners and gatherings. The Americans, in return, bombarded us with gifts — soap, chocolates, nylon stockings.

The only problem with the Americans was their tendency to drive on the right-hand side of the road, whereas the standard in China was the British left-hand drive. As the Japanese standard was the same as the British there had been no problems during the occupation. But the Americans were the conquerors, the liberators, and as far as they were concerned they could drive on any side they damned well pleased, scattering the local traffic in the process. Friday nights were especially hazardous, when a few drinks made the Americans forget which country they were in. The resultant accidents brought in additional business for Dr Nathing, our venerable Russian doctor.

Whereas Tientsin and Shanghai were liberated by the Americans, Harbin was liberated by the Russians. On 8 August 1945, two days before Japan surrendered, Soviet Russia declared war on Japan and the Soviet army entered Manchuria and Harbin.

Most of the Japanese army retreated from the Russian onslaught. But a number stayed back, rather than return home in disgrace, and continued their fight as guerillas, inflicting as much damage on the Chinese and Russians as they possibly could. The Japanese guerillas often wore civilian clothes and mixed with the Chinese, believing, correctly, that the white people would not be able to tell the races apart. In one incident a guerilla masquerading as a shoeshine boy plunged a dagger into the throat of a Russian soldier. There were also instances of Kamikaze-style attacks, where a Japanese armed with grenades would run into a group of Russian soldiers, blowing himself up and killing many of his enemies. It is alleged more Russian soldiers died in Manchuria after the war than during the initial battles against the Japanese.

On the civilian front, however, the occupying Russian soldiers were eager to associate with the local Russians and the Diakonoffs made many friends with them — after all, the whole family carried Soviet passports. Kolia, in particular, took every opportunity to be with them and talk fondly about 'Mother Russia'.

An unfortunate consequence of the end of the war was the loss to Natasha of her Japanese husband Matsuda. He and the rest of the Japanese War Ministry were forced to flee from the Russian onslaught. To stay would have meant possible execution. There was, of course, no way Natasha and the two daughters could have followed him.

Boris' father was deported to Russia for trial and found guilty of treason. His crimes were that he had been a White Russian officer and that he had collaborated with the Japanese by working as a teacher of English in the Japanese War Ministry. As far as the Soviets were concerned, these were acts of treason and he was sentenced to twenty years of hard labour. He died in a prison camp five years later.

As a postscript to the above, it was recently made known that in 1938 the Japanese built a vast complex just south of Harbin for the purpose of biological warfare research. It was named Unit 731 and staffed by some 3500 military personnel and civilians. This facility was used to carry out grotesque experiments on Chinese, Russian and Mongol prisoners. The experiments included injections of cholera, typhus, and bubonic plague; freezing of limbs; infection with syphilis; prolonged exposure to X-rays; and vivisections. The insiders, apparently, referred to the human guinea pigs as *maruta* (logs of wood). These experiments are estimated to have caused the death of at least 3000 prisoners. Other sources suggest that biological warfare experiments were also being carried out on entire Chinese villages by airborne spraying, with a total death toll being closer to 100,000.

At the end of the war, as the Soviet army was sweeping south to Harbin, the Japanese gassed the remaining prisoners and destroyed the facility. There is some evidence to suggest that, if it had not been for Hiroshima and Nagasaki, the Japanese could have commenced a germ warfare campaign against the Allies.

PLAYING GOD AGAIN: 1946

After the war, the Soviet government made a determined push to encourage White Russians to take up Soviet citizenship and return to their homeland. There were all sorts of advertising campaigns promising amnesty and a meaningful, fruitful life back in Mother Russia.

Many White Russians took up the offer of Soviet passports. There seemed to be nothing to lose by doing so — it was better than being stateless. But not as far as Aida was concerned. As the wife of a White Army colonel who had endured so much during the civil war she was dead against taking up Soviet citizenship. 'I would rather die on the street from hunger than be ruled by those Antichrists,' she declared.

The Soviet government arranged for the Russian ship *Gogol* to dock in Tientsin twice during 1946, and those with Soviet passports were urged to apply for visas for their free passage home. Many took up the visa offers, and among them were Nadia and Boris Kozlovsky. Boris had been without a steady job for some time. There was no call for mechanical engineers and he had to take on whatever part-time work he could find. Nadia's small salary at Kiesslings helped keep them afloat, but the future did not hold out much promise for them in Tientsin. All this eventually brought them to the belief that it was really not much of a gamble to migrate to Russia.

Aida was aghast at the thought. She tried talking her daughter out it, but her arguments fell on deaf ears. So in late 1946, just after the Kozlovskys received their visas, Aida sprang into action. In desperation, she stole their passports — yes, actually stole them — setting the following conditions for their return: Move to Shanghai and try your luck there. If, after six months, you still feel like going to Soviet Russia your passports will be returned and you can leave.

This action resulted in an uproar, lasting several days, but Aida refused to budge. Eventually there was nothing left for them to do but to agree to her conditions. Boris went to the Soviet consulate, told them some story about pressing business in Shanghai, and then boarded the *Li-Kung* for the journey there. He soon found a good job and, shortly after, Nadia and their son George followed him to Shanghai.

Once again, Aida had saved the day and averted a family disaster.

THE RETARDED CHILD: 1946

Back in Harbin, Nusia was about to make her life even more difficult. A friend of hers dropped in to see her. She was very distressed.

'You must help me save a child from a fate worse than death,' she told

Nusia. 'A tenant of mine, a woman, has an eleven-month-old boy, Alexei, whom she treats worse than a stray dog. She goes out for the whole day and leaves him sitting on a sack on the cold floor, without any food. When she returns, she boils some gooey mess and forces it into his mouth. As a result, his stomach is not working properly. As soon as he eats anything, it all comes out the other end. For the last two days she has been screaming that she wants him dead. Today she even tried to strangle him. I had to rush in to save the child.'

She begged Nusia to take the boy into her family and away from this cruel and uncaring mother. Kind-hearted Nusia was moved by the story and asked Diakonoff if she could adopt the boy.

'You're the one who will have to look after him,' was his offhand reply. 'Take him if you wish. I really don't care.'

Nusia took that to mean approval. She gave her visitor a blanket and sent her off to get the child. When he was brought in and Nusia uncovered the blanket from his face, she received the shock of her life. He looked like a savage little animal — dirty, unkempt, frightened, bruised, whimpering. A terrible sight. But her original shock soon turned to pity and she clasped the child to her breast.

The boy was in a dreadful state. He had bruises and scratches all over him and his feet were covered with sores. Nusia had to soak them in a bath for a week before he was able to stand. As she continued to lavish care on him, he started looking less animal-like and more human. His name was Alexei, but with jet black hair and dark brown eyes, he looked more Mongolian than Russian. When Nusia first took him to church for communion, the sudden appearance of this unusual-looking baby gave the gossiping ladies of the congregation a field day. However the parish priest was most sympathetic.

'You are a good woman,' he said to Nusia. 'God is smiling on you for saving the baby.'

But when Nusia embarked on this wonderfully humanitarian venture, she had no idea what was in store for her. It soon became obvious Alexei was severely retarded. Either he had been brain-damaged at birth or the early mistreatment had caused this impairment. His mental age never developed past the age of about six months.

Nusia cared for him for the next four years and it proved to be a huge burden for her. He could not learn to speak. He would not respond to toilet training. He had to be spoon-fed. Although he was able to walk, he had to be watched at all times to ensure he did not hurt himself by touching the stove with his hands or walking out into the snow in his bare feet. Her son Vova had to erect some barricades in the room to keep him from wandering about.

Had Nusia known he was retarded, she would have certainly thought twice before taking the child. By the time she realised the extent of Alexei's mental problems, his mother had disappeared and there was no way she could return the child to her.

The rest of the family treated Alexei as if he were a pet. In other words, he was largely ignored, sometimes played with, and often yelled at. The bulk of the caring load, of course, fell on Nusia. As for Diakonoff, he was especially unsympathetic. 'I warned you,' he would say. 'You elected to pick up the cross and you must now bear it.'

OFF TO MIANDUHE: 1947

The end of the war did not improve the fortunes of the Diakonoffs. The eldest son Kolia was still unemployed. He spent much of his time with his Russian soldier friends talking about life in Mother Russia. And of course he was still very much interested in the fair sex. As he was bereft of income, he would scrounge the odd dollar from his father, but mostly he would allow himself to be entertained by his Russian military friends. The bottom line was that he was living a useless, parasitic life and of no help to the family.

Although Diakonoff still harboured faint hopes that his first-born would someday amount to something, he was afraid the temptations of the 'big smoke' in Harbin would continue to lead him astray. The solution, he thought, would be to move the family to some smaller town or village. Life would be cheaper. Maybe they could even buy a small farm, have a cow, do some farming. Perhaps Kolia would be useful on a farm.

Diakonoff did some investigating and settled on a place called Mianduhe, 600 kilometres northwest of Harbin and just 300 kilometres from the Russian border. It is not clear what attracted him to this village, which was quite ordinary and similar to all the other villages strewn along the Chinese Eastern Railway. It had a population of about 2000, the majority of whom were Russian. All the roads were unpaved. There was no electricity or piped water or sewerage. The countryside around it, however, was quite picturesque — lush and green, a large hill overlooking the village with a cemetery on its lower slopes.

The property Diakonoff selected was on 4th Street. The land was fifteen metres wide and 150 metres deep and contained a well, a small vegetable garden and two tiny houses, one of which was a converted stable, having previously been used to house cows and horses during the freezing winter months. It will be livable after we clean it up, he thought optimistically.

The other house was a tiny one-room hovel containing a kitchen and a sleeping area. Good enough for a new beginning, he said to himself.

Diakonoff knew the move would be a hard sell to Nusia. She would not want to move from a city like Harbin to some godforsaken place in the middle of nowhere. To soften her up, he returned from his trip with a large bunch of flowers.

'I've picked these from the fields around the farm,' he lied.

Plunging into his sales pitch, he extolled the virtues of moving to this paradise-like location, this Garden of Eden. The houses are a bit small, he told Nusia, but he promised to build her a larger one. 'You'll live like a queen,' he promised her.

He must have done a good selling job, for she actually believed him and even began to look forward to the move. Their plentiful belongings and furniture nearly filled a whole railway goods wagon. In Mianduhe the railway porters were amazed to see all these goods and chattels. 'You must think you've come to Moscow,' they laughed.

When Nusia saw their new abode — the tiny house and the stable — she could not believe her eyes. It was nothing like what Diakonoff had described. What she had expected were two charming houses in a pretty village, but what she saw was a dilapidated hut and a small stable set in a ramshackle plot of land in an ugly little village in the middle of nowhere. Her disappointment was palpable and she cried for days. In fact she never forgave her husband for this deception.

Still, they had made the move, and there was now no way to undo it. As it was impossible to fit all the furniture into the two tiny shacks, a lot of it had to be given away. It was obvious they would also have to split the family between the two houses. Nusia decided she would stay with Misha, the youngest, and Alexei, the adopted boy, in one, and her husband and the other two boys would occupy the converted stable. You could tell it had been a stable, because the windows were set so low you had to bend down to see the sky from the inside. The doors had a very low clearance and Nusia was continuously banging her head against the doorjamb. The whole environment was very depressing.

Diakonoff bought two horses, a wagon and a cow and the family's first business endeavour was that of collecting and selling hay. Once again, Kolia proved himself to be of little use. He could not even mount a horse. It was both hilarious and pathetic to see him place his stool alongside the beast, get up onto it, start to climb into the saddle, have the horse move off before he was able to mount, reposition the stool, try again …

At the same time, Diakonoff found that manual labour was becoming too much for him — after all, he was already sixty-two, an old man in those days. He was often sick or just plain tired, and would stay home playing solitaire. In addition, he had developed a massive hernia of the bowel, an affliction that was to be with him for the rest of his life.

With Kolia being no help, ten-year-old Misha in school and his father often incapacitated, it was Vova, aged seventeen, who carried most of the workload.

The hay business was only operational during the warm months and, coming in to winter, Vova realised he had to find alternative work for the cold months ahead. Their neighbour suggested he try the timber business. 'The forests around here don't belong to anyone,' he assured Vova, 'and everybody needs timber. You've got two horses. All you need is two sleds and you can go to the forest, chop down the trees, cut them up and sell them for firewood. Minimal financial outlay required. Just some muscles and sweat.'

So Vova tried it and it worked. There were no conservationists around at the time and nobody seemed to care much about the destruction of the environment. The forest was about fifteen kilometres away. The fir trees were big and straight and easy to cut. Vova would fell them with an axe, remove all the branches, cut the trunks into sections and take them home on the sleds. It took two hours of travel each way and he would leave home at 4 a.m. and return in the late afternoon. The load was heavy and the distance long, so the horses had to rest for a day between trips. During this day of rest, Nusia would help him saw the wood into shorter lengths — Misha would often help after school as well — and Vova would then split the timber into firewood, load it on a sled and take it to the railway station. It took three trips to the forest to get enough timber to fill one sled with firewood.

In the meantime, Kolia had established a circle of friends and continued his carefree ways. He was quite a charming, nice-looking, sociable type whose weakness was limited to his inability to do any useful work. Soon he had a steady girlfriend and many pals among the Russian military, who were still in force in Manchuria. Talking to them about Mother Russia eventually developed in him a yearning to go there. He began to believe life in Russia was wonderful and that he would be welcome there, even though he came from White Russian stock.

This mistaken belief was to cost him dearly.

The cow they had originally bought was a cantankerous beast. Nusia could not get any milk out of her. She asked her neighbour, a *Zabaikalka*, for help. These were descendants of Cossack and Mongolian unions centuries earlier, and were often credited with special healing powers. Surprisingly the neighbour had no trouble milking the cow. Nusia tried again the next day, without success. The neighbour came every morning for three days to teach her how to do it, but Nusia was still not able to get any milk. On the fourth day she managed to squeeze out just one glass, whereas she should have been able to get a whole bucketful.

Another neighbour suggested that Nusia seek the advice of a woman she knew, who could cast spells on cows — a specialist dairy spell-caster, no less. She was apparently credited with all sorts of successes. For example, after a cow gives birth to a calf, its milk is initially unfit to drink by humans, being bitter and foul smelling. Nine days after the birth of the calf, this woman would be called in and she would cast the appropriate spell. Lo and behold, the milk would immediately turn sweet again.

After hearing Nusia's story of woe, the spell-caster diagnosed the problem as follows: 'Your neighbour is a native *Zabaikalka*, and they are a sneaky race. She has obviously managed to steal your cow's milk, transferring it to her own cow. I'm sure hers now gives her twice as much milk as before, while yours has become barren.'

The analysis was not very constructive and there was nothing else left to do but sell the beast to a slaughterhouse. As the proceeds were insufficient to buy another cow, Diakonoff took Nusia's sewing machine and on the weekend he and Vova went to the next town to sell it. The price he managed to get was higher than expected and this prompted him to buy not just one cow but two.

Diakonoff thought Nusia would be happier with two cows — more milk, more income — but he was wrong. As far as she was concerned, one cow was necessary to provide the family with milk, but the second would be a rod for her back. She did not relish tending the extra beast, milking it, and then having to sell the spare milk, so the second cow was promptly sold. However, the remaining one was a good beast, her long teats making the task of milking very easy. The milk was rich, sweet and plentiful, more than enough for the family, and they were able to sell most of it. One of their neighbours owned a milk separator, and Nusia used it to make cream, cream cheese and butter. For this she paid the neighbour in kind, giving him a bucket of milk for every fifth use of the separator.

During the cow-buying exercise, Diakonoff and Vova had to stay overnight in the next town.

And that was the night that Kolia decided to abscond to Mother Russia.

GONE WITHOUT A WORD: 1947

Nusia was waiting for Kolia to come home that Saturday night so they could go to evening Mass, but he did not show up. When Nusia and Misha returned from church he was still absent. Nor did he come home at all that night. Beside herself with worry, Nusia ran around the village, looking for him in the obvious places, but he was nowhere to be found. Worried and downcast, she sat down to await Diakonoff and Vova's return.

In the afternoon, a girlfriend of Kolia's came by the house to pay him a visit, and Nusia told her of his disappearance. 'Oh, so he did skip across the border,' the girl said. 'I thought he was only joking.'

Nusia was horrified. He had never mentioned any such plan to the family. Could he have really done this? Soon another girl dropped by and told Nusia she had farewelled Kolia and three of his friends at the station the previous night. The visitor was amazed at Nusia's reaction. She could not imagine Kolia doing such a thing without telling his family.

Nusia was devastated. Her immediate reaction was to rush after him, but her neighbours dissuaded her. When Diakonoff and Vova finally returned that evening, Nusia broke the dramatic news to them. Diakonoff's first reaction was also to rush after him and stop him before he went across the border. But on reflection, he decided to let him go.

To add insult to injury, they discovered Kolia had taken all of the family's meagre valuables — two gold wedding rings, a gold bracelet and a thick gold necklace in the form of a snake which was a favourite of Nusia's and the most expensive item among the family possessions.

A SAD TALE: 1947

The winter after Kolia's departure to Mother Russia, Vova went to work for a logging company in the northern part of Manchuria. As his father was feeling reasonably well at the time, he joined Vova in the venture.

The huge coniferous forests in northern Manchuria are known as *Taiga*. These forests were, and still are, home to the largest tiger of them all, the great Siberian tiger – the 'Mighty *Vahn*' as the Chinese called him. This cat, which grows to up to three metres long (plus a one metre tail), is the only tiger living in a cold climate.

Since the forest was a long way from home, Diakonoff and Vova were to stay in the company's forest camp through the winter. The promised pay was quite lucrative, provided you brought your own horses and sleds, which they did. Unfortunately the owner reneged on the deal, announcing payment would only be made in the spring after the timber was sold. He would not even give them a small advance. Undoubtedly this was done to ensure the workers stayed for the whole season.

So there they were, all winter long, working for just their board and lodging, and not able to send any money home. Nusia therefore had a very difficult time making ends meet. She did not even have enough money to buy firewood and was very worried about the wellbeing of her twelve-year-old son Michael and the adopted child Alexei. Had she still had her jewellery, she could have sold it and made her life more tolerable. But Kolia had taken it all. As a last resort, she appealed to her mother and sisters in Tientsin who immediately sent her some money.

That winter was a rough one for the men as well. Besides the freezing cold and the hard work, their life was made more unpleasant because Vova and his father were not on speaking terms. The basis of the conflict was Diakonoff's displeasure with Vova's courting of a girl called Tonia (short for Antonina).

Behind this displeasure was his selfish fear that, once Vova got married, she would come to live with them and there would be one more mouth to feed.

The feelings from Tonia's side were reciprocated in full. She believed Diakonoff exploited his son. Vova gave all his earnings to his father for the family, and the 'miserable scrooge', as Tonia called him, never even gave him any pocket money for a drink or a date. And yet there was never a shortage of vodka or *Hah-nah* (a coarse, vile-smelling Chinese brandy) for Diakonoff's own use. If Vova ever went out to a party and came back late, his father would berate him for this, complaining he would be tired the next day and not able to work as hard.

Vova disliked his father — for his miserly attitude, his bossy nature, his grumpiness, his weakness and his inability to work. At the same time, he pitied him. His father was ageing very quickly. Having been very well off in the past, with a successful business and a good income, he was now unable to provide for his family. This was obviously weighing heavily on his father's mind, making him moody and irritable, and driving him to drink.

Which brings us to a nasty incident which happened that winter.

One cold night, as old Diakonoff sat near a stove in the barn, a drunken young Russian merchant came in and asked him some question or other. Diakonoff did not answer — maybe he did not hear him or maybe he just did not feel like talking. The drunk became annoyed, called him a stinking old fart, unbuttoned his pants and started urinating on Diakonoff's boots.

Vova, who was sitting nearby, immediately saw red. Being solidly built, he grabbed the drunk by his private parts with one hand and the scruff of his neck with the other and threw him over the stove on to a pile of straw. Lunging at the prostrate drunk, he began to pummel him with his fists.

Just then, in walked a major of the Chinese Communist Army, a highly respected military man, a pistol on his hip.

'Stop it!' he yelled. 'You have no right to treat a fellow human being like this!'

'Yes I have!' Vova screamed back.

The major came up to him and slapped him hard across the face. Vova let go of the drunk and was about to lunge at the interloper when the major slapped him again. Vova was now ready to kill. At that moment, someone grabbed him and stopped him from doing a very stupid thing. Had he attacked the major, he would have undoubtedly been shot dead.

After the officer walked out, followed by the frightened drunk, Vova turned to look at his father. The old man was sitting there, crying his eyes out.

The following day Diakonoff could not be found anywhere. He had disappeared. Searches proved fruitless. Days and weeks passed, but there was still no sign of him. Vova decided he must have been eaten by wolves, or perhaps even by the Mighty *Vahn*.

No great loss, he thought.

At the end of the season Vova was paid off, including the money owing to his father. On the way home, he began to think about his own miserable life. He had just gone through more than three months of hard work in freezing weather, with no money, little food, and a father who would not talk to him — and who had finally disappeared. And now he was going home to more poverty and back-breaking work, with no relief in sight.

'What's life all about?' he asked himself. 'Isn't it about time I had a bit of fun? Don't I deserve something better for my pain and suffering?'

As his answer to his own question was a resounding 'yes', he decided to sell the horses and have a bit of a splurge. On the way back to Mianduhe, he stopped over in Harbin, bought some good clothes, went to a few restaurants, had more than a few drinks and experienced some of life's pleasures. He did not spend all the money. There was still enough left to take home.

Of course he had to break the news to Nusia that her husband was missing, presumed dead. Although there was no love lost for him, the news was still a shock to her system. And, unexpectedly, it really upset Misha, the younger one, who had developed a surprising attachment to his ailing father. I say 'surprising' because the attachment had not previously exhibited itself in any show of tenderness or love from either party. A *panihida* (memorial service) was organised and the family began to adjust to the prospect of life without Diakonoff.

However, all this turned out to be premature. A week later the missing man reappeared. The effect on the family was one of astonishment rather than relief, except for Misha who rushed over to hug his father.

Diakonoff refused to tell anyone where he had been. This secret remained with him to his dying day.

BEST OF FRIENDS: 1945–1948

The best friend I ever had in my life was Andrew Morozov. He was the same age as I, but was a couple of years behind me at the college. His father had an important position with the Customs Department and his mother was a kind and hospitable person. They were quite well off and had a beautiful large apartment on the French Concession. It was so big it had three huge unused rooms in which we often played games, the most memorable of which were mock sword fights with bamboo sticks, under the influence of films such as *The Mark of Zorro* and *Captain Blood*.

For reasons that will become obvious later, Andrew used to come to my house more often than I came to his. By that time, my mother, Vasia, Elena and I had moved to my grandmother's Yang-Ho-Li address and I had a room to myself for the first time in my life. It was tiny, about two metres by three, situated on the third floor with a window overlooking the entrance lane. In it were a bed, a desk and a small cupboard,

Andrew would ride over to our place on his fancy multi-speed bicycle with thick balloon tyres, similar to today's mountain bikes. Pausing in the lane below my window, he would whistle our special, secret three-note whistle and I would open the window and throw him the keys to the front door. After parking his bike in the hallway, he would climb up the stairs to my room.

The two of us were on the same wavelength. We never got tired of each other. We shared a love of music and girls, liked the same movies and had no secrets from each other. We spent

Andrew Morozov, Tientsin, 1948

endless hours together in my tiny, cocoon-like room, away from the rest of the world, discussing anything and everything — the future, the past, our aspirations, our desires. Often we just sat there silent, communicating through osmosis. The only time we quarrelled was when I tried to wean him off a girl with whom he was in love, but who did not care for him.

Our tastes in music were compatible as well. Andrew had a rich aunt who owned a radiogram — an electronic method of playing records through a speaker, as opposed to the purely acoustical horn of the wind-up gramophone. Once he took me and another friend of ours, George Wagner, to his aunt's place to listen to this wonderful instrument. We sat there, mesmerised, listening to a 78-rpm recording of Rossini's 'The Thieving Magpie Overture'. I still remember the thrill of it. A more realistic sound was unimaginable. It was a most moving experience.

George Wagner was a bit of a genius. He became the youngest person ever to graduate from St Louis College, some two years ahead of the norm, and he was also an electronics buff. He loved to build all sorts of electronic gear, with large valves, condensers and the like. The experience with the aunt's radiogram inspired him to build his own audio amplifier from some circuit diagram he saw in a magazine. And it had even better sound!

I remember when Andrew and I first went shopping for records in a second-hand bazaar in the French Concession and bought

Self, just before leaving Tientsin, 1948

ourselves the Lalo 'Symphonie Espagnole' on four twelve-inch 78s — our first record purchase ever. Later we also bought the first two records of a three-record set of Rimsky-Korsakov's 'Capriccio Espagnole'. The third record was missing, so we were able to negotiate a good price for the first two. We spent many hours listening to them on George's set, marvelling at the reproduction. George splurged and bought Tchaikovsky's First Symphony, 'Winter Dreams'. It is the least interesting of all his symphonies, but as we had never heard any of the others we thought it was marvellous music, and the reproduction was awesome!

One of the major stimuli to my love of classical music, besides my piano lessons, was the radio. Uncle George, who was then working for Brynner's Customs Agency, presented me with a beautiful, modern short-wave radio (it had no doubt been confiscated by the Customs Department). It was a marvellous instrument, the envy of all my friends, and Andrew, George and I spent many hours listening to it. The Hong Kong station was my favourite. It played a lot of classical music. Once I wrote to the station and requested an airing of the Rimsky-Korsakov 'Capriccio Espagnole' so we could hear how the work ended. They did play it and even provided some mirth when they pronounced my name as Eye-vashkoff, instead of Ee-vashkoff.

Andrew also studied the piano at Sajin's, but his heart was not in it. His mother often asked me to play the piano for her, which I did with the greatest of pleasure. I liked to perform and I was flattered by her request.

SEX EDUCATION, LACK OF: 1945–1948

My sex education was non-existent. I did not get it in college, as the Marist Brothers did not include it in their curriculum — nor, being celibate, would they have been experienced enough to teach it. And my mother never raised the subject, maybe because she was always at work, or maybe because it was not considered necessary in those days. My school buddies were similarly unendowed with knowledge on this important subject. But being healthy growing boys full of testosterone, we could not stay off the subject for long.

To illustrate our level of ignorance on this matter, I remember, at the age of twelve or so, having a heated discussion with my friends about how babies were conceived. We all knew they were carried in the stomachs of women, but we did not really know how they actually emerged from the mother's body. And what we certainly did not know was how they got there in the first place.

One of the group told us he had it on good authority from one of the seniors in college that the conception process was as follows: 'The male and female both pass water into a chamber pot, it is mixed, and the female drinks it down.' As no-one else was able to come up with a more plausible story, we accepted that version as the truth, with some revulsion and pity for the poor female. I was relieved when the truth turned out to be much more palatable.

The big breakthrough came when one of my classmates, Kostia, discovered a thick book on his father's shelf entitled *The Encyclopaedia of Sexual Knowledge*. Overnight he became the most popular boy in our class. We used to go over to Kostia's home on Wednesday afternoons when school was out and his parents were at work, and hungrily devour the chapters and study the graphic illustrations. In a very short time, we were transformed from ignoramuses into experts.

In the end, one of Kostia's mates stole the book from his house, for which Kostia was beaten black and blue by his father. In addition, the poor kid lost all his ill-gained popularity. The thief was a real blackguard to have done this to a friend who must have added immeasurably to his knowledge of sex.

St Louis College was a segregated school and I was a student there from the age of eight to fifteen. For four of those years I was a boarder, I did not have a sister so, apart from my mother and my aunts, I was deprived of regular female company for just about all my formative years. Thinking back, this was not at all healthy. One of the penalties I paid for this deprivation was that, in my teens, I was very shy and awkward in female company. I was not used to being with girls or women or communicating with them. To me, they were shrouded in some sort of mystery. They constituted half the world's population and yet I felt they were some sort of untouchables.

Isn't that weird? It is certainly unnatural. Why do this to a growing boy or girl? And why are many schools segregated? Maybe it emanated from the various religious orders that operated schools run by celibate Brothers, Sisters and the like. I suppose it was unthinkably risky for them to mix Brothers and Sisters in the same school. And of course there would perhaps be an even greater risk if a bunch of Brothers were to look after young girls (perish the thought) or a cast of Sisters were to look after a bunch of horny boys ...

At any rate, I was well into my puberty before I was able to overcome my shyness and feel at ease with females. Consequently I vowed that, if I ever had any children, I would send them to coeducational institutions — which is what I did do, without any detrimental effect to their scholastic results.

The desk in my room belonged to Vasia, my stepfather. It had one large full-width drawer, plus three small ones on the side. The large drawer was always locked and therefore off-limits to me, making me intensely curious to find out why it merited such strict security. I tried picking the lock, without success.

But one day I found an old bunch of keys somewhere and decided to try them out. To my surprise and delight one of them opened the drawer. Imagine my amazement when I discovered the forbidden fruit to be a comprehensive collection of erotic magazines and books. I have no idea where Vasia obtained them, as I had not seen their like in any bookshops or anywhere else, but there they were — and here I was, at the age of fourteen, with an unimaginable collection of erotica right in my own room, and accessible at will! For some unknown reason, the book I remember most was *The Autobiography of a Flea*, a collection of vivid stories told by a flea which jumped from one person's pubic hair to another's during intercourse. Now you can understand why Andrew spent more time at my place than I did at his!

Many years later I told Vasia about my stroke of luck, but he did not believe me. He said he had always checked the arrangement of the materials in the drawer to satisfy himself they had not been disturbed. Which just goes to show how careful I had been in replacing the goodies.

A CRUEL PUNISHMENT: 1946

I was fourteen when my mother bought me a bicycle for my birthday in June, just before the start of the three-month summer vacation. It was a nice bike, not as fancy as my friend Andrew's but eminently serviceable. I loved it. For three whole days I enjoyed this wonderfully exciting mode of transportation. And then tragedy befell me.

Each month the Marist Brothers issued a report card rating the students' scholastic record and conduct for the month. The maximum mark was 100. The card came in one of four colours — Gold for marks of 90–100, White for 80–89,

Yellow for 70–79 and Blue for a mark below 70. Two Blues resulted in expulsion.

My record up to then was either Gold or White, but this time I received a Yellow, my first ever. I don't remember whether it was my school marks or my conduct that gave rise to this situation, but whichever it was I knew Mum would kill me for it. What was I to do? In panic mode, I embarked on a rather drastic and risky plan. Stealing a blank White card from Brother Charles' desk, I asked an older friend of mine to fill it out and forge the Brother's signature on it. When mother saw the card, she berated me a bit for not getting a Gold, but otherwise it all went off pretty well. I was reprieved, but not for long.

My bad luck arrived in the form of Brother Charles, who met my mother in the street shortly afterwards and inquired if she had been distressed at the sight of my first Yellow card.

'What Yellow card?' she asked. 'You can't be referring to Igor. He brought home a White card. That was bad enough.'

'That's not quite right, dear madam. This time I had to give him a Yellow one. You must have mixed up the colours. Have another look at it.'

Mother knew she had not made a mistake.

'Guess whom I met on the street today?' she asked me when she came home.

By the tone of her voice, I sensed something was up, something unpleasant. 'Who?' I asked innocently.

The story of her meeting Brother Charles shattered me. I was sure I had got away with it. There should be a rule preventing the Brothers roaming the streets, I thought. They should stay indoors and pray in their spare time. Anyway, the jig was up and I confessed the whole thing.

Mum was not a terribly strict person. She never put a belt to my bottom. But this time I felt she had every right to do so. However, she decided I was too old to receive my first hiding and instead — oh, horror! — she prohibited my use of the new bike for the whole summer. And that was the period I needed it most. This was 1946 and with Kiesslings now in Chinese hands and many of the foreigners gone, the Peitaiho branch did not open for the summer. So I would be staying in Tientsin for the whole of the summer holidays. The only consolation was the fact that I would at least be mobile. Without my bike, was life really worth living? I was devastated.

To add insult to injury, the bike just stood there in the hallway, a vision of speed and beauty, continuously reminding me of what might have been. I begged Mum to give me a good hiding instead or to take away my pocket money, or both — anything but the bike. But she remained firm. I even volunteered to do all sorts of unpleasant chores around the house, in the hope she would weaken and forgive me, but to no avail.

It was the most severe punishment I had ever received. It was, of course, fully deserved.

On my beloved bike, Tientsin, 1946

When school re-started, the bike embargo was lifted, and this transformed my life. I rode the bike to school, visited my friends and relatives more often than I used to, and went for rides in the countryside. The feeling of limitless mobility was wonderful.

After a year or so the bike began to show some signs of wear and tear, especially in the brakes department. In fact, they did not work at all. To compensate for this minor problem I learned to skilfully apply the sole of my shoe to the front wheel when the situation demanded it.

One day Mum saw me doing this and was aghast.

'You're going to kill yourself!'

'Don't worry, Mum, it works fine,' I assured her.

'What if you are going fast? Will you be able to stop in time?'

'Absolutely!' I replied, full of confidence. 'Let me give you a demonstration,'

At the time, she was walking on the footpath and I was riding on the road beside her.

'Just stand here. I'll ride to the end of the street, pedal back as fast as I can and brake to a dead stop right in front of you. Trust me!'

As I came past her at about thirty kilometres an hour, I jammed the sole of my right rubber-soled sneaker against the front wheel. It stopped dead, the back wheel rose off the ground and I went flying over the handlebars past my screaming mother, landing heavily on the paved road about five metres ahead. Mother led me away, scratched and bleeding, and I was not allowed to ride the bike until the brakes were fixed. This incident probably saved my life. Had this happened in an emergency on a busy street, I am sure I would not have seen my fifteenth birthday.

RISK-TAKING: 1947

I am a risk-taker by nature. In my maturity, I think the risks I have taken were calculated ones, but in those days I used to do some pretty stupid things. Two incidents come to mind.

The first concerned my bicycle. The Tientsin traffic laws decreed that bike riders should stay close to the curb, leaving the rest of the street for motor vehicles. I thought it was a pretty stupid law, as the vehicular traffic in those days was very light and the roads were pretty wide. So I used to ignore the rule and hurtle down the middle of the road.

One day, the police decided to mount a blitz on erratic bike riders like myself. In Victoria Road, the main thoroughfare, they brought in scores of police cadets and lined them up on both sides of the road, about twenty metres apart and two metres from the curb. The cadets had their arms outstretched, parallel to the curb, thus forming a human bicycle lane, and bike riders were supposed to comply by riding between them and the curb.

Unfortunately nobody had told me about this blitz and I came hurtling into Victoria Road from a side street. There I was, riding pretty fast, no hands, in the middle of the road, wondering what all those funny uniformed Chinamen were doing on the sides of the road, and why they were gawking at me with incredulity. It took me a while to twig to the situation. But, instead of immediately moving across to the designated bicycle lane, I decided I would risk it to the next intersection. There I would duck into the side street and pedal away like mad. They would never catch me.

However, this blatant disregard for the law provoked the police cadets into frenetic action. They yelled and screamed, pointing at me. All hell broke loose. You'd think I was a serial killer on the run. The ones ahead of me waved their arms wildly, those in the back screamed their heads off — while I went on pedalling furiously, weaving between them, trying to reach the intersection. Regrettably, the force of numbers was too great for me and they trapped me about ten metres short of my escape route.

I thought I would get away with a lecture, but the head cop decided I needed to be taught a lesson. Triumphantly he marched me off, past the jeering cadets, to the police station about three blocks away. There I was interrogated by a stern-looking officer who yelled at me for a while and then instructed I be taken to a cell! Yes, that's right. A jail cell! Once the cell door slammed shut and my eyes adjusted to the dim light, I realised I was not alone. Three fierce looking Chinese were staring at me. I could tell by looking at them that they were not fellow joy-riders. They looked like real criminals to me, with nasty, snarling faces. They stank, the place stank, it was dark and dingy, and I was frightened, very frightened.

Two hours later — the longest two hours of my life — I was released and the stern-looking officer gave me a lecture and extracted a promise I would never ever do it again. After deflating my tyres, they let me have my bike back, and an equally deflated Igor walked home, pushing his bike.

Fortunately, my mother did not find out about this incident or I would have been in even deeper trouble. The stay in jail did sober me up and I was a more careful bike rider from then on — at least for a while.

The second incident that comes to mind was the water-balloon-bombing episode.

At that time we were living on the Italian Concession in Vasia's apartment, which was in a residential complex where every unit had a window or two looking out on to an internal courtyard. This courtyard was used as a playground for small children.

One of the European tenants had two small children who were looked after by a young Chinese amah. They were cheeky brats and I didn't like them. So I used to tease them a bit. Because of this, their amah developed an intense and unreasonable dislike for me. She used to yell at me to stay away and would generally make herself a pain in the neck. And I was powerless to retaliate. After all, you can't really get into a fistfight with an amah.

Our bathroom was on the second floor and its window overlooked the courtyard. Whenever I went there, I used to look down into the courtyard out of curiosity to see what, if anything, was happening. Often the nasty amah was there, tending her brood. The sight of the unprotected top of her head always prompted fantasies, such as throwing something heavy, like an anvil, on top of her. The anvil idea was, of course, impractical, but one day I remembered the movie in which Harpo Marx dropped a balloon filled with water on the baddie's head. Thus was hatched a nefarious plan to pay the amah back, with interest, for her malevolence.

The balloon was bought and hidden in the bathroom. Now it was only a matter of the right opportunity. And one summer evening it presented itself. We were at dinner — Mum, Vasia, his mother Elena and I — it was still light outside. As I needed to go to the toilet, I excused myself and ran up the stairs. As usual, I looked out of the window and there in the courtyard below was the hated one. And her head was just below the window. It was too good a chance to miss.

Quickly, I filled the balloon with about two litres of water, quietly opened the fly screen, took aim and let the missile go. As it dropped, I could see it was going to score a bullseye. By the time it hit her, I had the fly screen closed and was halfway down the stairs. Mother and Vasia were engaged in conversation and I quickly sat down to continue eating, innocence personified.

A minute later there was a loud banging on the front door. Normally I would have jumped up to answer it, but the banging was louder than normal and accompanied by Chinese screaming and swearing, so Vasia went. There stood the beastie, sopping wet, her hair dishevelled, her clothes soaked. And she was yelling and pointing at me and demanding retribution. She would get her master to call the police, she screamed.

Fortunately for me, Mother and Vasia had been engaged in some heated conversation and had not noticed my brief absence. Both of them told the girl it could not have possibly been me, as we were all sitting there having dinner together and I had never left the table.

'Look, there he is, quietly eating his dinner.'

I had an ironclad alibi!

'Hi! You're all wet. What happened to you?' I asked politely.

The beastie, of course, did not believe them, but who was she to argue with my parents, who were steadfastly denying the possibility of my guilt? She left.

'Fancy blaming you, Igor,' Mum said, patting me on the head.

Many years later I told my mother the truth and she was amazed at the revelation. She honestly believed I had not left the table that night. But Vasia's mother, Elena, knew I had, though she had never said anything.

GROWING UP, TIENTSIN-STYLE: 1945

Movies were the main escape mechanism of the day. There were three theatres within walking distance of our apartment — the Empire, the Majestic and the Grand. The first movie I ever remember seeing was *The Wizard of Oz*. I must have been about eight and I recall sitting in the front row with my friend Keshka, who was at least ten, and screaming with terror every time the witch appeared. In the interests of peace and quiet, Keshka covered my face with his beret every time the witch made an appearance.

Later, before the war, Andrew and I would revel in the escapism of Errol Flynn's *Captain Blood* and *The Sea Hawk*, and in Tyrone Power's *The Mark of Zorro*. During the war, the occupying Japanese did not permit the showing of Yankee movies so it was a cinematically dull period.

When the war ended I was already thirteen and the testosterone was beginning to build up in my eager little body, re-focussing my cinematic tastes on subjects of a more romantic nature. And Hollywood was able to oblige with the right sort of material.

My first love was Esther Williams in the watery extravaganza *Bathing Beauty* (my first glimpse of a slinky bathing suit). She was soon replaced by the redheaded Rita Hayworth in *Gilda* ('Put the Blame on Mae, Boys' sent me crazy). Rita was followed by Lana Turner in *The Postman Always Rings Twice* and finally by Joan Leslie ('Who's she?' you ask) in a film called *Hollywood Canteen*. There was something about Joan that ignited not just my sex drive, but a genuine *love*. I dreamt of cuddling her, stroking her hair and murmuring 'It's all right, sweetheart. I'll look after you.'

Mostly I went to the movies with my friends. Due to a lack of funds I could not invite girls that often, but arranging to meet them inside worked nearly as well — the same benefits for less cost. Sitting in the very back row with your arm around a girl was what movies were all about. The arm got very tired, but it was very adult and risque.

I think my social life started at about the age of fifteen. We were all mad about girls, and the single most important outlet for these feelings was the party. The most popular parties were in the homes of friends whose parents trusted them not to misbehave, and therefore left the premises.

Food was not important at these events, nor was liquor. As a matter of fact I don't ever remember drinking alcohol at them. Dancing and special games were what they were all about. The music for dancing came from the trusty wind-up gramophone, with 78s of the crooner Leschenko singing tangos. This Russian tenor had a beautifully romantic voice, somewhat like Julio Iglesias, and dancing in the dark to his tangos — with titles such as 'Confess to Me', 'Blue Eyes' and 'Miranda' — was the closest thing to heaven.

Our favourite party games were spin the bottle and monks.

The first one is well known in most circles: the spinner kisses the girl at whom the bottle points when it stops spinning, and then it is the recipient's turn for a spin.

Monks, however, was the ultimate in sexy games and was always played during the dancing, which meant just about all night. These were the rules: A boy and a girl go into a separate room and canoodle; then the boy tells the girl whom he would like to see next; the girl taps the new girl (who is dancing) on the shoulder and takes her place, while the chosen one goes into the room for her thrill; she then tells the boy whom she would like to see next, and the boy goes out and gets him. And so it goes.

This could go on all night, and it often did. The only frustration was the wait to be chosen. As one would expect, those who were popular saw a lot of action, and the others considerably less. Fortunately I was in the popular category. During large parties we would play double monks — two rooms at the one time.

The partygoers were normally in one of two categories: those who were going steady with their girl or boy friends, and those who were loose. The former had to give preference to their steady during monks and ensure their time with others in the private room was kept to a minimum. The most popular girls were, of course, the 'broad-minded' ones who not only let you kiss them but also fondle them. That's as far as we, or at least I, went in those days. Sex between teenagers was definitely not the norm.

A girl named Vera liked me. She was a student at St Joseph's College, a girls' school run by Catholic Sisters, which was close to St Louis College. One day as I was pedalling to school, I saw Vera walking with some of her friends and stopped to say hello. She asked me to give her a lift to school on the bike — a popular form of togetherness in those days — and I agreed. Unfortunately, she was a solidly built girl, while my build, on the other hand, was slight in those days. Anyway, she climbed sidesaddle on to the bar and waved goodbye to her friends.

As soon as we moved off, I knew I had made a grave error of judgment.

The road was uphill. There were no gears on the bike and the task of pedalling was excruciatingly difficult. Even though it was winter, I was soon perspiring and my legs were ready to fall off. It was horrible, but I had to go on, and I had to give the appearance of enjoying what I was doing. As we overtook pedestrian students we waved happily to them, and all the time I had to look debonair and relaxed.

My first love —Tanya, Tientsin, 1948

Vera caught me again the next day and I had to repeat the performance. After that, I changed my route to school. She was okay to kiss and pet, but definitely not to cart around on a bike.

I was about fifteen when I first fell in love. Tanya (short for Tatiana) was a shy but pretty girl who lived on the French Concession with her parents and a younger sister. Her shyness beguiled me. I felt I was placed on this earth to protect her and make her happy. We went to parties together, to the movies, for walks. I remember those romantic rides on a double rickshaw from the cinema to her home, especially cosy in winter, with the two of us rugged up under a blanket, our bodies touching ...

In the year or so that we were going steady the furthest point on the sex scale we got to was kissing — no petting, no hanky-panky. And it seemed right to keep it at that level. I did not have visions of her without her clothes on, or us having sex. She appeared to me to be too pure for all that.

A MARRIAGE IN CRISIS: 1946–1947

After years of doing odd jobs and earning a pittance, Len landed the job of manager of the Astor House Hotel, which was one of the most prestigious establishments in Shanghai. A fringe benefit was the use of one of its large apartments.

Although Len's financial position became quite reasonable, his family life was still in a mess. When he married Galya, his second wife, in 1940 they were quite happy. But it did not take long for Len to get back to his philandering ways. Galya knew of his affairs — he was not terribly discreet — but she still loved him and hoped he would eventually change his ways. When she fell pregnant in early 1943 she saw the coming child as a possible glue for their disintegrating marriage.

Svetlana was born on 25 November 1943. She was a lovely girl and both parents doted on her, but unfortunately the birth of a child did not turn Len into a devoted family man. He continued his old ways and paid little attention to the family. His girlfriends and his mates meant more to him than his wife or child. Galya felt herself alone and neglected, and for company she relied increasingly on her mother. And she also realised her mother had been right. Len was not, and would never be, a faithful husband or a caring father.

But divorce seemed to be out of the question. After all, she had a small child to rear, the divorce process was expensive, and they had little money. They were stuck together by default, an unhappy couple with a toddler.

But worse was to come. At the age of twenty-two months, Svetlana contracted cholera. The Indian doctor in the casualty department of the local hospital misdiagnosed the illness as gastroenteritis and sent her home. She died the following morning. It was 30 September 1945.

Len and Galya were grief-stricken. They would have probably divorced there and then, had it not been for the fact that Galya was pregnant again. This time it was to be a boy, Len Jr, who appeared on the scene on 16 March 1946, six months after Svetlana died. And on 30 September 1947, two years to the day after Svetlana's death, Liz was born. But nothing else changed between Len and Galya. They were still an unhappy couple.

Then, in 1947, a Chinese businessman bought the Astor House Hotel, and Len was fired. Not only did he lose his job, but also his apartment. At that time accommodation was not easy to find and Galya spent much time and effort in that pursuit. Len, as usual, did very little to ensure the welfare of his family. Galya's mother helped in the search and discovered an empty apartment opposite her own in Route Freulupte on the French Concession. Initially, Len would not have a bar of it — he despised his mother-in-law and did not want to live anywhere near her — but a lack of alternatives eventually cleared his mind and they moved in.

The relationship between Len and Galya continued to deteriorate and, with Len out of work, their financial situation was precarious. Following in the footsteps of his father, Len felt many of the available jobs were below his standing in life. It seemed he preferred to have his family starve rather than take on menial jobs. He did some part-time work here and there, but the money coming in was paltry and they survived largely through the financial assistance of Len's sister Nadia Kozlovsky and Galya's mother.

Len began to spend more and more of his time away from home with his buddies and his girlfriends, and Galya spent more and more of her time with her mother.

The marriage was in crisis.

MILLIONAIRES GALORE! — 1946–1949

When Boris Kozlovsky arrived in Shanghai in late 1946 after Aida's passport stealing episode, he stayed for a while with Len and his family in his Astor House Hotel apartment. Boris had been exceptionally lucky on the job front. A friend of a friend, Mr Evseyeff, was the engineering manager of the Chinese Aluminium Rolling Mills, a Canadian–Swiss Company, and he had a vacancy for a draughtsman. Boris was readily available and within ten days of his arrival he was employed and earning a good salary. Nadia and little George were brought out from Tientsin and the family settled down in a small apartment in Route des Sœurs. Life looked promising again.

The end of the war saw the re-emergence of civil war between the Chinese Communists and the Nationalists. It had quietened down during the Japanese occupation, but the defeat of the Japanese and the growing exodus of foreigners had restarted it in all seriousness and the situation became extremely fragile. Fragility causes inflation, and that's what happened here, and happened in spades, right across the country. Galloping inflation.

Boris' salary was originally paid in CRBs (Chinese Reserve Bank), but as inflation escalated his salary was paid in all sorts of stable currencies — US dollars, English pounds and even Mexican pesos. As the Yankee dollar was the only currency anyone trusted, the CRBs were immediately exchanged into that currency and, when needed, converted back again into local currency for everyday use.

In 1948 the Chinese government decided to stomp out inflation by decreeing that, from 1 August, a new 'stable' currency would be introduced — the FRB (Federal Reserve Bank) — and that it would be pegged against the US dollar at a rate of four FRBs to the US dollar. The stability of this new currency would, allegedly, be guaranteed by the US Federal Gold Reserve. Furthermore everyone was instructed to hand in their old CRBs and all foreign currency and precious metals for conversion into the new FRBs at a prescribed rate. Anyone disobeying this order would be publicly executed — yes, executed!

Many people believed what the government said and handed in their money, receiving the appropriate number of FRBs in exchange. Among those unfortunates was Galya's mother who converted all her savings, which were in silver bars, to FRBs. However, the Kozlovskys decided to take a risk and abstain, which proved to be a wise decision.

Within a month, inflation was rampant once again, indeed so much so that the government was forced to establish an inflation index. This index was based on an international comparison of the price of vital food products. Initially, the index was published on a weekly basis, then on a daily, and finally twice daily. Unsurprisingly, the inflation caused immense problems. Everyone who converted their foreign currency and bullion to FRBs now saw their money lose value at a breathtaking speed. Most rushed back to convert the FRBs into something more stable, but the losses in the process were considerable. Galya's mother was a significant loser.

Shopkeepers adjusted their prices twice a day. Nobody knew, in advance, how much anything would cost. As soon as one had any FRBs, one would rush to change them into US dollars. Even an hour could make a difference to the rate. Small denominations of FRBs disappeared completely. Not only did the government printing presses work twenty-four hours a day, but every available private printing institution was also contracted to print money.

At that time, Boris' monthly salary was the equivalent of $US300. It was paid in FRBs in three instalments, on the 1st, 11th and 21st of the month, with the amount adjusted each time for inflation. But because of the time gaps between the calculation of the wages, the receipt of his salary and the time he could change it into US dollars, he was in danger of losing money. So he and his money changer worked out a deal. At 12 noon on payday, when Boris was told how many FRBs he would be getting, he would ring his money changer and they would agree on the rate of exchange for a 6 p.m. transaction. This rate was adhered to irrespective of the afternoon fluctuations in the official rate.

Just before the Communists took over in 1949, the rate had reached three million FRBs to the US dollar. Compare this to the four-to-one rate set for the new 'stable' FRB just a year earlier. Boris' monthly pay had climbed to 900 million FRBs!

On payday dozens of big trucks would roll into the company yard, loaded to the brink with money. The cash would be unloaded into a special warehouse cleared for the occasion, and the payroll staff would spend the whole morning arranging it into individual piles, surmounted by a printed envelope with the employee's name. Boris would bring an empty twenty-kilogram rice bag to carry the bundles of cash to the company bus for the journey home. Getting off at the money changer's office, he would exchange his pay for US dollars. If Nadia had some minor expenses the following morning, she would ask him to keep a few million FRBs back for her.

To give you an idea of the value of the money, it cost one million FRBs to take a three-kilometre ride on a rickshaw — the equivalent of thirty-three US cents. Everyone was a millionaire, but nobody felt like one.

SUMMER JOBS: 1945–1947

After the Kiesslings Peitaiho branch ceased to operate in 1943, I spent the summers doing odd jobs and earning a little bit of money in the process. The pay was meagre, but the jobs chosen for me by mother and Vasia were supposed to give me some training in a useful trade or two. The first summer job was with a sort of jack-of-all-trades repairman. Georgian by birth, he was quite a gruff hunk of a man who could repair anything, from cars to tea kettles. However, I was not allowed to touch anything he was working on. I could only watch and ask questions.

What saved me from being bored to death was his ownership of a motorised bike, a cross between a bicycle and a motorcycle. Whenever he went off in his truck for a service call — he never took me with him — I would hop on the bike and go joy-riding around the streets of Tientsin. The sensation of speed was exhilarating. I would overtake everything in sight, screeching around corners at speed without any regard for my safety or anyone else's. It was a foolish and dangerous pastime, but it was a wonderful release from the boredom of the job.

He never found out about these escapades. I always made sure I checked how long he would be away and the address of his service call. This determined how long I could bike around and in which direction I should go to avoid any chance of him catching me in this illicit activity. My closest call was when I once ran out of petrol about two kilometres from the workshop. Not having any money with me, the only thing I could do was drag the bike back, while worrying that my boss would return before me. Although I did make it, this taught me a lesson. From then on, I always checked the level of petrol before a new outing.

For the following two summers, I became an apprentice motor mechanic. But instead of learning the auto trade as I was hoping to, I was given the job of greaser and oil changer. As cars had to be regularly greased in those days, their undersides were covered with grease nipples, to which one would apply a pneumatic grease gun. There were two major problems. One was that the undersides of cars were normally covered with dirt and the nipples were hard to find, and the second was that different brands and models of cars had their nipples in different locations. It was necessary, therefore, to familiarise oneself with these differences. After two summers I was probably the greatest young greaser and oil changer in the business. I knew the exact location of every nipple of every car known to man.

'How many nipples on a 1939 Chrysler?' my workmates would yell out to me.

'Twelve,' I would yell back confidently.

'But I can only find nine.'

I would come across and find the missing three in ten seconds flat. Admiring eyes would follow me out of the pit.

It was an extremely dirty and, in the long term, useless job, but it did give me some pocket money and kept me off the streets.

TOWARDS GRADUATION: 1947–1948

It was interesting to be a non-Catholic in a Catholic school run by Catholic zealots. I remember having long religious discussions and arguments with the Brothers, especially Brother Charles, during the last year of school. These discussions normally occurred during Religious Studies classes and ranged from the alleged infallibility of the Pope through to the existence of heaven, hell and purgatory — and, of course, limbo.

I remember how we used to bait the Brothers about the criteria for mortal and venial sins. In the Catholic belief of the day, a mortal sin, if unconfessed and unforgiven, sent one straight to hell. Mortal sins ranged from murder to missing Mass on a Sunday. How ridiculous, we thought. You miss one church service, fail to confess this terrible sin and you are damned for eternity to the flames of hell! This was certainly fertile ground for discussion.

A venial sin, however, was a misdemeanour and resulted in an indeterminate period of cleansing in a place called purgatory before going to heaven. We would come up with weird examples of unsavoury activity and ask the Brothers to adjudicate on the category of the sin — and, if it were categorised as venial, the length of stay in purgatory. Whichever way they answered, we were intent on giving them a hard time and used to argue the point.

Limbo, on the other hand, was supposed to be the depositary for unbaptised infants and the mentally defective. It was not heaven, nor was it hell. So what was it? Did one suffer there or have a good life? If suffer, then how much? If a good life, then how good? And anyway, why should a child be punished for something his parents omitted to do? The whole idea seemed stupid and unfair, and it was obvious the Brothers did not have any sensible answers. Their discomfort added impetus to our desire to embarrass them.

Being of the Russian Orthodox faith, I also remember being dismayed at being required to attend Catholic services, even though the Catholic faith forbade its own believers from entering a non-Catholic church for prayer. You could go there for a wedding ceremony or a christening, as a spectator, but not — definitely not — to pray. Praying to a non-Catholic God was a no-no. This seemed to be a blatant case of double standards, and I argued that point on many occasions.

'But this is different. Ours is the only TRUE religion!' was the standard answer. 'We're doing you a favour by taking you to our Church and offering you a chance for salvation and eternal happiness.'

I graduated from St Louis College in 1947 at the age of fifteen.

My mother was smart enough to realise we were not likely to stay in China for the rest of our lives, and she wanted to ensure that, wherever we went, I would have the necessary qualifications to enter a university. Having been deprived of a proper education herself made her determined to give me the opportunity for a higher education and she therefore insisted I sit for the Cambridge University matriculation exams by correspondence. This was done under the surveillance of the Brothers. I passed them well, though not brilliantly.

This decision on my mother's part was very wise as the Tientsin St Louis College graduation certificate was not recognised in Australia and I would have had to repeat the last year of high school and sit for the Leaving Certificate before entering university.

When I look back at my years in the college I realise that, although the Brothers all had their weak points and a few were despicable characters, the majority were fair and reasonable and the education we all received was the best available in Tientsin, and perhaps in all of China. Besides giving us a broad educational base, we were taught the difference between right and wrong; the value of integrity and morality; respect for elders, parents and authority; and the importance of being a contributor to society.

The majority of the graduates became productive, upstanding, law-abiding citizens, and many excelled in their chosen professions in their lives after China.

WELCOME TO RUSSIA! — 1947

Kolia Diakonoff had not been happy in his family life. He knew his father was ashamed of him, constantly taunting him and making fun of his weaknesses, calling him sickly, clumsy, inept, a first-born son gone wrong. His younger brothers too had little respect for him. In no way did he live up to their image of the 'big brother'.

Only his mother Nusia still seemed to have some love left for him. She believed most of his shortcomings were not his fault — maybe they were even her fault — after all, she had hated the idea of bearing her husband's child and was very depressed during the pregnancy. Perhaps that was the reason he was born prematurely, she thought. Could that have affected the quality of the finished product?

The bottom line was that Kolia felt unloved and unwanted. And he hated Mianduhe. His friend, Venka Shchelokov, was also unhappy with his life and it was he who suggested they skip across the border to Russia. Neither of them would probably have taken the plunge on his own, but, with each of them feeding off the other, they built up considerable enthusiasm for the idea. The more they talked about it, the more exciting the prospect became. Their girlfriends also agreed to join them.

Kolia did not tell anyone at home of his decision. He was, to all intents and purposes, running away from home — from his father's mockery, from his brothers' contempt, from his mother's tears. Why bother telling them?

The train took them 300 kilometres to Manchouli on the border of Manchuria and Russia. Palina, Kolia's girlfriend, had some friends there and they stopped over with them for a day or two. Her friends told them the border was only three kilometres away but warned them that the Chinese border police would not let anyone through without appropriate documents. And even if they did, the Russians would certainly arrest the interlopers and deport them.

All this was a surprise to Kolia and Venka. Naively, they had thought it was just a matter of getting on the train in China and getting off in the USSR. Now it seemed that they would have to sneak across the border somewhere. But relationships between the USSR and China were strained at the time and the border was heavily patrolled by the Chinese and the Russians. If caught by either side, Kolia and his friends could easily be taken for spies and shot. But, as the alternative of going back home to face the ire of their respective families was even less appealing, they decided to press on.

The way to the border was across open fields, with only occasional clumps of trees. Making quick dashes from tree clump to tree clump, Kolia and the other three frequently stopped to reconnoitre. After a few kilometres, they saw a Chinese guard patrolling the length of a trench which they decided was the border. It looked to be about two metres wide but they could not see how deep it was. On each side of the trench was a bare strip of ploughed land. This side was China, the other Russia.

They stayed in hiding until the guard was out of sight and then made a dash for the trench and jumped into it. It was about a metre and a half deep and, although Venka had no trouble clambering out, Kolia and the others had difficulties. As Venka was pulling them out they must have made a bit of a racket because the Chinese guard suddenly reappeared.

'Halt or I'll shoot! Hands up, all of you!' he yelled.

By now the four of them had clambered onto the Russian side of the trench. And there they were, standing in Russia, with their hands up and a Chinese guard pointing his rifle at them across the trench. Luckily, a Russian border guard appeared out of nowhere and pointed his gun at the Chinese soldier.

'They're on our side already. Get the hell out of here, you yellow-faced degenerate!'

It's unlikely the Chinese understood the Russian words, but he certainly understood their intent and retreated.

'And what exactly have we got here?' the Russian guard asked.

'We have come to our motherland,' they replied.

'Your what?' he yelled. 'Your motherland, you say? We'll see about that. Until we sort this out, you're under arrest for violating our border!'

And off they were marched to the nearest pillbox, where the guard made a phone call. Soon a truck appeared and they were whisked away to a command post about forty kilometres away. Here an officer questioned them and their documents were examined. They all had Soviet passports. In the meantime the guards relieved them of anything remotely valuable, including all the items Kolia had stolen from his family. The only item of value he was allowed to retain was the tiny gold cross hung around his neck.

'Why have you come here?' they were asked.

'Because we want to be in our native land; because we are sick and tired of living among the Chinese; because we have seen Russian films and life here seems to be great.'

'Well it's certainly better than living among the Chinks,' the interrogator said. 'But why the hell do we need the likes of you? We've got more than enough idiots here already. You should have come here during the war. Then you could have helped your country. But what can you do for us now? Nothing! I think the only place for you now is one of our holiday camps.'

The four illegal immigrants could not believe their ears. A holiday camp, they thought, with amazement. What a great way to start a new life!

They were led to a large hut, where there were another thirty or so Russian fugitives from China, all keen to live in the motherland. And that is where they remained for the next two days, under tight security and on meagre rations. On the third day, an officer came in and announced they would all be moved to Chita, 400 kilometres away. There, he said, they would stand trial and the court would determine their final destiny. 'And good luck to all of you stupid misfits,' were his final words of encouragement.

Visions of a holiday camp quickly disappeared and rumours began to fly around the group. Some said the guards were only trying to scare them, that they were going to be released. Others said the average sentence was seven years of hard labour. Others even thought they could be shot as traitors or spies.

A prison train brought them to Chita and the court heard their pleas — that they had Soviet passports and that they were not spies — just stupid patriots who crossed the border to come to the motherland. It was touching stuff but the judge found them guilty of crossing the border illegally and sentenced the two girls to six months, and Kolia and Venka to three years. The three years were to be split into four months in prison and the rest in a labour camp.

'The camps will be of therapeutic value to you,' said the judge in his summing up. 'They will flush out all of your nasty capitalist thoughts once and for all.'

Welcome to Russia!

THE 'HOLIDAY CAMP': 1947–1949

Venka, the girls and Kolia were separated, and Kolia was carted off to a prison in Kuibishev in European Russia. After the appropriate 'welcoming' procedure, he was taken to his cell, which was huge, with three levels of bunks and about thirty inmates. Most of them were real hardened criminals — thieves, murderers and rapists — and as Kolia walked in someone threw a dirty towel on the floor at his feet. He picked it up.

'Whose towel is this?' he asked innocently.

That was clearly not the right thing to do or say. Apparently the prison custom was for a new inmate to take off his shoes and socks, and wipe his feet on the towel before entering the cell. This was deemed to be a sign of respect for the old-timers. But how was Kolia to know this? Nobody had warned him. The reward for his ignorance was a solid beating.

When he regained consciousness, he found himself lying naked under one of the bunks. They had stripped him of his clothes and also relieved him of the gold cross from around his neck. The head prisoner, the cell boss, pointed to the bunk at the far end of the cell next to the toilet bucket, indicating it was now Kolia's. He added a few words of warning.

'If you want to stay alive, keep your mouth shut at all times. You don't see or hear anything that goes on in here — ever! Understand?'

Kolia understood. Dragging himself to his bunk, he just sat there, not knowing what he should do next. He asked for his clothes, but this was met with derisive laughter. Shortly afterwards a guard came through on his rounds. Seeing Kolia sitting there naked, he grabbed him by the hair and hauled him off to see the warden. And there he stood in front of the furious official who proceeded to accuse him of losing his clothes playing cards. Still naked, he was then led to a small underground cell, no more than three metres long and one and a half wide. A bunk with a straw-filled pillow stood at one end, with a toilet bucket alongside. And that was it. Kolia collapsed on the bunk and wished he were dead.

As he lay there, he noticed the ceiling had been drilled with a pattern of large holes. I wonder why, he thought. He did not have to wait long for the answer. Without warning, a torrent of water came pouring down on him. Apparently the ceiling was the bottom of a water trough and the guards amused themselves by pouring water at irregular intervals over prisoners in solitary. There was no place in the cell where one could escape the water and the guards helped things along by yelling out appropriate obscenities and taunts.

'Would you like some nice soap to wash yourself with, you filthy mongrel?'

'Would you like an umbrella, you spineless bastard?'

Sometimes, they even relieved themselves into the trough. They obviously had a well-developed sense of humour.

Kolia's daily food ration was 150 grams of black bread and a litre of water. When he returned to his cell after three days in solitary, now clothed in some prison rags, the cell boss informed him that from then on his main duty was to empty the cell's toilet bucket. The fact his bunk was next to the toilet bucket made him admirably situated for that role, he was told.

'And if you spill any of it on the floor, not only will you have to clean it up with your towel, but we'll also beat the shit out of you for being sloppy!'

This brought back memories of how his father had told him he was useless at everything and that he should get a shovel and become a shit cleaner. Here I am, Dad, he thought, doing it in bucketfuls.

On top of his cell job, Kolia had to help the guards distribute food to the inmates. The daily ration was 500 grams of bread, plus some vile-smelling stew made of rotten meat or fish.

Life in Mianduhe was beginning to look like Paradise Lost...

After four months Kolia was moved to a 'holiday camp' in Krasnoyarsk, 1800 kilometres away in Siberia where the state was using prison labour to build a large plant on the outskirts of the city. All the inmates of this prison camp had been detained under the infamous Section 58 in Soviet law which was used to incarcerate citizens found guilty of anti-Soviet activities, such as criticism of the regime, capitalism, anti-patriotism and the like. In other words, political prisoners. It was not difficult to gain admittance to these camps. All you needed was a jealous or annoyed neighbour with an invented story about you, and you became an immediate candidate.

Some of the inmates were there on twenty-year sentences. The work was backbreaking — seven days a week, long hours, in all sorts of weather. However, the living conditions were somewhat better than in prison, with more rations and sleeping in barracks rather than cells. But they were still prisoners and guarded every moment.

Two years and eight months to go.

TWO YEARS OF MISERY: 1947–1948

In the meantime, on the Ostrouhoff front, Volodia's father had sold the goat farm Volodia had bought for him in Peitaiho and moved to Shanghai, where he married a rich widow with a large apartment. As they had a spare room, he urged Volodia to move to Shanghai and live with them. Jenia was not keen on moving from Tientsin, but Volodia was anxious to be close to his father. Throughout his life he had little opportunity to be with him, and now felt it was time for some togetherness. So, in 1947, Jenia, Volodia and their four-year-old son George left Tientsin for Shanghai.

By now, the only members of the Tarasov family left in Tientsin were Aida (and Chelpanov), my mother (and Vasia and his mother Elena) and I. The rest were in Mianduhe or Shanghai. Aida felt most uneasy about this. She always felt uneasy when her whole brood was not close by.

Meanwhile, Volodia found a job as an assistant bookkeeper for a Jewish businessman. Although it was not well paid, there was at least sufficient money for them to live frugally and even to pay a nominal rent to the mother-in-law. Unfortunately, after a year or so the mother-in-law decided to sell her apartment and move to Chile. The Ostrouhoffs were given a months' notice.

The timing could not have been worse. Shanghai was suffering a massive shortage of rental accommodation. The Communist forces were advancing steadily from the north, resulting in a huge influx of Russians and other foreign refugees from Harbin, Peking and Tientsin. The price of any decent accommodation had become exorbitant and was far beyond the means of the Ostrouhoffs. Volodia's initial salary had been $US70 dollars a month. When inflation hit, his boss started paying him in FRBs, and as the rate of inflation accelerated to triple digits per month his salary did not keep up with it. In fact at the time he was looking for accommodation he was earning the equivalent of $US9 dollars a month. (Compare this with the $US300 dollars a month Boris Kozlovsky was earning.)

Accommodation in the city was completely beyond their means. The only affordable place they could find was a small humpy in Chinatown, some distance away. It was basic in the extreme — thatched roof, no water, no electricity, a charcoal-fired hibachi in the street outside the humpy. The place was renting for $US10 dollars a month for the summer only, and the owner was demanding four months' payment in advance. As they were penniless, Volodia had to borrow the money from a friend. His salary was barely sufficient to keep the three of them from starving. Their Russian neighbours owned a couple of goats and were kind enough to donate a pitcher of their milk for little George every day. That helped. But what were they going to do when the four months were up? Where would they live then?

In desperation, Volodia went to his boss and told him of his plight. Surprisingly, the man showed a tiny streak of human kindness, the first ever. For the winter, he let them move into one of his empty warehouses in Chinatown, rent-free. And that is where they began to live — in a corner of this damp, cold, cavernous structure. It was the toughest period of their lives.

Living away from the rest of the foreign community was not a pleasant experience. By that time the Chinese were beginning to publicly exhibit their growing anti-foreign feelings, and this was especially evident in Chinatown, where the appearance of a foreigner normally elicited rudeness and profanities, especially from the children, who were obviously mirroring the feelings of their parents and had fewer inhibitions.

As George was only four at the time, Jenia could never leave him alone, as the mere sight of the little boy was enough to bring out the worst in the Chinese children. They would taunt him, spit on him and act most aggressively. This despicable behaviour was once witnessed by a Chinese man who owned a small block of apartments next to the warehouse. Distressed by the children's behaviour, he offered to look after George whenever Jenia had to go out. At first she was apprehensive, but he seemed like a nice man and she finally took up his offer. From then on he became a sort of godfather to her, helping whenever he could, without asking anything in return.

One may very well ask why it was that Jenia's family was living in abject poverty while her sister Nadia's family was living in the same city and doing very well. Boris Kozlovsky was earning thirty times as much as Volodia Ostrouhoff, and yet no help was forthcoming. How could this happen within the Tarasov family which had been so close-knit over the years?

Jenia's recollection was that they visited Nadia one Sunday, but felt unwelcome and decided not to come again. However, Nadia did not recall any such incident, nor did she remember ever seeing the Ostrouhoffs during the year and a half they were in Shanghai. This breakdown in communication remains one of the mysteries of this story.

5 EXODUS 1948–1951

THE EXODUS BEGINS: 1948

For China, peace was slow in coming. The end of World War II sparked an escalation of the civil war between the Nationalists under Chiang Kai-shek and the Communists under Mao Tse-tung. The Nationalists controlled all the main cities, but the Communists were dominant in the hinterland of the north and in Manchuria. Gradually the tide turned in favour of the Communists and they began their advance to the south, towards Peking and Tientsin.

At that time, it was estimated there were some 3000 Russians in those two cities, and they had split themselves into three groups: The first consisted of those who were still stateless; the second were the Whites who had taken out a Soviet passport (there were no strings attached to becoming a Soviet citizen, and many had made the change even though they had no intention of going back to Russia); and the third were those with Soviet passports who had been impressed with the Soviet victories of the war and the propaganda promises of a good life, and had every intention of returning to the mother country.

For the first two groups, the prospect of a Chinese Communist occupation, likely repatriation to Soviet Russia and potential incarceration was not welcome. These two groups totalled some 750 people, and they were the ones who had to get out before the Communists came. The Tarasovs were among that lot.

Shanghai boasted an active Russian Emigrants' Association. Headed by Grigori Kirilovich Bologoff, an ex-colonel of the White Russian Army, the association's purpose was to coordinate the evacuation of the White Russians from China should that become necessary. It kept a complete record of all the affected people and maintained contact with sister organisations in Tientsin, Peking and Tsingtao. Colonel Bologoff was an excellent organiser and communicator, and kept the White population constantly apprised of the developing situation. And he maintained contact with the various international humanitarian organisations whose role it was to assist in the evacuation of war refugees.

One such organisation was the International Refugee Organisation (IRO) whose main mission was the resettlement of war refugees who had no home country to return to, such as the White Russians in China. The IRO was an agency of the United Nations and had its headquarters in Geneva. It had commenced its operation in 1947, taking over from the United Nations Relief and Rehabilitation Administration (UNRRA). Colonel Bologoff was in constant communication with the IRO to organise suitable asylum countries for the White Russians. However, the IRO was significantly understaffed and worked on the basis of managing crisis situations only. To the IRO, the gradual Communist takeover of China did not appear to constitute an immediate crisis. After all, who knew how long it would take them to reach the southern cities.

But the Communist armies advanced faster than anyone had expected and by the middle of 1948 it became obvious it was only a matter of months or even weeks before they overran Tientsin and Peking. At that time, the IRO still had no plans to evacuate the Whites and Colonel Bologoff was forced to take matters into his own hands. He sent an emergency request to Admiral Oscar Badger of the US Pacific Fleet stationed in Japanese waters, asking him to urgently evacuate some 750 Whites from Tientsin and Peking. The admiral's response was an agreement to evacuate 500 — that was the maximum number he could fit on a landing craft (LST) — but the colonel told him it was 'all 750 or no-one'. The Admiral finally agreed to have the LST make two trips.

An announcement was made to all the Whites in Tientsin and Peking that two vessels would be arriving, three weeks apart, each capable of taking 500 refugees. All families would be limited to just one suitcase per person. And, most important of all, this would be the only chance to leave before the Communists came. After that, the Whites would be on their own.

A mass exodus quickly destroyed the opportunity for selling one's possessions at a fair price. Goods and chattels were sold for a fraction of their value. Possessions which took years of hard work to acquire were sold for peanuts. It was heart-breaking.

As Aida and Chelpanov had lived together since 1933 but were still not married, it was considered prudent for them to do so before leaving. The wedding was a proper one, in a church, with a few select guests. I had the rare honour of being the best man, giving my grandmother away in holy matrimony.

Although we were all going to leave together on the first LST, Vasia's mother Elena fell ill and could not go. My mother decided that, to be on the safe side, I should leave with Aida and Chelpanov on the first LST and they would follow on the second one. Vasia spent a lot of time farewelling his friends and colleagues, especially the Chinese with whom he had worked for many years.

Farewelling meant drinking, and that resulted in him being drunk every night. Fortunately, because his mother was ill, he did not do his drinking at home. Nina and Elena were at least spared that unpleasantness.

The new Chinese owners of Kiesslings were sorry to see Nina go. She had worked there for twenty-two years and was like an institution. The management gave her a good bonus and loaded her up with boxes of chocolates, cakes and biscuits. They even took her home in the company car.

Many of my friends were leaving Tientsin with us, but my best pal Andrew was not. His parents were among those who decided to return to Russia. The parting was very painful as his friendship had meant so much to me. Another sad parting was with my piano teacher. My lessons with him continued right up to the time we left Tientsin, but unfortunately the wonderful Nicolai Sajin also elected to return to Russia, where he died shortly afterwards.

I owe all my love of music to him. He was inspirational.

Our trip by sea to Shanghai was only memorable because the LST went through a hurricane — or at least it seemed like one. The LST is a flat-bottomed vessel which bobs around on top of the waves like a cork. Just about everyone on board became seasick. The accommodation did not help. We were all housed on folding army camp beds in the huge warehouse-like hold. The hold, which was normally used to carry vehicles for beach landings, was huge — maybe 200 by 20 metres and eight metres high. All sorts of pulleys and rope contraptions hung from the ceiling, and these swayed erratically as the ship bobbed up and down and to and fro. I remember lying on the bed, sick as a dog, watching the swaying paraphernalia and getting sicker.

My mother, Vasia and Elena arrived on the second LST, three weeks later.

All 750 refugees were housed in the old unused French military barracks on Route Freulupte to await further developments. Conditions there were very basic. We lived in large dormitories with double-decker wooden bunks. There was a communal dining room and communal washing and toilet facilities. For privacy, families strung bedsheets and blankets between the bunks.

But what worried the refugees most was the future. Everyone knew the stay in Shanghai would only be temporary. It was obvious that the Communists would soon occupy the whole country and we would all have to get out of China to go … where?

However, Aida was happier than most. To her, family was everything, and all her children except Nusia were now with her in the same city.

Let us now pause a moment and take stock of the situation in Shanghai at the end of 1948:

The Kozlovskys were reasonably well off, with Boris in a good job with a foreign company.

The Ostrouhoffs were living in a warehouse, with Volodia earning a pittance and the family close to starvation.

Len was working part-time only, his family was in dire financial straits, and his marriage was on the rocks.

Aida, Chelpanov, Vasia, Elena, my mother and I were living in the French barracks, awaiting the next phase of the evacuation from China, courtesy of the IRO.

Besides the refugees in the French barracks, there were another 5000 or so Shanghai White Russians in a similar situation. Before long, all of them would have to leave China or face an uncertain future under the Chinese Communists. Already the political situation and living conditions were deteriorating. The Communists had taken over Tientsin on 15 January and Peking on the 23rd and were now only weeks away from entering Shanghai. There was galloping inflation. And the Chinese were becoming increasingly hostile to the foreigners who, in turn, saw no future for themselves and their businesses in an emerging new xenophobic China.

TUBABAO, A HAVEN FOR REFUGEES: 1948

Imagine this scenario: The IRO realises they have to evacuate a few thousand White Russians out of Shanghai, and they have to do it quickly. They try the USA, the main sponsor of the IRO through the UN, but it refuses to accept them. It has a long queue of refugees trying to get in already. Various European countries are approached, plus Hong Kong and South Africa — no luck. Nobody wants them. South America would probably take them, but it's too far. So the IRO sends a few of its best salesmen to the Philippines and the following exchange takes place:

'What about giving asylum to a few thousand White Russians?'

'You must be joking! We're in the process of rebuilding our own country and there's no way we can afford such an influx of refugees. And anyway, what have the Russians ever done for us?'

'But these guys are desperate! If they don't get out, the Commos will eat them alive! It's only for about four months. By then, we'll be able to find some countries to take them permanently.'

'Well, we've got a lot of uninhabited islands around here. You can dump the lot on one of them if you wish.'

'Okay, we'll take it! Do you have one that will fit about six thousand?'

'Sure. But there's no way we'll feed them or house them. That's your problem.'

'That's okay. We'll handle that part of it. Which island do you have in mind?'

'Give us a day or two to select one. We'll get back to you.'

It would obviously be an act of kindness to help the IRO, they think. Maybe they can give them some deserted ex-US base? They look at the possibilities and decide Manikani looks the most promising. An ex-US Navy base, now deserted, it is well equipped with huts, warehouses and officers' quarters on land of about 600 hectares (1500 acres).

Then one of the Filipino officials suddenly remembers a small island called Tubabao, not far from Manikani, which housed a US Navy Receiving Station. It is nowhere near as well equipped as Manikani, but the overwhelming advantage of selecting it is that it now belongs to a friend of President Quirino of the Philippines. The owner should be able to squeeze the IRO for a per-head rental, which will please the President. He likes to be magnanimous to his friends.

Thus, the island of Tubabao is offered to the IRO. They point it out on a map. It is off the southern tip of Samar, 600 kilometres southeast of Manila, and eleven degrees north of the equator. It's about three kilometres by four— more than enough space to fit 6000 refugees. It's separated from Samar by a narrow channel spanned by a bridge, which leads to the town of Guiuan about five kilometres away. As an ex-US Navy base, Tubabao has a lot of excellent facilities — electricity, water, huts, roads. It seems ideal for everyone's needs. The IRO officials are delighted with this offer and readily accept it.

Nobody bothers to visit the island to check out its alleged facilities.

FLEEING FROM CHINA: 1949

By January 1949 it was deemed to be time to organise the exodus of the Whites from Shanghai to Tubabao.

Fifty able-bodied single men were selected to be flown there to ready the place for the refugees. Oleg Miram was placed in charge of this working group. IRO officials told him the island had electricity, running water and huts, and it was just a matter of cleaning the place up in readiness for the first batch of 500 evacuees who were leaving on the *Hwa-Lien* the following day. As the working party was being flown there, they would have a full two weeks to get the place ready. IRO officials would of course meet them in Manila and accompany them to Tubabao.

What actually happened was quite different. Nobody met them at Manila, nor did they have any luck in contacting any IRO officials. Miram had to arrange the transportation to Guiuan himself. On arrival there, eight Philippine army jeeps transported them to the island and dumped them on a clearing in the middle of the jungle. On exploring the island, they found the remains of a tiny US base, with one large quonset hut and several other small huts — and nothing else. There was no electricity or water. They were told there would be a store of army tents, but there were none. Nor did they have any tools to work with. And 500 evacuees would be arriving there in a fortnight!

Having borrowed some basic tools from the Filipinos, the team cleared some of the jungle and dug pits for the toilets. And they managed to get word to the IRO that there was no accommodation on the island. In reply, they were assured that a pile of tents would be loaded on to the *Hwa-Lien* when it docked in Manila.

The arrival of the ship in Tubabao on 24 January 1949 was a scene of complete chaos. The refugees found themselves in a jungle, with their luggage dumped in a pile in a clearing. In another clearing was a huge pile of US army surplus tents. The refugees were told to find their luggage, select a tent, clear an area in the jungle, put the tent up and settle down. It is almost impossible to describe their sense of shock and of disappointment, having been told by the IRO that the camp was all set up for them, with all the necessary facilities.

It took a few days for all the tents to be erected. They were of different sizes, haphazardly placed, without any master plan. The end result was a camp that resembled a shanty town. Subsequently the additional manpower was able to make better preparations for future shiploads of refugees.

The *Hwa-Lien* made another two trips, the *Cristobal* also brought evacuees, and many more were flown in. The last group arrived in late May 1949. At its peak, Tubabao camp housed 5600 refugees.

LIFE ON A DESERT ISLAND: 1949

The camp was laid out into fifteen districts. The original working party and their families, plus the first *Hwa-Lien* group, settled in Districts 1 to 4. Aida and Chelpanov were among them. My mother, Vasia, Elena and I arrived in February and settled in District 5. The Ostrouhoffs followed in March and lived in District 12. Each district had a district officer responsible for the welfare of its population, who was also the communication link to the camp director, an IRO official. We the inmates were called 'displaced persons', or DPs for short.

Our home in District 5 consisted of two tents joined together by a canvas awning. Each tent had two folding camp beds. Elena and I slept in one tent and mother and Vasia in the other. We were given one small table, four folding chairs, a crate in which to store our possessions, a bucket for water, and a mosquito net for each bed. The floor was bare clay. And that was it.

Single people and childless couples were housed in communal tents, each of

Entry to the Camp, 1949

which held about twenty. Every district had two communal toilets, a kitchen and a hot water dispensing facility worked with kerosene stoves. The only water supply on the island was a stream in the gully, and the water had to be carted up from there and boiled before drinking. The toilets were simply large holes in the ground covered by planks. There was no privacy, one just squatted there alongside six or seven strangers, and tried to get away as quickly as possible.

To wash, one had to either bathe downstream from the water collection point or bring the water up to the tent in a bucket. The eventual installation of a diesel-powered pump and a large elevated water tank made the task a lot easier. Later, some communal showers were built. Initially there was no electricity, but generators were eventually installed, allowing the use of one, and only one, 25-watt globe in each tent. The electricity was switched off at 10 p.m., with an extension to 11 p.m. on Saturdays.

The IRO provided a small amount of timber for the handymen, who built additional tables, shelves, wardrobes or whatever. Some built personal showers. Some even constructed floors for their tents. Vasia was not a handyman and therefore none of these features graced our tent. But our 'home' did boast an elaborate bamboo fence, which I constructed. It served no useful purpose — it was just a decoration — but it gave the place some individuality. Ours was the only 'home' in the 'street' with a fence.

The DPs did all the work and maintenance in the camp. Every adult was rostered for various duties. Vasia was on garbage patrol. My mother worked in the kitchen two days a week. I was exempt because I was too young. Elena was exempt because she was too old.

The climate was hot and muggy, always. Most of the time the sides of the tents were rolled up to let in whatever breeze there was. Although this eliminated any hint of privacy, we all got used to it very quickly.

The island itself was one big jungle with plenty of palm and banana trees. There was a myriad of unpleasant insects — scorpions, poisonous centipedes —and mosquitoes, mosquitoes, mosquitoes. There were also snakes but there was only one instance of a bite by a poisonous one. The seawater was always tepid, and it would have been a pleasure to swim in it, except there was no sand, just sharp coral. One had to be very careful to avoid injury. In the humid, jungle atmosphere, cuts and scratches quickly turned septic. At best, they took a long time to heal.

It rained in abundance, sometimes two or three times a day. Although all the tents were surrounded by ditches, which were supposed to keep the water out, they were only partially successful during the heavier downpours. Two typhoons swept through the island while we were there. Very exciting! There were torn tents all over the place and coconuts raining down from palm trees. Fortunately the typhoons were not severe. A serious one would have flattened the whole camp.

Hot water station, 1949

General view of the camp, 1949

(Below) 'Red Square', 1949

The communal kitchens provided two meals a day — lunch and dinner. For breakfast, one went to the hot water station and then had tea with whatever leftovers there were from the previous day. The meals were mainly macaroni with tinned 'Hash' (a mixture of minced corned beef and vegetables) left over from World War II, but the enterprising Russian women were able to create reasonably tasty dishes from them. Although the food was not very nutritious, no-one went hungry. For some, like the Ostrouhoffs, it was an improvement on their previous lifestyle. At least there was no worry about where their daily bread would come from.

Later some fresh meat was added to the menu — fifteen kilograms, including bones, per district per day. That was roughly forty grams per person. The women used it to make soup, which was then served for lunch as a first course. Sometimes we were even spoiled by a dessert — maybe some rice with sultanas. After some representation to the camp authorities, a nutrition centre for children was opened, supplying the young with milk, peanut butter and fresh fruit.

Before our departure from Shanghai we were told there was no need to pack any crockery or cutlery. It would all be supplied. Like many other promises, this one was unfulfilled. Until a shipment of army-surplus mess kits and metal mugs arrived, we had to use empty hash tins and the like, eating with chopsticks fashioned from bamboo.

The initial living conditions in the camp were not far removed from those of a concentration camp and the IRO officials felt guilty about this. They had made many mistakes: not checking the place out before moving us out here; not supplying the necessary tools and equipment; inadequate supply of food. Their initial reaction to this situation was to censor all outgoing letters for any negative comments, hence decreeing that all letters be written in English so they could read them. There is even evidence to suggest that letters with critical comments were destroyed rather than censored. Some months later, when conditions had improved, the censorship regime was rescinded.

The camp boasted a largish public square. It was no more than a large slab of concrete but it became the cultural centre. The DPs called it Red Square, showing they had not lost their sense of humour. On one side of the square was a stage and on the other a large movie screen. This was the venue for concerts, lectures, dances and movies.

The camp orchestra was a brass band under the direction of P.F. Tebnev who had been the conductor of the French Police Band in Shanghai. Forty-five strong, all its members and their families lived in District 11, which was known as the Musicians' District. Tebnev was an energetic man and he came up with all sorts of innovative musical programs. The orchestra was immensely popular with the DPs and even gave concerts in some of the nearby Filipino towns.

A stroller in typical Tubabao attire, 1949

Movies were supplied by the IRO and were shown about twice a week. The audience had to bring their own chairs, stools, crates or whatever. Some enterprising people even constructed special covered two-seaters to protect against the frequent showers. Plays were regularly staged and even an operetta once. Lectures on a wide variety of subjects were often given. Humorous skits about life in the camp were always popular, as were the dances which were held most Saturday nights. The music was either recorded or played by a dance band headed by Mickey, the drummer. He was a crowd favourite, especially in Latin American numbers such as 'Tabou' and 'Amado Mia'. Mickey was our neighbour. When he was not playing he was drinking himself silly.

There was a weekly newspaper written by an ex-newspaper editor, which kept the citizens up-to-date on events. A school was also built, boasting some twenty teachers, all from the DP ranks. It was interesting to note that the history lessons focused on American history. After all, everyone was hoping to get a visa to that wonderful 'land of milk and honey'.

The Filipinos opened some outdoor shops close to the camp and those with money could buy things like liquor, cigarettes, fish and fruit. They even opened a small restaurant and a movie theatre — US 25 cents was the entrance fee. I remember seeing John Wayne in *Reap the Wild Wind* several times.

The evening stroll became an institution. After dinner, many of the DPs, especially the young at heart, would put on the their best clothes and go for a walk along the main street. There they would meet their friends, exchange stories and gossip, find out who had obtained a visa and to what country.

Scouts on parade, 1949

Scout troop and church, 1949

Those with money would buy a San Miguel beer (US 20 cents) or an ice-cream (US 10 cents).

A large dilapidated wooden building, a remnant from the old US base, was completely renovated and transformed into a Russian Orthodox church, complete with onion-shaped cupola and a belfry, with empty gas cylinders instead of church bells. In those turbulent days, churchgoing was especially popular, and weekend services were well attended. They also brought out the best of sartorial elegance in the DPs — a huge contrast to the standard, ragged-like tropical appearance of most of the refugees during the heat of the day.

There were no opportunities for the DPs to earn much money — certainly no regular jobs. However, my enterprising mother Nina used to make some money from her sewing skills, and every so often she would give me a US dollar or two. This made me feel very rich.

Once, Mum decided to splurge on some extra food and bought a chicken from a local villager. We were looking forward to this change of diet but, unfortunately, the chicken was practically inedible, extremely tough and smelling of fish. Apparently, the diet of the local chickens consisted of whatever they could scrounge from the seashore — clams, small crabs and the like. Even their eggs tasted fishy.

Mother's earnings were also used to subsidise Vasia's drinking, and he certainly did a lot of that. He was drunk nearly every night. He and the drummer Mickey made great neighbours. The booze most people drank was a cheap liquor called Majorca made by San Miguel — a sickly, aniseed-based brandy, but one with quite a kick. It only cost US 70 cents a half-litre bottle and gave the maximum bang for the buck.

Vasia was not a pleasant drunk. Instead of quietly dozing off, he would become agitated and insist on going walkabout. Mother and Elena would try to stop him — they were worried he would either fall over and hurt himself, stumble drunkenly into someone else's tent or get arrested by the police for offensive behaviour. But the process of stopping him caused rowdy scenes and, of course, their voices could be heard all over the district, which embarrassed the two suffering ladies a great deal. I used to urge mother to just let him go — perhaps we

Aida and friend at communal water tap, 1949

In the middle (top to bottom) George Chelpanov, Aida and George Ostrouhoff—with friends outside their tent, 1949

would be lucky and he would fall over a cliff and break his neck — but my pleas were ignored.

I did mention the police. Yes, the DPs formed a local police force, made up from ex-policemen and bodyguards. Dressed in US khaki uniforms and matching desert helmets, they sported a red band on their left arm. There was even a small jail and an arbitration court.

Overall the mood of the DPs was surprisingly upbeat. There were few fights (the unavailability of vodka and the general lack of money for liquor probably helped), no suicides, few scandals and hardly any crime. There was a great spirit of cooperation, of pulling together in times of adversity. The common bond of homelessness seemed to unite us into a peaceful, friendly group.

To me, a boy of seventeen, Tubabao was like a big holiday camp. I had completed high school, so there was no schoolwork, and I was too young to be rostered for any duties. I had fallen through the cracks, so to speak, and had tons of spare time on my hands.

My primary involvement was with the Scout movement, which had a strong following in the camp. We were fortunate to have outstanding, motivating leaders — Alex Kniazeff, our Scoutmaster and Donat Kobelev, our troop leader. I was a member of a patrol called the White Eagles, which was acknowledged to be the best on the island. In competitions, such as knot-tying, racing or tent building, we always came first. This gave us all a tremendous feeling of camaraderie, of pride in ourselves and a desire to strive for excellence. We also used to go camping and on extended hikes, and we formed working bees for different projects.

The Sunday campfire meetings were wonderful events. They were even popular with the non-Scouts, who often outnumbered us. Oleg Levitsky, an assistant Scoutmaster, was a brilliant satirist who wrote delightfully humorous sketches and skits on life in Tubabao. The one I remember best was called 'Carmen in the Kitchen', which satirised the trials and tribulations of a rostered kitchen helper, sung to the tune of the 'Habanera' from *Carmen*. Another was a poem recited in English called 'The Funeral of Hash', which made fun of our terrible diet. That meeting was attended by the camp director, an IRO official by the name of Captain Combs, and this poem was the catalyst for the allocation of fifteen kilograms of fresh meat per district per day.

My musical life did not hibernate. I founded a six-piece orchestra consisting of five Scouts playing paper combs with one on drums. I was the conductor and we often performed, with some success, at the Sunday night campfires. Although rehearsals were great fun, they had the odd tense moment. Once I slapped our drummer, Vitya Goustavsky, across the face because he couldn't keep time. Immediately embracing him, I asked his forgiveness. Fortunately, we remained friends. To make sure I had not wasted my years of piano study, I practised daily on the camp piano. To add to my involvement in the arts, I joined an amateur theatre group and even once played the role of Eugene Onegin in a scene from Pushkin's play.

A scene from Pushkin's *Eugene Onegin,* with Ludmilla Rubanova as Tatiana and me as Onegin, 1949

My girlfriend Tanya — my first love from Tientsin — came to Tubabao as well, but, for reasons unknown, the old passion had died down and our relationship was reduced to that of friendship.

All in all, I made a lot of friends, chased a lot of girls, did a lot of swimming in the warm tropical waters and generally had a great time.

However, the adults did not have much fun. The main problem for them was the sense of insecurity, the feeling of a complete lack of control over one's life. Here they were, DPs, on an island in a foreign land, not knowing which country if any would give them asylum; dreading the thought of starting life again from scratch, perhaps having to learn another language, perhaps not being able to find a job — perhaps, perhaps … In addition, there was no way to earn any money in the camp, no way to escape the life of communal handouts, no way to do something special, something different for your loved ones. The feeling of a lack of personal contribution was pervasive. Most of the adults' time was free — free to worry about the future

Before leaving Shanghai, the IRO promised the refugees their stay in Tubabao would be no longer than four months. By that time, they said, asylum countries would be organised. That did not eventuate. Countries were not quick to rise to the challenge of offering the DPs entry, especially not America which was, of course, everyone's preferred destination. On the US visa front, Congress took a long time to agree to the acceptance of Tubabao refugees. When it did, it was on the condition they were sponsored by a US citizen, guaranteeing them jobs and accommodation. This proved to be very difficult to organise. To make things worse, Congress later stipulated that children born in China would be classed as Chinese citizens and allowed in under a different quota system, resulting in the possible split-up of families.

Even though Brazil and Australia were willing to accept DPs, the general feeling towards those countries was negative. Who would want to go there? In Brazil, they spoke Portuguese, and Australia appeared to be a backward country, full of kangaroos.

THE GREAT TB SCAM: 1949

What was common to most of the likely asylum countries was their requirement for proof of absence of any serious illness among the applicants, especially tuberculosis. To check for the presence of this scourge, the medical administration decided to X-ray everyone.

Although the hospital was staffed by doctors and nurses from the Russian DP ranks, the hospital administrator appointed by the IRO was Chinese, Dr Han. There were also a few other IRO people in key medical positions. Dr Han was not popular among the DPs. He was dogmatic, unapproachable and

TB protest march, 1949. The placards say *'Recognize our representatives—the TB committee.'* *'Save us from incompetent dictatorship.'* *'First re-examination, then treatment !'*

arrogant. He treated the DPs as members of those despicable foreign races which had dominated and exploited China over the centuries. In one report to the IRO in Geneva, which later came to light, he referred to the DPs as 'unpleasant refugees, the majority of whom are mentally deranged from worry about their future'. He then defended criticisms by saying that 'because of their background, they still look down on us, the Chinese, and expect us to be their servants'.

A friend of ours was diagnosed with TB, which was a terrible shock to him and his family. They had just obtained approval for entry into Australia, subject to medical clearance, and here was this bombshell. He was informed it would take a year or more for him to be cured and it was suggested he let his family go to Australia and then join them when he was clear of the disease. Surprisingly, he was not warned the disease was contagious. However, it was recommended that he keep the news of his illness to himself, as he could otherwise be ostracised by the rest of the community. He shared the terrible secret with us because we were close friends and he needed to tell someone. Other DPs also found to be infected were told the same story by the medical authorities.

As you would expect, secrets like these cannot remain under the table forever and news of a TB epidemic began to gather strength. Surprisingly, most of the infected patients showed none of the symptoms (coughing, expectoration of blood), and this convinced many of the 'ailing' they had been misdiagnosed. However, the medical authorities ignored demands for re-diagnoses. Just accept it and get on with the treatment, they were told. The treatment consisted of a daily injection of some unknown substance.

Finally, the disbelief and discontent among the ill was so great that a mass protest was organised. Everyone who had been diagnosed with TB was asked to gather in the main square at a given time. To everybody's amazement, nearly a thousand residents appeared — an unbelievable 20 percent of the camp population! The matter was raised with to the IRO management outside the camp and arrangements were made for a team of Filipino radiologists to come and re-examine the patients.

The new team arrived, complete with its own X-ray facilities, and their re-examinations cleared 90 percent of the 'infected' patients, including our friend. Only a hundred or so of the 5000 in the camp actually had TB.

Following an IRO investigation, it was alleged Dr Han and some of his medical cohorts had cooked up an elaborate scheme. Knowing how concerned world medical authorities were about an outbreak of TB, they falsified the records of hundreds of DPs and advised the IRO headquarters in Geneva of a massive epidemic in the Tubabao Camp. They demanded and obtained huge supplies of the drug streptomycin, which they then sold on the black market for a healthy profit. The daily injections given to the 'patients' contained some useless placebo. The perpetrators were arrested and removed and were, hopefully, sentenced to long jail terms.

Dr Han was replaced by Dr Altemirano, an Italian. The new doctor was a wonderful humanitarian who enjoyed immense popularity and trust with the DPs. When he finally left, he said in his farewell speech that, 'I have only cried three times in my life. The first was when I left home for school; the second when my sister died; and the third is now.'

A LONG WAIT FOR ASYLUM: 1949

We too applied for a visa to America and became frustrated with both the delay and the US Congress rulings. Fortunately, an Australian mission arrived in Tubabao, indicating that Australia was willing to give asylum to the DPs, provided they were young and healthy. They gave many speeches extolling the virtues of the country, which they said was prepared to accept two types of migrants—unsponsored and sponsored.

With unsponsored migrants, the government would pay their fares and provide free accommodation in camps strewn across the country (Bathurst, Greta, Parkes, Bonegilla to name but a few). In exchange, the migrants would be required to sign contracts to work for the government for two years. These were paid jobs, but one could not pick and choose between them.

General view of the camp, with a hot water station in the middle, 1949

A sponsored migrant, however, was one whose welfare was guaranteed by an Australian citizen. The sponsor would take it upon himself to ensure the migrant would not be a burden on the Australian government. The sponsor's guarantee covered the first two years, by which time it was assumed the migrant would be able to stand on his or her own two feet.

Before leaving, the Australian mission left a large batch of copies of the *Sydney Morning Herald*, encouraging the prospective migrants to familiarise themselves with the country. We were amazed to see the huge number of jobs listed in the 'Employment' section. By examining the salaries offered and checking the prices of cars and houses in the 'For Sale' section, we calculated how much we could earn and how quickly we could buy a car and a house. The figures looked great, and we could speak the language. Australia suddenly became an eminently desirable destination.

Vasia remembered he had an old friend in Australia, Boris Kandaoorov, who had migrated there some years back. He operated a chicken farm in Galston on the outskirts of Sydney. Vasia contacted him to see if he could be our sponsor. Kandaoorov consented and the IRO agreed to pay our airfares. Vasia also asked Kandaoorov if he could find some sponsors for Aida, Chelpanov and the three Ostrouhoffs (Jenia, Volodia and little George, then six). Kandaoorov searched around and found a friend in Brisbane prepared to sponsor them. This meant the family would initially be split between Brisbane and Sydney, but at least we would all be in the same country.

Just as we were about to leave, I fell ill with dengue fever and was hospitalised for a week or so. The Russians pronounced it 'donkey' fever, which amazed me, as I had not been in touch with a donkey since my days in Peitaiho five years earlier.

Finally, we took off for a new life in a new country. The whole family was on the same plane, a Qantas Constellation. It was the first time any of us had travelled by air. At our refuelling stop in Darwin we had a light meal in the small airport cafe, and were taken aback at the sight of white waiters and waitresses. We had been so used to seeing Chinese in these roles that this unexpected sight astonished us — a shameful but accurate depiction of our reaction.

We landed in Sydney on 7 December 1949, where we were met by the Kandaoorovs. The rest of the family proceeded to Brisbane.

Our DP status had been finally terminated.

Although our stay of eleven months in Tubabao was long enough, some others were there for nearly three years. The majority of those were the DPs who steadfastly refused to go anywhere but America. With its slow rate of intake, this proved to be a long wait. Towards the end, the IRO threatened the DP stragglers with deportation back to China if they did not select a willing country for asylum. This helped accelerate the exodus.

In December 1951 a violent typhoon swept through Tubabao. At that time, there were still 120 DPs in the camp. The typhoon destroyed the facilities, killed two people and injured a score of others. The stragglers were evacuated by IRO to Manila, where they continued their wait for asylum.

Of the total population of 5600 DPs, about 3000 went to America, 1500 to Australia, 500 to France (including 68 people suffering from TB — a great, humanitarian gesture), and the rest to Brazil, San Domingo, Paraguay, Chile and Surinam.

Thus ended the extraordinary saga of the displaced persons' camp in Tubabao. How true is the saying: 'Man has such a need for freedom that he would go into exile to keep it.'

SHANGHAI: 1949–1950

Now the Tarasov family was fragmented into four locations — the Kozlovskys and Len's family in Shanghai, Nusia's family in Mianduhe, Kolia in Russia, and the rest in Australia. Aida had tried very hard to get both the Kozlovskys and Len's family to come with them to Tubabao, but they had both refused, for different reasons.

Nadia and Boris were living reasonably well and had decided to wait things out. Possessing a Soviet passport, they had no fear of the advancing Chinese Communists and, for that matter, no worries of the possibility of being evacuated to Russia. They felt there was no need for any precipitous action and wanted to keep their options open.

Nadia in relative luxury, Shanghai, 1949

Len was experiencing a different set of circumstances. His marriage was very shaky and the family's financial situation was precarious. In addition, there was disagreement on the subject of Soviet passports. Len was all for getting them and Galya was dead against the idea. Her father had been executed by the Soviets and there was no way she was prepared to be a citizen of a barbarous regime. As they could not agree, Len obtained a Soviet passport for himself only and told Galya that he, as the family head, was planning to take all of them to Russia. Galya, on the other hand, remained resolutely stateless and said she would never go there or allow her children to go. It was difficult to see a resolution in the short term.

Aida had always wanted to have her family safe and close by, and she now had a challenge on her hands — that of getting the rest of her brood to Australia. She knew it was going to be tough, but she was determined not to rest until that happened.

By the time we arrived in Australia the Communists had overrun all of China. Tientsin had fallen in January 1949 and Shanghai in May. The Nationalist forces under Chiang Kai-shek had fled to Taiwan and on 1 October the People's Republic of China (PRC) was proclaimed under Mao Tse-tung.

In Shanghai, foreign businesses were either closing down or being taken over by the Chinese, and the foreign population was leaving at an accelerated pace. The Chinese were becoming increasingly hostile to foreigners. There were signs everywhere proclaiming 'Out with the Foreign Devils!', 'China is for the Chinese!', 'Go home, greedy whites!'. Foreigners were often accosted in the streets and treated in a humiliating fashion.

Moreover, the fortunes of Boris' employers, the Chinese Aluminium Rolling Mills, began to suffer. As the People's Republic had not yet been recognised by many foreign countries, there was an embargo on the export of aluminium ingots to China and there was no way the company could continue to operate.

Hundreds of workers were retrenched, so it looked like the writing was on the wall for the future viability of the company. The prolongation of the good life for the Kozlovskys was now in serious doubt.

When Aida heard of the latest developments, she intensified her efforts to lure the Kozlovskys to Australia. 'Australia is beautiful, full of nice friendly people,' she wrote. 'Forget about Soviet Russia. Why would you want to go to a country full of Communist butchers? [Aida did not mince words] Come here. We're all waiting for you. You'll have a good life.' Eventually, Nadia and Boris capitulated. The future in China did look bleak and the future in Russia was uncertain, so they applied for a visa to Australia.

Len's wife, Galya, and her mother were also impressed by the news of life in Australia, and Galya obtained the necessary emigration forms, but Len refused to sign any of them. Then one day he came up with a startling proposition which he hoped would end his unhappy marriage and sort out the whole mess. The deal he put to Galya was that he and Len Jr (aged four) would go to Soviet Russia and Galya could then take her mother and Liz (aged three) to Australia ... or anywhere else for that matter. This would give them all a new start. How's that?

Galya refused. There was no way she would let her son go. When Aida heard of this plan, she too was horrified and begged Nadia and Boris to do everything possible to change Len's mind. They put in their best efforts and Len finally put forward a compromise plan. He would come to Australia only on the condition that Galya's mother stayed behind! This left Nadia and Boris with the task of convincing Galya this was the right thing to do. You can always bring your mother out later, they told her, adding that this was a worthwhile sacrifice if she wanted to keep her family together.

Galya finally agreed and then went about persuading her mother to accept the condition. In late 1950, Len affixed his signature to the Australian visa applications.

FAREWELL, YELLOW BABYLON! — 1950–1951

The Kozlovskys obtained their Australian visas and were now ready to leave. It was only a matter of arranging passage on a ship. But an unexpected event halted the process when, in June 1950, North Korea invaded South Korea. The UN immediately condemned the invasion and the US came to the aid of the South. In November 1950 the People's Republic of China joined the Communist North Koreans in the conflict and the war went into full swing.

Rumours of American retaliation against China began flying around Shanghai and there was a panic exodus of the remaining foreigners. All outgoing ships were booked out for the foreseeable future and those destined for Australia were re-routed to other destinations, mainly Europe. The only method of transportation still available for the Kozlovskys was rail to Hong Kong and then air to Australia. But there was no way one could buy airline tickets in Shanghai for the Hong Kong/Australia leg, as money could not be transferred out of the country to pay for them. The Kozlovskys had the money for the tickets but could not buy them.

In fact the Communist authorities imposed a number of strict regulations on exiting foreigners. Firstly, one had to apply for permission to leave. Dozens of forms had to be completed. If permission was granted, a fixed date was set for the departure. If that date were missed, the whole cumbersome process had to be undergone from square one.

Secondly, there was the matter of what valuables could be taken out. Only a tiny amount of foreign currency and very small quantities of gold and silver were allowed. Although there was no limit to the amount of personal jewellery one could wear, all the other portable valuables had to be submitted to the government bank for inspection and weighing. There, the permitted quantities of gold, silver and foreign currency were sealed in a bag with special government wax seals. Breaking the seal before reaching Hong Kong was punishable by immediate cancellation of the exit permits.

In addition, there was an embargo on taking out any photos considered to be demeaning to the Chinese or showing them in a bad light. All photo albums had to be submitted to the bank for inspection, where offending photos were removed. Thus Nadia and Boris lost all their photos of the Tientsin flood and any photos showing rickshaws.

Regarding payment for the air passage, Aida's helping hand came into play

Galya's mother, Katya Gracheva, with her grandaughter Liz, 1949

(Left to right) Nadia, Len jr, Liz, Galya and George, Shanghai, 1949

yet again. She scraped up enough money to pay a deposit for the tickets in Brisbane, with the idea the Kozlovskys would pay the balance when they arrived in Hong Kong. But there was another catch. The sum required to pay the balance for the three tickets exceeded the maximum one was permitted to take out of China. The currency rule was strictly policed and all departing passengers were thoroughly searched to ensure compliance. It was the classic Catch-22 situation.

The solution came in the form of their Russian friend Mr Kichii, who had just received a significant termination payment from his company and was also on his way to Australia. In his search for a solution, he had found a Jewish businessman who claimed to have an illegal but safe process of transferring money to a bank in Hong Kong. Kichii offered Boris the opportunity to add the Kozlovskys' kitty to his own for the transfer. Boris agreed and gave him the money.

Len, Galya and their two children had already left Shanghai about a month earlier and had arrived in Australia on 23 April 1951. Galya's mother had funded their passage to Hong Kong and the IRO funded the flight to Australia. Although this was not the norm in 1951, Galya had convinced the IRO that they were penniless and needed this assistance. Galya's mother followed them to Australia some months later, and mother and daughter were soon reunited, much to Len's annoyance.

A few days before the Kozlovskys' departure date of 9 May, Boris received some good news. His employers had decided to give him a termination payment. This was a pleasant surprise, but it now left him with a bundle of money he could not take out of the country, nor was there enough time to have it transferred to Hong Kong via Kichii's Jewish channel. The only thing left to do was buy some expensive, saleable items they could take in their personal baggage or wear. So out they went to buy up big — two fur coats (for Australia?), diamond earrings, a high quality set of draughting instruments and an Exacta camera (which subsequently proved to be a fake).

Many of their friends came to see them off, but strict security rules prevented them from entering the departure platform. The baggage was meticulously searched before it was loaded. Kichii was on the train with them. The trip to Canton (now called Guangzhou) lasted three days and two nights. Before being taken to a hotel for an overnight stop, their baggage was searched again. The following morning, at the station, it was scrutinised yet again, and this time there was a personal search as well.

A couple of hours later, the train stopped at the river bridge marking the border between China and Hong Kong. Here everyone was asked to disembark and enter a large thatched hut, where the most thorough luggage and body search of all took place. The officials worked in pairs and had a novel approach. One would do the searching, while the other engaged the passenger in small talk, arranging himself in such a way as to allow the passenger to clearly see what the first official was doing. If the searched passenger showed any signs of agitation, the search would be intensified. The Kozlovskys had nothing to hide and got through all right, but this technique did uncover many illegal items among other passengers, even though all had been searched several times before.

In the late 1930s the population of Shanghai had been close to four million of whom nearly 100,000 were foreigners, 40,000 of them Russians. It was without doubt the most cosmopolitan city in the Far East. But by the time the Kozlovskys left the city in 1951 it had changed from a vibrant metropolis to a dull, grey, lifeless city. Most of the foreigners had departed and most of the foreign shops and establishments had closed their doors. Motor traffic was sparse, except for military vehicles, and night life virtually non-existent.

The Communist advance in 1949 saw the gradual disintegration of the Russian community. The majority migrated to Russia — where they had been promised amnesty for their 'Whiteness' and a good life in Mother Russia — but most soon regretted that choice. The rest, who still felt that White was better than Red, were either evacuated by the IRO to Tubabao or stayed and eventually found their way to other countries.

Thus, over a period of twenty-six years, the Russian presence in Shanghai rose from a handful in 1923 to a thriving, vibrant community of 40,000, only to be dismembered by circumstances completely outside its control.

It was a fascinating and memorable period in the history of the 'Yellow Babylon'.

On arrival in Hong Kong, the Kozlovskys were astounded by the sight and feel of the place. Here life was proceeding at full bore, just the way it had been in the good old days in Shanghai. This filled the new arrivals with optimism for the future.

Unfortunately, this feeling was quickly undermined by some unexpected financial events. On 14 May, the day after their arrival, Boris and Kichii went to the bank to check on their money transfer. To their horror, none had come through. As Kichii had been given a phone number in case of an emergency, they called it immediately. There was no answer. Repeated calls during the day bore no fruit.

A telegram was urgently sent to Shanghai asking where the money was. 'It will be there tomorrow,' came the reply. It was not there tomorrow either and a follow-up telegram was hurriedly dispatched. 'There has been a minor change of plans,' came the reply a day later. 'The money will be deposited in a bank in Sydney in your name [Kichii's], all in time for your arrival there. Don't worry. Everything will be okay. Trust me.'

This seemed to satisfy Kichii — he had already paid for his airline ticket to Sydney — but what were Nadia and Boris to do? Aida had only paid the deposit and they now needed money for the balance. It was 17 May and the Qantas flight they were booked on was leaving on the 19th. The airline's policy was that passengers forfeited their deposit if they did not come up with the balance in time.

When in trouble, get in touch with Aida was the well-known cry of the Tarasov clan, which is exactly what the Kozlovskys did. A telegram was dispatched and, within a day, Aida had scrounged up enough money from her friends and relatives to pay the balance to the Qantas office in Brisbane, and at 4 p.m. on 19 May, four hours before the departure time, they were phoned and cleared for take-off.

The Kozlovskys arrived in Sydney the following day. My mother and I met them at the airport and we had a great Welcome to Australia party for them in our rented rooms in Waverton. Shortly after their arrival they sold the two fur coats and paid back the loan to Aida. Eventually, they also received the transferred money, although it came in dribs and drabs over the period of a year.

Now only Nusia's family, the Diakonoffs, remained in China. And, of course, Nusia's son Kolia was still somewhere in Russia.

6 THE STRAGGLERS
1950–1954

LIFE WAS NOT MEANT TO BE EASY: 1950–1952

Life in Mianduhe was harsh. It lacked even the most basic facilities. There was no electricity — naked flames were the sole means of illumination. The richer people used kerosene lamps, but the Diakonoffs could not even afford the kerosene. Sometimes they used candles, but these too were generally outside their means. On winter nights they opened the door to the small stove in the middle of the room. The flames cast a flickering light into the room and Misha would sit on the floor by the stove to do his homework.

There was no toilet. They just used the fields around them. There was no running water; Nusia would cart buckets from a well. In winter, with temperatures of -45^{0}C, the well froze over. A lid kept some of the cold out, but the water still froze and a long sharp stick was used to punch a hole through the ice cover before a bucket could be lowered.

A side benefit of the ice in the well was the fact that, by keeping the lid on in summer, they were able to maintain the ice cover through the hot months when temperatures often reached 30^0. The well thus became a natural refrigerator. Perishable foods were lowered into it by ropes which were then attached to hooks on the side of the well.

Most of the meat they ate was mutton, and often, in summer, they cut it into strips, salted it and hung it up to dry in the sun. They claimed it was very tasty, a sort of mutton jerky.

Diakonoff's original promise to build Nusia a big house never came to fruition. 'Don't worry,' he continued to say. 'You will get your mansion.' But although some timber for the house was eventually delivered, he never got around to the building stage. 'I'll hire some help and we'll get stuck into it,' he would say, but the only thing he ever got stuck into was his vodka. So they continued to live in these shabby little houses, and Nusia felt betrayed and angry. But she had to bear it. There was no alternative.

To add to his ailments, Diakonoff developed asthma and this ended his ability to do any work at all. With Kolia away in Russia and Misha still in school, Vova was the only breadwinner in the family. He continued to collect hay in the warmer months and cut trees for firewood in winter.

One winter's night he was attacked in the forest by a pack of hungry wolves. They showed up out of nowhere. He was in the middle of cutting down a tree and had just taken off his warm jacket when they attacked. The horses, which were not tied up, ran off in panic and Vova clambered up the tree he had been felling. Sitting on a branch, he watched the wolves running around the base, looking hungrily up at him, howling and salivating. It was about 20^0C below freezing and all he was wearing was a pullover. The bitter cold began to permeate his clothes, and his bare hands began to feel like blocks of ice. But he was afraid to rub his hands or move his limbs for warmth as he had already cut a large chunk out of the tree trunk and it could fall any moment, especially if he were to move or there was a wind gust.

Suddenly he thought he heard the bells of an approaching sled. Yelling as if his life depended on it (which of course it did), he was able to attract the newcomer's attention. Seeing the wolves, his saviour fired a few shots and dispersed the hungry pack. Vova climbed down and thanked him profusely. The man said he saw Vova's horses a few kilometres back with their reigns entangled in some shrubbery and Vova soon found them. They were still standing there, calmly, as if nothing had happened.

One mild day in winter, Vova asked his father if he wanted to come to the forest with him. Diakonoff readily accepted, deciding to treat the outing as a picnic. Taking a few blankets, some tomatoes and a bottle of vodka, he was looking forward to an enjoyable day — eating, drinking and watching Vova work — which is what he did. By the time Vova loaded the two sleds with the cut wood and was ready to start back, Diakonoff was pretty drunk.

Most of the homeward journey was downhill. Normally Vova would walk alongside the lead horse, making sure it kept a steady pace and the sled with the heavy load was under control. This time, however, his father took up the front position and Vova walked alongside the rear sled. Suddenly Diakonoff clambered up on top of the load and, spurred on by the vodka, took a whip to the horse, urging it to gallop downhill.

'Stop it, you idiot! You'll kill yourself!' Vova yelled after him

But Diakonoff was not about to be stopped. He spurred the horse on, yelling at the top of his lungs as the sled with its load of timber careered downhill, completely out of control.

By the time Diakonoff realised they were going too fast no amount of frantic pulling on the reins could slow the horse down. Luckily, on the next curve the sled veered off the road onto the grass and the thick snow-covered mat slowed it down and eventually stopped it. Diakonoff hopped off and, spurred by fear and guilt, began to whip the poor horse for its allegedly erratic behaviour. Vova rushed to his father, tore the whip out of his hands and threw him down on the snow. It took all his self-control not to give the true villain a few well-deserved whacks.

A BRUSH WITH DEATH: 1950

The authorities eventually outlawed the destruction of the forest. The new decree prohibited the felling of any living trees. All you were allowed to do was to pick up dead trunks and branches from the forest floor. If caught breaking the law, a big fine or even jail awaited you. How was Vova now going to earn any money?

There seemed to be only one option — break the law. To minimise his chances of being caught, Vova began cutting timber at night. In the past he used to leave home at 4 a.m. and return at about 4 p.m. Now he reversed the procedure, leaving home at 4 p.m. and returning before daybreak.

It was during a night visit to the forest that he had a terrible accident.

Vova left home at the usual time, arriving in the forest after darkness had fallen. It was a bright moonlit night, with the moon reflecting off the snow. Quiet. No wind. The horses standing harnessed to the sleds, wolves howling somewhere in the distance. It did not take Vova long to select a tree and cut two deep V-shaped cuts, one on each side of the trunk. Then he stepped back to let it fall. Nothing happened. It would not move. It just stood there on a very thin wedge, supported by the trees around it. Vova gave it a nudge but it remained standing. He tried again, but it would not budge. In desperation, he put his shoulder to it and pushed with all his might. Suddenly, instead of falling sideways, the tree slipped off the wedge — and pinned Vova's right foot to the ground. And there the tree stood, dead upright, supported by the branches of neighbouring trees, with no intention of toppling. The weight of the tree was crushing his foot. Vova tried pushing the trunk, tried to make the tree fall to the side, but all that did was cause him excruciating pain.

As he stood there, pinned to the ground, Vova felt the icy cold burrow its way into and through his clothes. It was only a matter of time before he either froze to death or was eaten by the wolves. He yelled for help at the top of his voice until he was hoarse, but there was no-one around to hear him. His limbs were beginning to feel numb from the cold and his foot was still firmly held by the upright tree, as if it were saying, 'You took my life, and I will now take yours.'

In desperation, Vova decided the only thing he could do to save his life was cut off his foot. He stretched for the axe, but it was out of reach. It was deathly quiet all around, except for the howling of the wolves. There was not a breath of wind. Snow, the numbing cold and the approaching wolves. Terrifying!

Finally, Vova prepared himself for the inevitable, horrible death. Remembering he had not been to confession for a long time, he prayed, asking God to forgive him and grant him entrance into heaven. 'I'm really sorry, dear Lord. You know how busy I've been …'

Suddenly, out of nowhere came a magic gust of wind — perhaps the only gust in the whole forest that night. The tree shuddered (excruciating pain) and then slowly toppled, setting him free. After lying on the snow for a while, Vova crawled painfully towards the two horses which were, as usual, untied, waiting for their master. But seeing an unfamiliar shape crawling towards them they became startled and moved away. He crawled after them but they moved out of reach again. With an almighty lunge, he grabbed one of the reins and, pulling himself up on the sled, promptly blacked out.

From sheer habit, the horses began to walk home. On the way, a group of Chinese workers travelling to work saw the two empty sleds, stopped to investigate and discovered the unconscious Vova. Piling some hay on the sled, they laid him on it, covered him with more hay and, not knowing where he lived, slapped the horses on the backside hoping they would find their way home — which they did.

Normally Vova would sleep on the sled while the horses trudged home, where they would stop at the gate and give their master a wake-up neigh. This time, when they gave their customary neighs, Vova was semi-conscious and the gate remained closed. They neighed again and again, until Nusia came out to investigate. When she saw Vova's condition she woke her husband and the two of them carried their poor son inside. The shoe was cut off his foot and Nusia spent the rest of the night bathing it with ice water.

Fortunately, there was no permanent damage and he was back to normal within a few weeks.

It is only when you have something to do with animals that you realise how smart they really are. Take horses, for example.

The forest where Vova did his lumberjacking was about fifteen kilometres from home. After harnessing them, all he had to do was slam the side of the sled with his axe. This was the signal for them to start the journey. Without guidance, they not only found the forest but the exact spot where they had been two days ago. And they could even do this in total darkness. On arrival, if Vova were asleep, they would just stand there waiting patiently for him to wake up. When wagons were used to collect hay, all he had to do was slam the side of the wagon with his pitchfork and they would unerringly go to the summer location.

Cows are also smart. The Diakonoff cow was also Nusia's pet. Whenever she went into the village to shop, the cow followed her like a dog. It was even capable of opening the gate with its horns. If Nusia dared to go out alone, it would open the gate by itself and trot after her. The residents thought it was a huge joke. 'I see you are with your pet cow again,' they would say, or 'Have you thought of getting a dog?'

Rather than taking out their individual cows to pasture, the Diakonoffs and their neighbours had a neat arrangement. They hired a herdsman who took their cow and a bunch of neighbours' cows out every few days to pasture, with all of the owners sharing the costs. On the way home the herdsman did not have to do anything to ensure each was delivered to the right property. As he walked back, the cows would stop at their own gate, open it with their horns and enter.

THE EX-CONVICT: 1950

When we last heard of Kolia, he was serving a three-year sentence in a labour camp near Krasnoyarsk. On 16 May 1950, two days before his twenty-third birthday and three months before the completion of his sentence, he was released. When the warden asked him whether he had any relatives or friends anywhere in Russia. Kolia answered in the negative.

'Then where would you like to go?' the warden asked.

'I was planning to settle down in Krasnoyarsk,' was the reply.

The warden informed him that Krasnoyarsk was a 'closed' city, off-limits to newcomers, especially ex-prisoners.

Kolia consulted a fellow inmate, who gave him some sound advice: 'Pick a place as far away as possible, say Leningrad [the renamed St Petersburg]. That way you will get the maximum amount of travelling money. Once you are out of here, you can go wherever you want to, including Krasnoyarsk. Who'll be the wiser?'

This sounded like a good idea. Kolia nominated Leningrad, collected his papers and 36 roubles in travel money and left the camp. However, settling down in Krasnoyarsk was not easy. The clothes handed to him when he left prison identified him as an ex-prisoner and made his presence unwelcome everywhere. Fortunately, he met up with two others who were in the same predicament, so at least he had some company. The three of them spent their days trying to find work and their nights sleeping on benches in the railway station. None of the locals wanted to have anything to do with ex-prisoners, especially political ex-prisoners.

Finally Kolia decided he must move to some place where his past misdeeds would not be so obvious. At someone's recommendation, he took a train to the coalmining town of Chernogorsk about 300 kilometres to the south, where he soon found a job. After working only two shifts, he was summoned to the manager's office. There, a stern-looking KGB agent asked to see his papers. The papers showed he was supposed to have gone to Leningrad and the KGB threatened him with arrest unless he followed the instructions in his papers to the letter.

'Yes sir. I will do so immediately,' Kolia said, but he had no intention of following the orders. Instead, he walked to Abakan about twenty kilometres away, and the following day began looking for work.

Abakan is on a river of the same name, near its confluence with the mighty Yenisei which winds its way through Krasnoyarsk and northern Siberia to the Arctic Ocean. Walking along the busy waterfront, Kolia saw an office with a 'Positions Vacant' sign proclaiming, 'Every job from stokers to sailors'. Kolia entered the office. He had always been fascinated by ships and had often dreamt of becoming the captain of a liner.

'What's your experience on ships?' he was asked.

'I've worked as a stoker on a steam train,' he said, remembering he had spent four days doing that back in Mianduhe. 'But I'd rather be a sailor, if you don't mind.'

'Show me your papers,' was the demand.

These, of course, revealed he was an ex-convict. The man sneered, but offered him a job as a stoker. 'Take it or leave it!' Kolia took it.

The contract was for two years, and the pay 560 roubles a month. On top of that, he was given a 300 rouble advance. The official gave him the money, new papers and a ticket to Krasnoyarsk — yes, Krasnoyarsk, the very town where he wanted to settle down in the first place!

Kolia left the office believing a new and positive phase of his life had just begun.

A MARITIME CAREER: 1950

The money in his pocket made Kolia feel very rich. He bought some new clothes, had a good feed and caught the train to Krasnoyarsk. There, the shipping company told him to report for duty in a week's time.

He rented a small room and sat down to write a letter to his mother, Nusia. It was just over three years since he had left, and this was his first letter. In it, he apologised for taking her valuables, related some details of his incarceration, and wrote that he now had a good job as a sailor on a big passenger ship. He said the future looked bright and he would write often.

When he reported back to the shipping company, he was given a uniform, placed on a passenger ship, the *Josef Stalin*, and sent 900 kilometres north to a place called Podkamennaya Tunguska[†], where he was to join the ship to which he had been assigned. When he arrived there, his ship was still up-river. He would have to wait for it.

He would have to wait for it.

The small, dingy town looked completely deserted. As he had no place to stay, Kolia set out to find a hostel or inn for the night, but there were none in town. It was getting dark and, even though it was July, it was surprisingly cold. As he walked the streets, he peered into the houses hoping to see a friendly soul who would perhaps wave to him and invite him in. But this was not to be. Suddenly Kolia had a moment of inspiration. Most Siberian houses have enclosed porches in front of their front doors. This enclosed area helps insulate the house against the cold and also serves as a convenient storage area. Why not sneak into one of them? he thought.

Selecting a house with a large porch, he tiptoed into it. Inside, he found a ladder leading up to a loft full of hay, where he lay down and immediately fell asleep.

He was awakened in the morning by the sound of a ship's horn blast. Springing up, he grabbed his belongings and stumbled down the ladder — and landed right on top of a startled old woman hunched over a milk bucket. There she lay spreadeagled on the floor, in a pool of milk. When she saw Kolia bending over her trying to help her up, she began to scream.

'Thief, murderer, rapist!'

She had a surprisingly loud and shrill voice. Kolia dropped her and ran out of the house, and she ran out after him, yelling and screaming. The neighbours heard the noise and rushed out to help the poor woman in distress. Before long, about twenty armed, vicious-looking citizens were chasing Kolia down the street towards the waterfront, waving pickaxes, spades and hoes.

On reaching the river, he had no hesitation in jumping into the icy cold water and swimming to an anchored barge. Climbing aboard, he was relieved to recognise the barge captain as a man he had met the previous day. After listening to Kolia's story of woe, the man rowed back to the wharf and pacified the vigilantes.

When his ship did eventually arrive, he was extremely disappointed with what he saw. He had visions of a large, impressive vessel, like the *Josef Stalin*. Instead, it turned out to be a rusty old tug. And he had just signed a two-year contract to be a stoker on it.

The job of a stoker did not require much skill and even Kolia was able to quickly master

Kolia as a stoker on a tug, 1950

† 'Podkamennaya' means 'Under a stone ' and 'Tunguska ' means a woman of Tungusian origin. The Tunguses were Mongoloid people living in eastern Siberia and Manchuria.

a passenger ship. He visualised himself walking among the passengers in a snappy uniform and wooing the attractive girls, who would succumb to his uniform and personal charm.

A few months into his contract, he applied for a transfer. The shipping company replied that one is normally expected to spend at least three years on tug duty before any chance of a transfer to something decent. Every time he raised the subject of a transfer, he was given the same answer.

About a year and a half later his tug was tied up alongside the passenger ship *Friedrich Engels*, and Kolia was able to make friends with the captain, who took an immediate liking to him. Kolia was a good-looking man with an honest face and a bright personality. Over a glass or two of vodka, Kolia asked him for a job as sailor. The captain agreed and arranged Kolia's transfer. 'But you'd better understand this,' the captain warned. 'Just one step out of line and I'll drop you off at the first village, and you can freeze to death for all I care.'

After a year on the *Friedrich Engels*, Kolia landed a job as helmsman on the *Borodino*, another passenger ship. Things were looking up.

SHAMANISM: 1952

In the warmer months at Mianduhe, Vova went away for up to a month at a time to cut hay for rich landowners. At other times he collected hay from farms and sold it. This was a more pleasant job than the winter one, but it too had its share of excitement.

Once, in the spring, he went off with the two horses and wagons to gather some hay. A short cut to the location was across a river which was frozen in winter and quite safe to cross. Even though it was spring, the ice looked firm and he decided to risk a crossing. That was not one of his wisest decisions. Vova was the first to fall through into the icy water, followed by the horses and wagons. Luckily they were close to shore and able to climb on to the bank.

Another time, the laden wagons were crossing a bridge over a raging stream when the flimsy bridge suddenly collapsed, plunging them all into the swirling water. The horses were still harnessed to the wagons and in danger of drowning, but Vova dived under the churning water to unharness them and they were all able to clamber out. This time, however, the wagons were lost.

One autumn day, Vova heard they were looking for hay-cutters in Mongolia for a couple of weeks' work and that the pay was good. Mongolia was not that far away and they needed the money, so off he went. They were long days of hard work but Vova enjoyed it. The autumn weather was balmy and the Mongols a nice bunch to work with. At the end of a working day they would slaughter a sheep and boil it in salt water over a bonfire.

One night, Vova was famished and ate with great gusto. The mutton was fatty

One night, Vova was famished and ate with great gusto. The mutton was fatty and salty and the salt made him very thirsty. He walked across to a mountain stream and drank a bucketful. The water was icy cold and beautifully sweet, but suddenly he felt an agonising pain in his stomach. Screaming, he collapsed on the bank, thinking he was going to die. All the mutton fat in his stomach must have solidified. His fellow workers heard his screams and ran to his aid. Carrying him back to the bonfire, they sent off one of the workers to get some help. But what help could he possibly find in the middle of nowhere?

After what seemed to be an eternity, the worker returned with a scrawny old Mongol in tow. The man knelt down and examined Vova, who was still in agony. After a few moments, the old man nodded to himself and waved his arms to clear a path through the throng of workers attracted by the screams. Entering the tool shed, he returned with a metal rod and placed it in the fire. When it was glowing red hot, he took it out and clenched it between his teeth.

A gasp escaped from the lips of the onlookers. But there was no burning of skin or lips, no smell of burning flesh, no discomfort on his face. As the mesmerised audience looked on, the old man began a slow dance around the fire, accompanying himself with strange, guttural sounds. Stopping abruptly after a few minutes, he fixed his intense gaze on Vova — and at that very moment, his pain suddenly disappeared.

Vova started laughing with relief, but another Mongol stopped him.

'No laughing at our shaman[1],' he warned.

Vova could not explain what had happened. All he knew was that there must have been some witchcraft associated with it.

That was not Vova's only experience with alternative medicine. One day, back home, he had some time to spare and decided to ride to his girlfriend's place. It was a perfect summer's day and he took his time, forgetting all his worries and simply relishing the moment, thinking how great it was to just be alive.

As he rounded a corner, he noticed some young girls in the distance, walking slowly down the street. Being young and impetuous, this seemed to be a great opportunity to engage in a spot of showing-off. Letting out a blood-curdling yell, Vova dug his heels into the horse and galloped towards them. The noise attracted their attention and they stopped to see who it was. As he approached, they started to laugh and clap, and this urged our brave Cossack into even more excesses. Faster and faster the horse galloped. By now, he had taken his cap off and was waving it above his head, while his yells became even more blood curdling.

---

[1] In Mongolia and other parts of northern Asia, the shaman is the equivalent of a medicine man or witch doctor. Shamanism is a religion embracing a belief in controlling spirits, which can only be influenced by shamans. The shaman's main function is to influence supernatural forces and to alleviate illnesses.

even more spectacular sight. The horse stumbled and our hero went flying over its head — and right on to his own. The startled girls ran to his help, but he was out to the world. Some passing men were kind enough to hoist him up on to a wagon and take him home.

He awoke with an excruciating headache. This, he thought, was understandable. In fact he was lucky to be alive. But as the days passed the headaches became worse and more frequent. There was no respite. He could not work. He could not think straight. He could not function. During the most severe attacks, he felt as if his brain was on fire. The pain was sometimes so unbearable that he would scream, rush out the door and plunge his head into a bucket of water in a vain attempt to ease it. But nothing helped. The doctor was baffled. He had never struck anything like that before.

In the meantime, Vova was gradually losing his mind and seriously contemplating suicide. A neighbour recommended that Diakonoff call in a shaman and, with no other alternatives available, he readily grasped at this hope.

The shaman examined Vova very carefully. He studied his head from all sides, twisted it with his hands and felt it with his fingers. Then he mumbled something to himself and asked Nusia for a strip of paper and a pencil. The paper was carefully tied around Vova's head and on it he marked the middle of the forehead, the middle of the back of the head and the position of the ears. Taking the paper off, he examined it carefully, measuring the distance between the marks.

Finally, grunting with satisfaction, he untied and removed his cloth sash, a twisted rope-like band worn by Mongols instead of a belt. He then proceeded to tie it very tightly around Vova's head, even using his knee as leverage to make it tighter. This made Vova's head throb even more and he was about to complain when the man stepped back, clenched his fist and slammed it with all his might into the side of his patient's head. Vova dropped like a stone, blacking out. But when he regained consciousness the headache had vanished — and it never returned.

The shaman told him that the fall had twisted his skull and dislocated his brain. The blow had forced it back into position.

THOSE LOST YEARS

About two years after they moved to Mianduhe, Nusia met one of her old Harbin friends in the village store. They had not seen each other for years and Nusia invited her over for a cup of tea. Seeing the retarded child Alexei, she exclaimed: 'So you're the one who finished up with the Eliseev kid! I heard the story, but I didn't realise it was you.'

Nusia told her all about it — the hard work, the frustration, the pity, even the love for the little creature. Alexei was about five and, although somewhat small for his age, he looked pretty normal. But he was still not toilet trained and he could not speak. Incoherent mumbles were the only sounds escaping from his lips. Nusia only heard him utter one word in all the time she cared for him. While patting their cat, he once lifted its tail and said *gorshok* (chamber pot), a word which Nusia often used to urge him to pee into the chamber pot rather than his pants.

'Did you know that his father is living in the next village with two of his children?' her friend asked. 'One is a girl who is very bright and the other a boy who is also retarded. Why don't you try giving Alexei back to Eliseev? After all, he is the father.'

That sounded like a good idea to Nusia. Caring for him for more than four years had been a huge burden, and Nusia was becoming more and more distressed with it. Giving the boy away to his natural father sounded like a welcome release from hell, so off they went to see him. Nusia related the whole story and offered him the boy, his son. The man showed a complete lack of interest.

'Why would I want to take him?' he asked. 'He's none of my business. Give him back to whoever gave him to you. I've got enough problems of my own.'

Having now seen his other backward son, Nusia was convinced that Alexei's affliction was hereditary and that he would never improve. Continuing to care for him would just make her life increasingly miserable. And that is when she decided to give him up, making arrangements for him to be sent to a special orphanage in nearby Yakishi. There he was registered as Alexei Diakonoff — they were not allowed to use his real surname as there was no proof of his true parentage.

By 1953 the only change in the Diakonoffs' life was that Vova had married his childhood sweetheart, Tonia. The family was still living in Mianduhe and still living in poverty; Diakonoff himself was too old and feeble to work; Misha was attending school; Vova was still the sole breadwinner, working his fingers to the bone; Kolia was in Russia — and Nusia was contemplating the ruins of her life.

Just think of it … Nusia, a nineteen-year-old girl — good-looking, sensitive, hard-working, a bit of a dreamer, attached to her family — gets married against her will to a man twenty-two years her senior, a man whom she not only does not love but practically despises. She does this at her mother's urgings, as a personal sacrifice, so her family could share in some of the trappings of his wealth. As soon as she marries, the family abandons her and moves to Tientsin which, to her, is a million miles away. She is now left for the rest of her life with an old man she did not want to marry and whose unwanted child she is carrying.

After a few years of financial comfort, things turn for the worse. The husband loses his business; they become poor; his new business ventures fail; they become poorer; and they finally move to Mianduhe, a godforsaken little village in the middle of nowhere. And now she is living the life of a destitute peasant. In the meantime, the rest of the Tarasov family has moved to Australia, leaving her completely cut off from the family she loved so much.

Poor Nusia. Right throughout her life, she hated her husband. It was not only the age difference. It was also his bossy nature, his lack of sensitivity, his miserliness, his drinking, his ill health, his broken promises. Sex was never of any interest to her, at least not with him. He had never seen her naked — she would not allow it. The sex act was performed in the dark, and she always felt violated, ashamed and disgusted.

Nusia loved her three children, especially the first-born, Kolia. He had been her favourite but had suffered from ill health and a lack of talent or interest in work. And he had stolen her valuables and run away from home, and she had not seen him since. In addition, she spent nearly five years looking after somebody else's backward child — an onerous chore, but one she had done out of the kindness of her spirit. Add to that the terrible living conditions, the poverty, the long cold winters, and one can understand her feelings of despair and anger.

She stopped looking after herself. She put on weight; she dressed shabbily; she did not care how she looked. As far as Nusia was concerned, life was not worth living. And yet, if she had loved or just respected her husband, she would have probably taken all these misfortunes and deprivations in her stride. Unfortunately, there was no such bond between them and she blamed him for all her misery.

I cannot imagine it being a pleasant life for Diakonoff either. He was in bad health; he could not provide for his family; his son had absconded to Russia without telling him; Vova, the breadwinner, despised him; and his wife loathed him from the time they were married. Is it any wonder he was driven to drink …

A MARRIAGE OF CONVENIENCE: 1952–1953

Kolia's ship, the *Borodino*, plied the Yenisei River between Krasnoyarsk and Dudinka, a distance of more than 2000 kilometres. The river was ice-bound from October to May and during those months the ship would be docked in Krasnoyarsk for overhaul — scraping, painting and repairs. Each of the crew had duties to perform. It was certainly not a paid holiday. And it was during

Yenisei River frozen solid

one of these winter overhauls that Kolia unexpectedly met Palina, the girl who had escaped with him to Russia.

Palina had been in love with Kolia in Mianduhe. When he informed her he was planning to leave for Russia, she begged him to take her along, saying she could not bear the thought of living without him. But on arrival in Mother Russia she had been sentenced to six months in jail. After her release, she was determined to find Kolia. When she discovered he was in a prison camp near Krasnoyarsk, she moved there. She could not see him. Political prisoners were not allowed visitors. Nor could she write to him. Knowing he had been sentenced to three years, she settled down to wait for his release.

On the third anniversary of Kolia's incarceration, Palina went to the prison expecting to welcome him to the outside world, only to be told he had been set free three months earlier and given money to go to Leningrad. She had waited for him all these years and now he appeared to be lost to her forever. Imagine her surprise and delight, then, when she bumped into her old flame in Krasnoyarsk.

Kolia was happy to resume their relationship. He had not seen her for over five years but he found he still liked her very much. She was an attractive girl and totally devoted to him. Although they did not live together, they saw a lot of each other during the winter months. Palina was kind and thoughtful and did everything possible to please him. During the sailing season, she would always be there on the wharf, welcoming him back home, a bunch of flowers in her hand. Kolia's feelings for her were not as strong, but he did resign himself to the idea he would eventually have to marry her — an award, of sorts, for her devotion.

But then, concerns about the marriage began to grow in his mind. Palina was very attractive. That was a plus. But it was also a huge minus. It would mean she would be constantly courted and pursued by other men. As he was away for long periods, she would have many opportunities and temptations to be unfaithful, which would lead to domestic scenes, dramas and divorce. Did he really need all these worries and hassles? These negative thoughts were on his mind as he departed Krasnoyarsk on the final journey of the 1952 sailing season.

When a ship called into a village or town on the river, it was a bit of an occasion for the residents. Living in the depths of Siberia, they did not get much passing traffic. Crowds would gather on the wharf and market stalls would be set up selling handicrafts and foods. A carnival-like atmosphere would prevail. The ship normally docked for an hour or so, allowing the passengers and crew to go ashore for a spot of shopping, giving the villagers the opportunity to mix with the visitors and make a bit of money.

A girl called Anna ran one of the village stands. She was a pleasant girl, somewhat solid in build and very plain. Her stall was filled with dairy products from her farm and Kolia always bought some of her sour cream. As his ship made five round trips a season, he would see her ten times a year.

After a couple of years of this business relationship, she began offering him the sour cream for free, because he was such a good customer, she told him.

Suddenly Kolia had what he thought was a brilliant idea. Why doesn't he marry Anna instead of Palina? She likes me, he thought. She looks healthy, she's probably a good worker, and she is very plain. No likely problems with other men.

The more he thought about it, the more the idea appealed to him. So on the outward journey of his last trip of the season he asked Anna to marry him.

She said that she would have to think it over and that she would give him her answer when the ship called in on the return journey.

After they parted, negative thoughts started flooding again into Kolia's head. What if she's a terrible cook or housekeeper? What will I do then? I haven't tested her out. Am I rushing into this? But Kolia consoled himself with the thought he could always leave her if she wasn't suitable.

When the ship docked at the village again, there she was, standing on the wharf, a small suitcase by her side. Kolia asked the captain if he could bring Anna on board for the journey to Krasnoyarsk, where he planned to marry her. The captain was delighted with the idea, but suggested they get married immediately and celebrate on board.

And that's exactly what they did. The Marriage Bureau was open and Kolia and Anna registered themselves as man and wife — it was as simple as that. There was no church ceremony (religion was not in vogue then), no lengthy service, bridesmaids, best men or anything like that. The captain was true to his word and they celebrated all night. In his inebriated state, the captain even offered Anna a job as a cabin girl for the rest of the journey and she accepted. The extra money would come in handy.

When the ship docked at Krasnoyarsk, Palina was waiting on the wharf, the customary bouquet of flowers in her hand. But someone must have broken the bad news to her before Kolia walked down the gangplank with Anna. Quietly, she congratulated him on his betrothal. Then as she turned to walk away, she threw the bouquet into the murky water.

The captain was very pleased with Anna's performance as a cabin girl and offered her a job for the next season. The fact she was a good worker seemed to vindicate Kolia's decision to select her for his wife.

Anna worked on the ship for two years, only leaving when she was pregnant with their first son, Vova.

THE SORCERESS: 1954

Shortly after the birth of their son, a strange thing happened to Kolia. Part way through a rowdy party, he suddenly felt himself passionately drawn to a woman he had met before but had never been interested in. Following her around all night like a puppy, he ignored everyone else, including his wife.

This was obviously most embarrassing for Anna, but she thought it was probably the vodka and that he would get back to normal the following day. But he did not. The woman became an addiction for him. Wherever he was — at home, at work, or with his pals — he would suddenly be seized by an uncontrollable desire to see her. Dropping everything, he would rush over to her place. And this was happening more and more often. As you would expect, the affair was making life for him and Anna miserable.

His boss noticed his peculiar behaviour and asked him what was wrong. Kolia broke down and told him the full story.

'You know, exactly the same thing happened to me in my youth,' the boss said. 'My infatuation with a girl was destroying my life, and I had to do something about it. A friend suggested I go and see a sorceress. Even though I thought it a bit weird, I was willing to try anything. And I'm glad I did. She cured me.'

Kolia did not believe the sorcery story, but he was desperate to try anything.

'You'll need a hundred roubles to pay for her services,' his boss said. 'Go and get an advance from the paymaster and I'll tell you how to find her.'

Kolia took the money and set out on his journey.

The sorceress lived in a small village a long way off, in an old ramshackle wooden hut surrounded by what used to be a garden but was now just a weed patch. Approaching the house, Kolia saw an old hunched woman sitting on the porch.

Before he could open his mouth, she said: 'Oh you poor wretch, you look awful. What have they done to you?'

'You know of my problem?' he asked.

'Of course I do. I can see it in your face. Come in with me.'

It was dark inside. The shutters were all closed.

'Why don't you open the shutters and let in some light?' he asked.

'What's the matter? Afraid of the dark? Don't worry. No-one will bite you here'.

They sat down and Kolia poured out his problems. The old woman nodded her understanding.

'Are you a Christian?' she asked. 'Have you been baptised?'

'Yes I have,' he replied.

'Well, then I might be able to help you.'

She poured a glass of water and placed it on the table. Selecting three small pieces of charcoal, she set them next to the glass and, closing her eyes, began to mumble some incantations. Finally she turned to Kolia.

'I want you to take these three pieces of charcoal, chew them and swallow them,' she instructed. 'Then I want you to wash it all down with three, and only three, sips of this water. No more, no less.'

He followed her directions. It was not a pleasant taste sensation.

'Let me tell you what happened to you,' the woman said when he had finished drinking. 'When you were at the party drinking wine, someone must have slipped a hair from the woman's head into your glass and cast a spell on you. This made you fall madly in love with her. I have now removed the spell and you are cured. Give me the money and go in peace.'

When he walked out of her hut, Kolia felt as light as a feather. In fact he felt he could fly. When he saw the woman again, he found he couldn't stand the sight of her. He was cured! It was another instance of the Diakonoff family benefiting from strange cures.

THE FINAL EXODUS: 1954

Now that the rest of the Tarasov clan was safely in Australia, Aida began the process of bringing out Nusia and her family.

As Soviet citizens, the Diakonoffs had to apply to the Soviet consulate in Harbin for permission to leave China. However, the Soviet authorities were not at all cooperative. At that time Khrushchev had initiated a campaign to turn the virgin steppes of Siberia into an agricultural wonderland. To obtain the necessary manpower for this formidable task (which eventually failed), the Russian population of Manchuria was encouraged to return to Russia. They were offered free passage, absolute amnesty for the Whites and attractive remuneration.

As the Soviet consulate's objectives were clearly aimed at discouraging the migration of its citizens to any place but Siberia, all sorts of obstacles were placed in the Diakonoffs' path — dozens of application forms, requests for non-existent birth and marriage certificates, interviews, delaying tactics. In fact the Diakonoffs had previously given the prospect of moving to Siberia serious consideration, but the thought of what this would do to her mother was enough for Nusia to reject the idea.

Thousands of expatriate Russians did, however, take the bait — and lived to regret it. The work they were given was excruciatingly difficult, the remuneration was inadequate, and those who had any association with the Japanese or held significant posts in the White community were persecuted and jailed.

After many frustrating delays, the Diakonoffs were granted permission to leave Mianduhe and Manchuria. There was much joy and happiness. The whole village was abuzz with excitement.

The Diakonoffs began selling their possessions. First the horses, sleds and wagons, then the cow, and finally the property. When all was done, they moved to Harbin and lived for a while with the Ponomariuk family, staying there long enough for Vova's wife Tonia to give birth to a baby boy. It was quite a dramatic birth. As the contractions began, Vova and Misha rushed Tonia to hospital in a taxi. As it screeched to a halt outside the hospital, Vova opened the taxi door and, as Tonia lifted her leg to step out, the baby literally fell out — landing right on its head on the floor of the taxi.

'I've killed it!' screamed Tonia, but the panic was premature. The hospital orderlies picked up the baby, cut the umbilical cord and all was well. The baby boy did not suffer any ill effects.

Two weeks later, the Diakonoffs obtained their visas for Tientsin. Komleva, the lady of the wonderful family with whom the Tarasovs stayed when they first came to Harbin thirty-two years ago, was one of those who came to see

Icon of St Nicholas *Chudotverets* (miracle-maker), Harbin railway station, 1954

them off. Before boarding the train, they all visited the station chapel to light candles in front of the icon of Nikolai *Chudotvorets* (St Nicholas, the Miracle-Maker). That would assure them a safe journey, they believed. It was 22 May 1954

A few days after arriving in Tientsin, Misha contracted pneumonia, followed by pleurisy. Although he soon recovered, it delayed the Australian visa approval process. At that time Australia was very particular about lung diseases and the whole family had to have X-rays to get medical clearances.

In Tientsin, they lived in a hotel for more than three months. This stay was funded by money borrowed from some rich people who were also migrating but were afraid to take large sums of money with them, thinking it would be confiscated. So they lent the Diakonoffs money on the understanding it would be paid back to them in Australia — which it was.

The next stop was Hong Kong, where they stayed a month waiting for a ship. The final crisis before Australia came in the form of a typhoon, which threatened to sink their ship. It certainly laid everyone out for three days.

The Diakonoffs arrived in Sydney on 29 October 1954, nearly five years after the first of the Tarasov clan landed in Australia. They were met by Nadia and Boris Kozlovsky, with whom they stayed for a few days before proceeding to Brisbane.

There was a funny story associated with their arrival. Before they left China, they had been told Australia was desperately short of timber, and all forms of wood were extremely expensive and hard to get. So they left China with every possible wooden implement they could lay their hands on, including chopping boards. Imagine their astonishment, en route to Brisbane by train, at seeing the east coast's endless forests of eucalyptus trees.

Brisbane is where Aida lived with Chelpanov, Jenia, Len and their families. There was much joy in the reunion and many hours filled with memories, tears and laughter. After all those years of grief and suffering, Aida had again gathered her flock around her. All of them here in this wonderful, peaceful country called Australia ... All, that is, except Kolia Diakonoff, who was still in Russia...

Aida and Nusia were, of course, both eager to get Kolia out of Russia, but there was no way he was allowed to leave. In those days, overseas travel was strictly prohibited.

Although Aida believed her objective of moving the whole family to Australia was not fully accomplished, she consoled herself with the thought that eighteen of the nineteen members of the extended Tarasov family were now here with her, and that's not too bad a record.

If it had not been for her endless persistence and unswerving focus on keeping the family together, this would never have happened.

7 AUSTRALIA, LAND OF OPPORTUNITY

SETTLING DOWN

It would be remiss of me if I did not provide a brief account of how the family members fared in Australia.

Nina, Vasia, his mother and I were sponsored for entry into Australia by an old friend of Vasia's, Boris Kandaoorov. This benefactor of ours also found another family, the Potanins in Brisbane, who were prepared to sponsor the Aida/Chelpanov couple and the Ostrouhoff family. Sponsors took responsibility for our welfare for two years, during which time we were not eligible for any unemployment or medical benefits. But of course this did not mean that we could now sit back and expect to be catered for by these generous people. Everyone's primary concern was to find a job, and find one quickly.

Potanin, who owned a caravan manufacturing business, offered a job to both Chelpanov and Volodia Ostrouhoff. Chelpanov readily accepted, but not Volodia. He had been told by someone that his knowledge of languages would suit him for a job in the government — this was the period of active migration to Australia, and many of the immigrants could not speak English — and he was attracted to the concept of a government job, its status and its long-term employment prospects. So Volodia applied for a job with the Taxation Department. Although they were impressed with his linguistic skills, he was informed that no job offer could be made until he became a naturalised Australian citizen, and that meant a five-year wait. So he too joined Potanin's business

George Ostrouhoff, then six, could not speak a single word of English and his early days in primary school were quite traumatic. This was exacerbated by the fact that he was immediately nicknamed Paw-Paw Face for his chubby visage. George thought he was being told that his face looked like a *Popa*, which in Russian is a colloquial term for backside, but he calmed down somewhat when the fruit connection was explained to him.

All five lived with the Potanins, occupying two rooms in their apartment. Unfortunately, Chelpanov and Volodia fell into the typical Australian blue-collar after-work pastime of drinking in a pub every day after work. This practice distressed both Aida and Jenia. Not only did the daily sight of partly inebriated spouses cause them offence, but there was the wanton flittering away of hard-earned money they desperately needed to build a new life.

Finally the women concluded that the Chelpanov/Volodia combination had to be split up. Jenia talked Volodia into moving into alternative accommodation and, four months after their arrival, they did just that. Volodia found work in a shipyard closer to their new place of residence, and with the Chelpanov/Volodia connection cut they could now start saving money in all seriousness.

Two months later, Aida found a large house advertised for rent at a surprisingly low price and, on inspection, decided that she could make a reasonable income by taking up the offer and renting out the spare rooms. They moved and were soon able to let three of the rooms. Aida thus became a landlady once again.

Jenia, who had been an expert knitter all her life, went into the knitting business. She showed samples of her work to various shops and eventually found a buyer who was interested in doing business with her. For the next four years, working from home, she produced knitwear to order. This meant she could still look after little George, taking him to and from school, while earning some income. It was not much, but every little bit helped.

It is interesting to note that the day after the Ostrouhoff family became naturalised, Volodia joined the Taxation Department, where he remained for fifteen years.

PIANIST OR ENGINEER?

On arrival in Sydney in December 1949, Nina, Vasia, Elena and I stayed with our sponsor, Boris Kandaoorov. He owned a five-acre chicken farm in Galston, thirty kilometres from the centre of Sydney. It had about twelve large corrugated-iron sheds for the chickens and a rickety old timber house for the owners. Nina and Vasia occupied one of the bedrooms, Boris and his wife Dusia the second, and Elena and I slept on camp beds in the living/dining room. By comparison with our tents in Tubabao, this was the height of luxury.

Boris immediately put me to work tending the chickens – feeding them, collecting the eggs, cleaning out the sheds. I performed these tasks with the greatest of pleasure, enjoying doing something useful and revelling in the beautiful summer weather and the lovely bush surroundings. Nina and Vasia found temporary pre-Christmas jobs in a factory in nearby Hornsby and my mother immediately began to make plans for my career. She had always dreamed of me becoming a famous pianist and of course that meant further study in a music conservatorium. I was not convinced I would ever be good enough to earn fame and fortune as a pianist, and my leanings were towards an engineering degree, either mechanical or electrical – I was always keen on physics. Fortunately, Kandaoorov, who was not a music lover and who had never heard me play (although I don't think that would have made the slightest bit of difference) thought the idea of a musical career was asinine. On the other hand engineering was a useful profession and, for reasons best known to him he also believed that the New South Wales Government Railways would provide me with the best career opportunities. On top of which they offered university scholarships.

How could I, a seventeen-year-old kid, argue against such profound wisdom? So I went to see the railway people, who informed me that all the current university sponsorship positions had been filled. I must have looked particularly downcast, as the interviewer asked me if I would like to take on a job as an apprentice electrical mechanic. I brightened up. The words 'electrical' and 'mechanical' were ones I liked, and Boris did say the Railways was the place to be, so I said yes.

'Okay,' the interviewer said, 'you can start on the first working day of the New Year.'

My ambition was still to obtain a Railway sponsorship to the university, but this would have to wait until the end of 1950 when the sponsorships were likely to be offered again. But how was I to make sure that I was selected when the time came? In a round table conference with Boris, Nina and Vasia it was decided that I should do the first year of a diploma course on top of whatever training I would get in my apprenticeship. As the course was four nights a week, there was no reason I could not fit the two in together. If I did not get a sponsorship then I would continue with the diploma course.

And so began a rather demanding year for me. I used to take the first bus from Galston to Hornsby at 6.15 a.m., catch a train at Hornsby at 7 a.m. and arrive at the railway workshops in Chullora by 8 a.m. After a full day's work and training, I'd catch a train back to the city four nights a week and walk to Sydney Technical College in Ultimo to do three hours of the electrical engineering diploma course, then retrace my journey to Galston in time to catch the last bus home at 10.30 p.m. On the weekends I worked on my diploma assignments and helped tend the chickens.

Looking back, this work/study/travel routine sounds like quite a feat of endurance, and yet never once did I consider myself to be either overworked or underprivileged. I just did it because I felt it was necessary for me to get on in the world. And it was worth it. In December 1950 I was one of four candidates selected by the Railways for sponsorship to a full-time degree course in electrical engineering at the University of Technology (now the University of New South Wales). I think the story of my daily travel schedule must have helped as well …

RE-CHRISTENING!

My first day at the Chullora Workshops was the most memorable. I had been told to report to Charlie Williams, a foreman in one of the departments.

'What's your name, son?' were his first words to me.

'Igor Ivashkoff,' I replied.

'Not another bloody New Australian! Christ! What have I done to deserve this?'

The term 'New Australian' was one the locals used quite a bit in those days. During that period of massive migration to Australia, the local population, which had been well insulated from 'foreigners', was now receiving an overdose of new arrivals. So it was not surprising that many were becoming a little fed up with this onslaught, and especially with encountering people who spoke a language other than English. And thus the term 'New Australian' was born. It was not meant as a racist slur or a derogatory term nor, for that matter, was it a complimentary one. It was just the Australian way of differentiating between the locals and the migrants, and making a bit of fun of the peculiarities of the new arrivals.

Anyway, I must say that I was taken aback by the foreman's reaction. I suppose I expected something more welcoming. It would have been even more humiliating had it not been for the twinkle in his eyes and the lack of malice in his tone.

'What did you say your name was again, son?' he asked

'Igor Ivashkoff,' I repeated.

'That's not all one bloody name, is it?'

'No, sir. My first name is Igor.'

'Igor!' he exclaimed. 'What sort of a bloody name is that?'

'Russian,' I said.

'Well you're now in Australia, son,' he said. 'And we'll have to give you a name that everybody can pronounce and remember.'

I didn't think Igor was difficult to pronounce or remember, but who was I to argue with my boss on the first day?

'Now, let's see,' he went on. 'I've got a John and a Peter and a Simon and two bloody Davids — and, let me tell you, that's causing a problem — and I'm Charlie … I know! We'll call you Eddie. That's my brother's name, and you look like a bloody Eddie anyway. So welcome to my team, Eddie, and we'll just forget about your bloody surname.'

And that's the story of my re-christening. I was called Eddie from then on. In addition, the pronunciation of my surname was also changed from Ivashkoff (correctly pronounced Ee-vash-koff with the accent on the last syllable) to Eye-vash-koff, with the accent on the first syllable. In those days it was considered un-Australian to pronounce foreign words correctly.

But I didn't mind. What's in a name anyway? At least I now felt I was one of them.

THE ALCOHOLIC

In early 1951 we moved to Waverton, a suburb quite close to the city. There we rented three small rooms in a little timber house owned by a Russian named Yudaev. He was content to occupy just the one room and let us have the run of the rest of the house.

Yudaev was a fine old man who ran a part-time smallgoods business from the back of his panel van. I remember him well for two reasons. Firstly, he was the ideal landlord, rarely seen or heard. And secondly, he was an extremely frugal individual — practically a miser. For example, he once asked me to help him with something or other in the city. It meant driving across the Harbour Bridge which, in those days, had a toll of sixpence per person. Approaching the toll gates, he insisted that I hide under the dashboard to avoid him paying the extra money. Another time, when my mother, Vasia and I were in his van, he suggested that all three of us hide in the back to avoid payment. When mother questioned the wisdom of us sharing the space with the sausages and cheeses just to avoid payment, he told her this was standard practice with all his friends.

My mother and Vasia found a job at Warburton Franki, a manufacturer of electric power meters, a short bus trip from home. Nina was on the assembly line and Vasia in the meter-testing section. The pay was low but there was a lot of overtime and, with both of them working, they were able to put some money aside every week. In addition, Nina, whose Tubabao sewing experience had made her an expert seamstress, began to take orders for dresses from Russian ladies who were obviously better off than we were. This helped the family coffers. The goal was to save enough for a deposit on a house. Owning a house was the great Australian dream, and it had also become my mother's dream.

I went to university full-time, and the Railways even gave me a small salary — more like an allowance. I think it was £5 a week. During the university vacations I had to work in various departments of the Railways to obtain some practical experience. My mother was generous enough not to ask me to pay any board and I therefore had some money to spend for incidentals.

Within a year of us moving, Nina bought a piano for me — a Beale upright.

This was an unbelievably generous act. It cost something like £400, about a year's salary for her, but she told me later that it had been her ambition to do this as soon as she was able to. It was, of course, bought on 'easy-terms', as the Australians called time-payment, but it was still a huge dent to the financial position. And she must have done a supreme job to talk Vasia into it. He was not a music lover, and I'm sure the thought of constant piano practicing at close quarters had little appeal for him. And she also had to obtain the landlord's permission.

So everything seemed to be going according to plan, and the future was looking bright, except for one problem — Vasia's drinking. By this time he had become a genuine alcoholic, and an unpleasant one at that. He would drink vodka or Scotch every night before, during and after dinner until he became inebriated. And then the nightly routine would begin.

Firstly, he would start singing 'Moonlight and Shadows', a song Dorothy Lamour chanted in the 1942 film *Road to Morocco*. It was always the same song. Then he would announce that he was off to Kings Cross, the red-light district of Sydney. And then Nina and his mother, Elena, would begin the task of talking him out of leaving the house. There would be arguments, yelling, he would be grabbing for his coat, they would be trying to take it off him. Most nights, he finally gave in and fell into a drunken stupor. Sometimes, though, he was able to avoid their grasps and leave the house. Never was he away for more than an hour or so, even less in winter. Once I followed him out and saw him just stagger aimlessly around the streets before returning home. I told mother this and implored her not to go through these traumatic nightly charades.

'Just let him go,' I pleaded. 'This Kings Cross stuff is just bravado. He likes the idea of the two of you begging him not to go. When he starts his stuff, just give him his coat and show him the door. He hasn't got the guts to go anywhere.'

But neither mother nor Elena were game to try it. I suppose they were mainly worried that, in his drunken state, he would get run over or arrested.

These regular scenes took their toll on my mother and Elena, souring their delight with their new life. And they made me despise him. Although we were civil to each other — my mother begged me to be so — the feeling of mutual contempt was always there, and it was exacerbated after he once pushed my mother so hard she nearly fell (he was drunk). I grabbed him by the shoulders and told him that if he ever did that again I would kill him.

NADIA AND LEN

When the Kozlovskys arrived in Sydney in May 1951, they stayed with us in our rented rooms in Waverton — all three of them, Nadia, Boris and eleven-year-old George. Six people in three small rooms was very, very cosy ('cramped' is a better word), but there was no alternative. They had no money. Kichii's businessman contact had not transferred their money as yet and they were penniless.

Boris was a qualified mechanical engineer, but his diploma from the Harbin Polytechnic Institute was not accepted in Australia. However hard he tried, even offering to sit for any exams or technical interviews, he could not get a job as an engineer. In the meantime, Nadia decided to visit her mother, Aida, who she had not seen for over two years, in Brisbane. She took George with her, which relieved the cramped accommodation at our place.

After a few weeks, Boris gave up on the prospect of working as an engineer and settled for a position as a draughtsman at Australian Forge, a steel company. The pay was quite good, better than either Nina's or Vasia's, and as soon as he started earning money Nadia returned and they began to seek rental accommodation. This was soon found in a home owned by a Russian couple named Goncharov who had just bought the house on easy terms, but found themselves short of funds to furnish it and decided to rent out one room. The Kozlovskys bought three camp beds and a small wardrobe and settled in. Nadia immediately found work in the Australian Woollen Mills, George went to school and their new life began in earnest

Len Tarasov, his wife Galya and their two children, Len Jr (five) and Liz (three and a half) had arrived in Brisbane from Shanghai a month before the Kozlovskys. After staying with Aida for a short while they rented a small house of their own. Unfortunately, the new country did not have any beneficial effect on their family life. Although they were living together, Len and Galya were, to all intents and purposes, estranged. To combat her loneliness and despair, Galya encouraged her mother to come to Australia as quickly as possible. This was, of course, done without the knowledge of Len, who would have had a fit if he knew what was happening.

Six months later, Galya's mother arrived and began to live with them. This, to Len, was the last straw. Not only did he feel that the earlier agreement had been violated, but he felt bitter at the fact that Galya and her mother had become inseparable. However, Galya needed solace and companionship, and she certainly could not hope to get it from her husband.

The relationship became more and more strained, and finally Len decided to move to Sydney on his own. He was always on good terms with Nadia and thought the move would do him good. It was a typical act of selfishness and callousness but he did it anyway. Joining Warburton Franki, where Nina and Vasia worked, he embarked on a bachelor's life with no care for his family in Brisbane.

Eventually, Galya and the children moved to Sydney and there was an attempt at reconciliation, but it did not last and they eventually divorced.

MY FIRST CAR

At the end of 1951, two years after arriving in Australia, I became the owner of a car. Is this not a Land of Opportunity, I ask you? Well, not really a full owner, but at least a part-owner. Two of my friends, Alex Marchevsky and Victor Shliapnikoff, and I pooled our money and bought a 1928 Willis Whippet. It cost us the princely sum of £105. It was not the fanciest of cars, but it got us around — and it gave us a new-found freedom. We often used the car as a trio, but we also had a sharing rule — one week each in turn. When it was my week, the car was delivered to my place on a Sunday night by the previous week's owner, and it was then mine, all mine, for the next seven days.

Being the first person in the Tarasov clan to even part-own a car made me immensely proud. I took great pleasure in organising outings for the family picnics in the country, visits to the beach, even a trip to Canberra. The Whippet

The 1928 Willis Whippet with (left to right) me, Nadia, Nina and Nadia's son George, 1953

could easily seat seven people and we had some great times.

Mind you, the car did break down regularly, and as the three of us had to do all the maintenance and repairs ourselves, we learnt a lot about cars and what makes them work. Particularly bothersome was a fuel connection which used to come loose at the most awkward moments, such as in the rain on the Harbour Bridge in peak-hour traffic.

But the most memorable event occurred one Saturday evening when the three of us and another friend, Vitya Goustavsky, were on the way to a dance at the Russian Club in George Street. We were dressed to the gills — suits, ties, the works. It was summer and still light as we cruised along York Street past all the underprivileged people waiting for buses. Suddenly there was a loud clatter as something detached itself from underneath our car and fell on the road. The engine began to race, and, not knowing what had happened, I applied the brakes. It was the laughter of the crowds and their pointing fingers which drew our attention to the fact that lying in the middle of the road behind us was our car's tail shaft!

The four of us sat in the car, too embarrassed to get out and retrieve it. The crowd was still laughing and pointing, and you could hear the screech of brakes as other vehicles tried to avoid the strange object. As no-one was about to volunteer to retrieve it we played a four-handed round of stone-paper-scissors — and Goustavsky lost.

Summing up all his courage and bravado, he stepped out of the car, walked slowly to the tail shaft, hoisted it on his shoulder and walked back past the applauding crowd, acknowledging their interest and involvement with regal waves. The car was then pushed to the side of the road and we proceeded to the Russian Club on foot, laughing all the way.

AN EARLY MARRIAGE

In those days the Russian Club was a tiny, snug little venue on the second floor of a narrow building in George Street near Central Station. Every Saturday night was party night. My friends and I used to go there regularly. It was a great place for the young at heart — a three-piece band playing romantic music for dancing, dim lights, a warm and snug ambience.

And that is where, one night in July 1952, I met the beautiful Marina, my wife-to-be. Although I had been to the club many times before, I had never seen her there. Later she told me she did not like to go out by herself, and the only reason she was there was that she felt she had to make an effort to mix with the opposite sex or be doomed to eternal old-maidship. After all, she had already turned eighteen …

So there she was, a vision of loveliness. I was completely enchanted with her — beautiful face, great hair, good figure, a warm feminine sensuality, a little on the shy side — everything I had always desired in a girl. This was love at first sight! And, fortunately, she liked me as well. From then on, we were inseparable.

Marina Dobrovidova was Russian, born in Harbin. She had lived most of her life in Shanghai and had come to Sydney via Tubabao. Although we had been on the island at the same time, I did not know her. This is not surprising — after all, she was two years younger than me, and let's face it, a sixteen-year-old boy is not normally interested in fourteen-year-old girls. Her parents had divorced in China and she had been living with her father. They arrived in Australia in 1949, but not having a sponsor they were sent to the Greta migrant camp. By the time of our first encounter, Marina had moved to Sydney and was living in a rented room in Burwood, while her father was working for the army and living in the military base at North Head.

Anyway, two years and four months after we met at the Russian Club, Marina and I became man and wife.

My mother had been very worried about my matrimonial plans. She thought I was too young to get married. After all, I was only twenty-two and Marina twenty. Moreover, I was about to undertake the last year of my university course. Would my marital duties cause me to do poorly or, worse still, force me to give up my studies? Was Nina's lifelong ambition to see her son receive a tertiary education about to be shattered? It took a great deal of effort to convince her that I would continue with my studies, and that being with my loved one would give me more time to concentrate on my university work, without the constant need to travel back and forth to see her. Finally, she gave me her blessing.

With Marina, 1953

Our wedding on 7 November 1954 was a simple affair. There was no money around to spend on anything elaborate. The Western tradition of having the bride's parents pay for the wedding did not apply in Russian society, and even if it had it would have been purely academic. Marina was then living with her father in a tiny fibro house in Forestville which he had just built and there was no money to splash around.

The ceremony was held in a small Russian Orthodox church in Cabramatta — really a converted house — and the guests were limited to close family and friends. Hiring a function hall for the reception was out of the question, so we all adjourned to the new Kozlovsky home in Parramatta after the ceremony. Yes, the Kozlovskys now had a house of their own, the first of the Tarasov clan to achieve that dream. However small it was, it was still larger than our living quarters and they were kind enough to offer it for the reception. There were about twenty guests including my grandmother, Aida, who had come down from Brisbane. My mother and Nadia cooked up some delicious food and there was certainly enough to drink.

Which brings us to the honeymoon. By that time I was without a car. A year earlier, I had bought out my two Willis Whippet partners, paying them each £25. I thought I had struck a good deal, but in reality they were the fortunate ones. The Whippet breakdowns became more frequent and the car was off the road for most of the time. By the time of the wedding it was completely inoperable for want of an unobtainable spare part. So, immediately after the reception our honeymoon began with a fifty-kilometre train trip to Gosford and then a twenty-kilometre bus trip to The Entrance.

When the train pulled into Gosford station it was already dark. Sitting at the bus stop, our small bag at our feet, we waited for nearly forty minutes before the bus arrived. As it pulled in, we saw that it was completely empty. Ah, a special honeymoon bus all to ourselves, we thought. Climbing up to the top deck we sat down in the front row and, embracing each other, remained in that position for the full thirty-minute journey, very much in love.

By current standards, the Charles Hotel in The Entrance would be a one-star hotel. It occupied a floor above the pub. Our room was quite bare — just a double bed and a wardrobe; no en-suite, no air-conditioning, no ambience, no nothing. But we thought it was great. We thought everything was great. We were together and we were in love. What else could one wish for? We even had enough money to hire a car for a couple of days from one of those 'hire a wreck' outfits.

Returning home to start our new life, we were distressed to learn that my grandmother Aida had suffered a stroke two days after our wedding. Fortunately, she had quickly recovered. And then there was the question of money, or lack of it. We were broke. Our total assets amounted to £7 10s. I still had a year to go at university and was getting a mere pittance of a wage, so we had to survive on Marina's salary as a typist in an insurance company. Fortunately, her father had offered us free accommodation in his house at Forestville.

I remember well his offer one could not refuse. 'Igor,' he said. 'Come and

THE TARASOV SAGA

live with me. I am already fifty-two years old, and I probably have another five years or so to live, no longer. After I die, the house will be yours and Marina's. You won't have long to wait'

And I believed him! Although he was extremely healthy, I really thought it was reasonable for someone aged fifty-two to leave this world five years later. Ah, the stupidity of youth! He actually died at the age of eighty-eight.

Anyway, we lived with him for two years in conditions which could only be described as primitive. Being in a newly developed area, the house had no electricity, water or sewerage — just gas for cooking and water heating. Light came from kerosene lamps. The water was rain water from a tank connected to the roof gutters. The toilet was outside — a 'dunny', as the Australians called it — consisting of a seat over a bucket. Heating in winter came from a kerosene heater called a Fyreside which was carried from room to room.

Which reminds me of the fact that, although the winters here were much milder than in Tientsin, I had never before felt so consistently cold as I did in the winter months of Sydney. In Tientsin, one dressed appropriately for the winter — coat, gloves, hat, boots. Houses were centrally heated. Here, however, because of the relative mildness of the winter, most people did not dress any more warmly in winter than in summer. It was especially evident among the Aussie males whose macho culture led them to walk around in the middle of winter in open-necked shirts. And I had to follow their lead for fear of being considered a sissy.

DIVINE INTERVENTION

During 1955, the last year of my University course and the first year of our marriage, I was earning the princely sum of £15 a week and Marina £7. We were forced to embark on a strict saving routine. We did not go out at all (that was beneficial to my studies). We used public transport. We did not entertain. Not paying rent certainly helped. The only furniture of ours in the house was the bedroom suite Marina had bought on easy terms before our marriage. The living room was furnished with a few packing cases covered with blankets, but it did boast the piano mother had given to me. Life was very Spartan.

By the end of the year we had saved £100 for a deposit on a block of land in Granville and I had completed my Bachelor of Engineering (Electrical) degree. In fact I did very well in my last year, considerably better than in the previous one. The graduation ceremony in March 1956 was the first held in the new Kensington premises of the university. My mother was extremely proud of my achievement, and it was of course also largely her achievement as well. Having only had a rudimentary education herself, she had unselfishly done everything possible to have her son obtain tertiary qualifications. She could now relax and look forward to her grandchildren.

The year 1956 was a happy one for her for another reason. In fact, for an act of God!

Vasia by that time had drunk himself to such a state that he began experiencing the DTs — in his case, hallucinations of snakes and spiders crawling over his body. My mother's life became a living hell, and so did Elena's. And then providence stepped in and gave Vasia a nasty duodenal ulcer. His stomach pains became unbearable and his doctor told him that if he did not stop drinking he would die. No-one thought he would have the willpower to give up the booze, least of all my mother, but Vasia had always been a hypochondriac and the fear of death was an immense shock to his system. So the unthinkable happened — he gave up drinking completely. Not a drop passed his lips. Instead, he drank gallons of milk and became a decent though colourless human being.

And mother's life changed completely. Gone were the nightly drunken dramas and the wanton waste of money on liquor. Life became normal, a state she had not experienced for years. They began to save money, and within two years had sufficient for a deposit on a house at Naremburn. For many years, Nina thanked the Lord in her nightly prayers for his divine intervention.

OUR OWN HOUSE!

After graduating, I was on a £500 bond with the NSW Government Railways. They had sponsored my education and it was only reasonable for them to expect me to work for them after graduation. The bond was for ten years, meaning that I would be up for an outlay of £500 if I were to leave earlier. So I resigned myself to a long career with them.

A year after graduation a friend of ours who was building a house in Northmead decided to migrate to America, putting up his unfinished house for sale. We liked the area and the position and made him an offer. He accepted £2000 and, after selling our block of land in Granville and obtaining a mortgage, we became owners of a partially built house. It took about a year to complete it, and in December 1957 we were able to move in.

By that time I was getting a reasonably good salary and was also able to buy a car — this time a 1938 Standard Tourer. That was definite progress. From being a one-third partner in a twenty-three-year-old car in 1951 I had now, a mere six years later, become sole owner of a nineteen-year-old car. The purchase was financed by a personal loan from a trusting colleague — the banks would not lend me any more money, believing I was overextended, which of course I was.

My second car, a 1938 Standard Tourer, in front of our newly bought, partly completed house, 1956

MY NEW NAME

By 1959, after working for three and a half years for the Railways, I had become disillusioned with my job. It was boring, repetitive and without any challenge. But I was stuck. We could not afford to pay out the £500 bond, and the banks would not lend us the money to pay it off.

One day, I saw an advertisement in the paper by IBM, the computer company, seeking graduates for technical and sales positions. What attracted my attention was the money they were promising. After an eighteen-month training period, during which the salary would be equivalent to the one I was getting, the company was offering earnings of over £1500 a year, which was more than double mine. At the time I had no idea who IBM were or what they did, but their offer was immensely tempting.

Our only possible source of funds to pay off the bond was Marina's superannuation, which could only be tapped into if she left the company she was working for, but we were keeping that in reserve. However, after much discussion we decided that this was too good an opportunity to miss. I had found out more about IBM and was excited at the prospect of working for them. After many tough interviews, I was offered the job. Marina resigned with £900 of superannuation money and I paid off the bond. The remaining £400 were used to buy a Victa lawnmower, lay floor tiles in the kitchen and buy a lounge suite.

Joining IBM was the best business decision I ever made and I spent thirty-one exciting years with them until my retirement.

And why did I change my name? Well, for years I had trouble with my name in the Australian business world. I disliked the name Eddie, the constant mis-pronunciation of my surname, and having to regularly spell my name over the phone. But changing it would not have been easy while I remained in the same company. However, I was shifting employment, and if I was ever going to do it now was the time. But to what name?

At the time I was playing a lot of competition tennis and often had to write my name down, in capitals, on the score sheets. And when one writes IVASHKOFF, the first two letters were often taken for a split N. So, for a joke, many of my tennis friends called me NASHkoff. Getting rid of the *koff* left me with my new name. For a while I planned to be Igor Nash, but Igor was also badly mis-pronounced by the Aussies so the name Gary was selected. It too had four letters and the Russians often used the name *Garrick* when referring to an Igor.

My mother was not very happy with my name change, but she understood the reasons. If this were happening today, a name change would have never crossed my mind. By now, the Australian people are well used to these 'weird' foreign names. In fact my original name would have been easier to cope with than most.

THANK YOU, AUSTRALIA

Australia has been good to the Tarasov clan. All of us were able to get jobs and build a new life. The initial fear and distrust by the Australians of the mass migration intake in the early fifties could not detract from the basic strength of its culture — the laid-back, uncomplicated, simple, un-elitist, friendly, positive nature of the Aussies.

The fact that most of us could speak the language made our life easier than most non-English-speaking migrants, although it did take some time for us to get used to the Australian accent — especially the pronunciation of the letter 'a'. There were many jokes about 'today' being pronounced as 'to die'.

We Russians are generally good integrators into the Australian world. Although we still have the Russian Club and the Russian Orthodox churches, and although we celebrate Easter and Christmas at different times to the locals, we still mix in well. Most Russians are fluent in English; there are no Russian districts or ghettos; Russians freely marry outside their ethnic group; and when Australia plays against Russia in tennis or soccer, we do not go out and barrack for the Russians.

Of the seven of Aida's grandchildren in Australia, three married Australians, and one lives with an Australian de facto. Every one speaks excellent English. All their children consider themselves Australian and all have married non-Russians. We love the country. None of us would want to live anywhere else.

Thank you, Australia, for taking us in.

EPILOGUE

The Tarasov clan: (sitting left to right) Nusia, Nina and Aida; (standing) Nadia, Len and Jenia, 1977, two years before Aida passed away

My grandmother Aida died in 1979 from a stroke at the age of ninety. This was her second and last stroke. The first one had occurred twenty-five years earlier, two days after our wedding.

Her second husband, George Chelpanov, passed away in 1967 from a heart attack at the age of sixty-six. Although he had always maintained it was his vodka drinking that saved him from certain death in Tientsin when his insides burst, his lifetime's intake of that elixir did not, regrettably, grant him a long life.

The next to go was Nusia, Aida's eldest daughter, succumbing to cancer in 1997. She too had reached the age of ninety. Her husband, Michael Diakonoff, died in 1960, a mere six years after their arrival in Australia. He was twenty-two years older than Nusia and had been in poor health for over ten years. Nusia's feelings towards her husband never changed, and she did not shed any tears when he died.

If it weren't for Nusia, this book would not have been written. After I had despaired of ever getting any useful information from my mother, uncle and aunts, it was she who wrote twenty-four pages of her memoirs while in hospital with cancer of the bladder. That first set of memories spurred her siblings into action and resulted in this story.

The next eldest of Aida's children was Nina, my mother. She remained an active and delightful person right up to the age of eighty-seven. Unfortunately she then succumbed to Alzheimer's disease and began a slow, relentless journey into that mental abyss. Her younger sister Jenia looked after her during those trying times, but eventually Nina had to be placed in a nursing home, where she died in August 2000 at the age of ninety-two.

My mother, Nina, in 1991 at the age of eighty-three. This is the photo on her tombstone.

Her husband, Vasia Artemieff, died of cancer thirteen years earlier. In the last year of his life, after he was diagnosed with the disease and advised that it was terminal, he displayed brave and stoic qualities. At first, he even kept the terrible news from my mother and she only became aware of it when it could no longer be hidden. And he never complained to anyone about his lot and the terrible pain he must have suffered. Nina nursed him with loving care through those final years.

Throughout her life, Nina believed that family was everything. Selfless in her relationship with her loved ones, she could be always relied upon to provide practical assistance or moral support. And she was a wonderful mother, and a loving grandmother to our children. I loved her very much.

The third in line of the Tarasov siblings was Len. He and Galya finally divorced in 1973 when their children, Len Jr and Liz, were young adults. Galya died in 1993 from a heart attack. She was seventy-three.

The last few years of Len's life were tragic. In 1984 he was diagnosed with severe glaucoma and underwent two unsuccessful operations, which damaged his eyes beyond repair. Gradually he began to lose his sight, and by 1995 he was totally blind. Over this period he was transformed from an energetic, optimistic person to a gloomy, miserable old man. In 1995 he entered a nursing home where, mercifully, he died in 1999. Like his mother and Nusia, he too was ninety.

Jenia lost her spouse early in their married life. Volodia Ostrouhoff died in Brisbane in 1970 at the young age of fifty-six from a heart attack. His death was an unexpected tragedy for Jenia. They had been very happy together.

A few years later, Jenia and Aida moved to a small rental apartment in Sydney, where they were soon joined by Nusia. The three of them lived together until Aida's death in 1979, after which Jenia and Nusia continued sharing the apartment. In 1987, after Vasia died, Nina invited both of them to come and live with her in her home. They moved in and Jenia, being the youngest of the three, became the devoted nurse and carer to her ageing sisters.

Jenia is now ninety. She is alive and well, and living on the Gold Coast.

Nadia's husband, Boris Kozlovsky, died from a heart attack in 1993. Theirs had been an ideal partnership — the witty, charming, obedient husband and the energetic, caring, dominant wife. Boris' sudden death was a devastating blow to her. But being a woman of great fortitude and courage, she was able to rebuild her life. At the age of eighty-eight, she now leads an active life in Sydney.

It is interesting to note that all of Aida's offspring outlived their spouses and that none died at an age earlier than ninety. Obviously either Aida or her husband Leonid had those long-life genes. I hope these lovely genes are the ones that get transferred from generation to generation ...

Nusia's first-born, Kolia, who fled to Russia, served on the passenger ship *Borodino* for thirty-three years, reaching the position of first mate. He retired in 1987 on a pension of 130 roubles a month, which was not too bad by comparison with his final salary of 173 roubles a month. Unfortunately,

Perestroika and the huge resulting devaluation completely eroded the value of his pension, plunging him into abject poverty. Looking back, he realises that fleeing to Mother Russia was not one of his smartest moves …

However, he saw his mother Nusia and the rest of the Tarasov family again in 1988 when he visited Australia, forty-one years after he had run away from home. His trip was funded by his brothers, Vova and Misha, his mother and his aunt Jenia. While he was here, he spent many hours telling me about his life in Russia.

Although his brothers were civil to him, it was obvious they had not forgiven him for his 'defection'. They felt he had run away from his responsibilities as the eldest son and had acted selfishly, without any regard for the rest of the family.

'I can't really blame them for feeling that way,' Kolia said.

Lena, my father's sister, left Tientsin for Canada soon after the end of the war. Much later, after we had migrated to Australia, my mother corresponded with her, but we never saw each other again. She died from cancer in 1978, leaving most of her estate to some religious order. A few thousand dollars were willed to me for the education of my children. She had been a good, kind person and she did provide most of the funds for my education. It was a great pity our relationship soured at the end. May she rest in peace.

Perhaps a few words would be in order about the fate of Irina and Marina, the two Eurasian children of Natasha (Boris Kozlovsky's sister) and Matsuda, her Japanese husband.

After the disappearance of Matsuda at the end of the war, Natasha continued to live with her children in Harbin until 1953. The Kozlovskys tried to get them a visa for Australia, but because of the White Australia Policy then in force, entry to her half-Japanese children was refused. She eventually settled in Sao Paolo, Brazil, where she re-married. Matsuda also re-married, and in the 1970s visited his daughters and ex-wife in Brazil, showering them all with expensive gifts.

Both Natasha and Matsuda have since died. Irina and Marina are still living in Sao Paolo.

Marina and I went to China in 1988, visiting Shanghai, Tientsin and Peitaiho Beach. It was a sentimental 'back to our childhood' journey for both of us.

Tientsin suffered a serious earthquake in 1976, when many of the buildings were destroyed, including Yang Ho-Li, St Louis College and Gordon Hall, the site of the old British Municipal Council. However most of the sturdy bank and insurance company buildings survived. The Kiesslings of old had

been replaced by a five-storey factory named Kiessling Food Factory. A large
Kiessling Restaurant now graced the corner of Race Course and Davenport
Roads on the old British Concession. Occupying the premises of the old
Victoria Cafe, it still possessed the old-world charm of the Victoria and had
an excellent Russian borscht on the menu.

During our visit to this restaurant I tried to find someone who would remember
my mother — after all, she had worked for Kiesslings for twenty years. Armed
with a note in English and Chinese, I showed it to every person working in the
restaurant. But no-one could help me. Finally the manager was informed about
this inquisitive foreigner and came up to offer his assistance. After reading the
note, he told me he knew someone who would probably remember her and
suggested I come back the following day to meet that person.

When I arrived the next day, the manager asked me to follow him to a private
room to meet this mysterious person — but there was no-one there. The manager
then turned to me and admitted he was the very man. He said he was sixteen
when he began to work for Kiesslings and he remembered my mother well because
he had actually spent one summer with us in Peitaiho. Apparently she called him
Max. We spent a wonderful hour conversing in broken English and Chinese.
'Madama Nina,' he said, remembering back some fifty years, 'was good woman.'

Another unexpected event occurred on the train from Peking to Tientsin.

The first-class carriage we entered in Peking had only one other couple in
it, a well-dressed Chinese gentleman with a Eurasian lady. When they saw us

The new Kiessling Restaurant, 1988

I LIVED IN TIANJIN FROM 1932 - 1948.

MY MOTHER, NINA, WAS THE MANAGER

OF THE KIESSLING CAKE SHOP IN

VICTORIA RD (JIEFANG ~~BEI~~ BEI LU).

IS THERE ANYONE HERE NOW WHO ~~HAS~~ WORKED

FOR KIESSLINGS DURING THAT TIME?

我曾于 1932 ~ 1948 年住在天津

我的妈妈，妮娜 曾是起士林东点心店的

~~老板~~ 经理（地址 解放北路）

现在 是在 ~~还有没有~~ 那时侯工作过的员工？

The note I wrote to find someone who could remember my mother, Nina. It was translated into Chinese by John Han-Yu Chi, 1988

having difficulty locating our seat numbers, the man addressed us in excellent English, offering his help. After the appropriate introductions, I was delighted to discover that the man, John Han Yu-chi, was a graduate of St Louis College, having gone through the school a few years behind me. His wife Rita was half Chinese and half Russian, and she and her husband were on the way back to

In conversation with the elusive Max, 1988

Tientsin, where they lived. We were privileged to spend some time with them in Tientsin. They were a delightful, hospitable couple and we spent many hours reminiscing about old times.

After the communist takeover, most of the foreigners left and there were not enough students to keep

St Louis College open. The Brothers departed, with the majority of them settling in the Hong Kong Marist community.

In 2001, the city of Tientsin ran an international event called 'The First China Western Style Food and Drink Culture Festival". As that year coincided with the centenary of the founding of Kiesslings, the mayor of Tientsin invited Werner Kiessling, the son of the founder of Kiesslings, and his wife to the festivities. The Kiesslings were at that time living in Germany. and, although Werner was already eighty-one, he had no hesitation in accepting the invitation. The trip was a highlight for them they were treated like royalty.

Also in 2001 I was able to establish e-mail contact with Brother Vincent in Hong Kong. To my query about the fate of the other Brothers, he replied as follows: 'All of them have been called to their Father's Home. Brother Konrad and my poor self are the only ones left behind. So we are trying to be more pure before we too get invited to such a magnificent reward!' Brother Vincent was ninety and Brother Konrad eighty-six.

Peitaiho Beach has had a dramatic change. After the foreign exodus, it became one of the official summer resorts for the workers of China. Many large ugly complexes were built to house miners, foundry workers and the like for their annual vacations. Concrete bunker-like changing rooms and showers were constructed right on the sandy beaches, thus polluting the beauty and charm of that wonderful resort. My wife and I were the first foreigners the locals had seen in years.

Shanghai — once the Yellow Babylon — became just a large Chinese city with only a small foreign business population. Although the impressive buildings of the Bund were still there, all other evidence of the presence of foreign Concessions had been obliterated. None of the old foreign street names remained and the impressive houses of the rich foreigners were now occupied by multiple Chinese families and looked neglected and shabby — broken windows, grimy facades, front and back yards full of rubbish. It was a 'Babylon' no more.

Nor was Harbin the Moscow of the Orient any more. After the exodus in the years after the war, only a few hundred Russians remained. But by the mid-1960s even they had dispersed, some to Russia, others to America or Australia. There was no reason left for any of them to live there any more.

Harbin had finally reverted to just being a large Chinese city — albeit one enriched by a vibrant Russian past.

ACKNOWLEDGMENTS

Grateful thanks is extended to the following who have so graciously made available their photos and illustrations:

Innokentii Soovoroff, Merrylands, NSW, Australia
Peter & Kyra Tatarinoff, Homebush, NSW, Australia
Desmond Power, Canada (Author of *Little Foreign Devil*)
George Nathing, Hastings Point, NSW, Australia
Rostislav Balandin, Annandale, NSW, Australia
Harbin Polytechnic Journal, Sydney, Australia
Olga Parr, San Francisco, USA

The source of many of the photos of Shanghai in the 1930s came from:

V.D. Jiganoff's *Russkie v Shanhaye* (Russians in Shanghai)

The rest came from the Tarasov family's private collection.

BIBLIOGRAPHY

Aylett, J.F., *Russia in Revolution*, GSCE, 1989.
Crow, Carl, *Handbook for China*, Oxford University Press, *1984.*
Encyclopedia Britannica, Britannica 99 CD-Rom.
Jiganoff, V.D., *Russians in Shanghai, 1936.*
Maxwell, Robin, *Merry-Go-Round*, Pangli Imprint, 1990.
Moravskii, N.V., *The Island of Tubabao*, 1949-51, Russian Historic Society in Australia, 1999 (in Russian).
Petroff, Nikolai, *Shanghai on the Whang-Poo River, 1*985 (in Russian).
Power, Desmond, *Little Foreign Devil*, Pangli Imprint, 1996.
Various, *Tubabao—Russian Refugee Camp—Philippines, 1949-1951,* Russian Historic Society in Australia, 1999.
Wagner, Ms, *Light and Darkness*, available on the Internet on http://www.netzone,com/~adjacobs/compare.htm.

INDEX